Ireland and the European Union

Manchester University Press

European Politics

Series Editors: Professor Dimitris Papadimitriou (University of Manchester), Dr Kathryn Simpson (Manchester Metropolitan University) and Dr Paul Tobin (University of Manchester).

The *European Politics* series seeks to tackle the biggest issues facing Europe in the twenty-first century.

Previously published under the *European Policy Research Unit (EPRU)* name, this long-established and highly respected series combines an important scholarly legacy with an ambitious outlook on European Studies at a time of rapid change for the discipline. Its geographical coverage encompasses the European Union, its existing and aspiring members, and 'wider Europe', including Russia and Turkey, and the series actively promotes disciplinary, theoretical and methodological diversity.

The editors particularly welcome critical scholarship on the politics and policy making of the European Union, on comparative European politics, and on contemporary issues and debates affecting the future of Europe's socio-political and security outlook. Key areas of interest include Brexit, the environment, migration, identity politics and the ever-changing face of European integration.

Previously published:

Regulating lobbying: A global comparison, 2nd edition
Raj Chari, John Hogan, Gary Murphy and Michele Crepaz

Towards a just Europe: A theory of distributive justice for the European Union
João Labareda

Made in France: Societal structures and political work
Andy Smith

Crisis and change in European Union foreign policy: A framework of EU foreign policy change
Nikki Ikani

Ireland and the European Union

Economic, political and social crises

Edited by Michael Holmes and Kathryn Simpson

MANCHESTER UNIVERSITY PRESS

Copyright © Manchester University Press 2021

While copyright in the volume as a whole is vested in
Manchester University Press, copyright in individual chapters
belongs to their respective authors, and no chapter may be
reproduced wholly or in part without the express permission
in writing of both author and publisher.

Published by Manchester University Press
Oxford Road, Manchester M13 9PL

www.manchesteruniversitypress.co.uk

British Library Cataloguing-in-Publication Data
A catalogue record for this book is available from the British
Library

ISBN 978 1 5261 6142 0 hardback
ISBN 978 1 5261 5959 5 paperback

First published 2021

The publisher has no responsibility for the persistence or
accuracy of URLs for any external or third-party internet
websites referred to in this book, and does not guarantee that
any content on such websites is, or will remain, accurate or
appropriate.

Typeset
by Sunrise Setting Ltd
Printed in Great Britain
by TJ Books Ltd, Padstow

Contents

Figures

Tables

Contributors

Anthony Cawley is a Senior Lecturer in Media in the Department of Media and Communication at Liverpool Hope University, UK. His research areas include the development of online journalism in Ireland, the response of legacy media (print) organisations to the emergence of the World Wide Web, and news media framing of the economic crisis and of Ireland's overseas aid budget.

Aideen Elliott is a PhD Researcher in the Department of Anthropology at National University of Ireland (NUI) Maynooth. Her research examines EU migration policy from the perspectives of policy makers, exploring the ways in which migration policy is perceived, conceived and lived by those charged with policy making and professionally implementing it.

Jonathan Evershed is a Postdoctoral Research Fellow in the Department of Government and Politics at University College Cork, Ireland. His research explores the consequences of Brexit for political relationships between Northern Ireland, Ireland and Great Britain.

Patrick Gallagher is a Postdoctoral Research Fellow in the Department of Management and Organisations at the Waterford Institute of Technology, Ireland. His research interests include comparative political economy.

Michael Holmes is Associate Professor at the European School of Political and Social Sciences (ESPOL) in Lille, France. His research focuses mainly on Ireland and the EU and on the impact of European integration on political parties.

Sheila Killian is Professor of Economics in the Department of Economics at the Kemmy Business School, University of Limerick, Ireland. Her research addresses issues of social sustainability, accountability and the common good, with a focus on professional expertise and tax policy.

Stephen Kinsella is Associate Professor of Economics in the Department of Economics at the Kemmy Business School, University of Limerick, Ireland, and former columnist for the *Sunday Business Post* (Ireland). His research areas include macroeconomics, econometrics and economic history.

Brigid Laffan is Professor of European Politics and Director of the Robert Schuman Centre for Advanced Studies at the European University Institute, Florence, Italy. Her areas of research include dynamic European integration, EU governance and Europeanisation and Brexit.

Giada Lagana is a Research Associate at the Wales Governance Centre, Cardiff University, UK. She works on the ESRC 'Between Two Unions' project examining the impact of the UK's withdrawal from the EU on the UK's internal constitutional and intergovernmental arrangements.

Madelaine Moore is a postdoctoral researcher in the Department of Sociology at the University of Bielefeld, Germany. Her research interests include critical political economy, eco-social policies, water governance and social movements.

Jane O'Mahony is Senior Lecturer in European Politics in the School of Politics and International Relations at the University of Kent, UK. Her research focuses on policy-making processes within the EU, how adaptation to EU governance affects domestic policy actors of EU member states and how they engage with EU policies. She has written widely on Ireland's adaptation to EU membership in this context.

Seán Ó Riain is Professor of Sociology at the National University of Ireland (NUI) Maynooth. His research interests are in the sociology of work and employment, comparative political economy, inequality and social change, and the global information economy.

David Phinnemore is Professor of European Politics and Jean Monnet Chair in European Political Science at Queen's University Belfast in Northern Ireland, UK. His research interests are focused on the EU – his current work is focused on the process and potential implications of Brexit, the form that a new UK–EU relationship might take, and the consequences of Brexit for the EU and especially for Northern Ireland and the island of Ireland.

James Pow is a Lecturer in Political Science in the School of History, Anthropology, Philosophy and Politics at Queen's University Belfast in Northern Ireland, UK. His research focuses on the way citizens interact with democratic decision-making, including through elections, mini-publics and referendums as well as public opinion towards Brexit.

Fergal Rhatigan is a Postgraduate Researcher at the Department of Sociology at the National University of Ireland (NUI) Maynooth. His research interests include political economy and the sociology of work.

Kathryn Simpson is an Associate Professor in Political Economy within the Future Economies Research Centre at Manchester Metropolitan University, UK. Her research focuses on public opinion, political behaviour and attitudes towards the EU, in particular in Ireland and the UK in the context of Brexit.

Ben Tonra is Professor of International Relations at the School of Politics and International Relations at University College Dublin, Ireland. He researches and publishes in European foreign, security and defence policy; Irish foreign, security and defence policy; and International Relations theory.

Silke Trommer is Senior Lecturer in Comparative Public Policy in the Department of Politics at the University of Manchester, UK. Her research focuses on the politics of global trade, global governance and development, and on social movements in the international political economy.

Lisa Whitten is a PhD Researcher in Politics and Law at Queen's University Belfast, Northern Ireland, UK. Her research interests include constitutional law, Northern Irish politics and Brexit.

Preface and acknowledgements

The initial idea for this book came as a result of discussions at the UACES Annual Conference in Krakow in 2017 on the need to update the interpretation of the relationship between Ireland and the EU. The last book to be published on Ireland and the EU was in 2008 (Laffan and O'Mahony) with the last edited volume in 2005 (Holmes). Subsequently, Ireland and the EU were shaken by a series of crises: the financial and Eurozone crisis starting in 2008, a number of foreign policy challenges, the migration crisis of 2015 and Brexit from 2016.

The key to a project of this nature is the ability to examine a wide range of themes in a comprehensive and cohesive manner. For us, it was crucial to examine key areas pertaining to the political, societal and policy aspects of the relationship between Ireland and the EU in light of these crises. We organised a panel on *Ireland and the EU* at the UACES Annual Conference in Bath in 2018 and a two-day workshop on *Ireland and the EU in a Changing World* at Manchester Metropolitan University in April 2019. The workshop brought all contributors of the edited volume together and provided an invaluable source of feedback, discussion and debate.

Firstly, we would like to thank all the contributors to this volume. They have produced outstanding chapters despite the unusual challenges they have faced (general elections in the UK and Ireland, the elastic nature of the Brexit negotiations, the Covid-19 pandemic). The book reflects and draws upon the academic expertise of established scholars as well as PhD and Early Career Researchers demonstrating the richness of research on Ireland and the EU. Despite the diversity of disciplines and opinions, they have produced what we believe is a coherent and insightful set of analyses.

Secondly, we gratefully acknowledge financial support for the workshop from the Manchester Jean Monnet Centre of Excellence and the Future Economies Research Centre at Manchester Metropolitan University. Michael Holmes started work on this project during a sabbatical year at the European School of Political and Social Sciences (ESPOL) in Lille that was funded by the Regional Council for Hauts-de-France. We would also like to thank UACES, Liverpool Hope University and Manchester Metropolitan University for supporting this timely research.

Thirdly, we owe a debt of gratitude to the anonymous external reviewers of our initial proposal and of the final manuscript for robust feedback from which we have benefited. We would also like to acknowledge the help and support from Manchester University Press throughout this project, in particular from Tony Mason and Jonathan de Peyer during the initial stages, and Rob Byron on the final delivery of the book.

Finally, let's return to our initial conversation in Krakow. It began with Kathryn commenting on how her path through university and into academia had been helped by Michael's 2005 edited volume. We would like to dedicate this book to the students who will, we hope, be using this book and benefiting from it over the coming years, in universities in Ireland, the UK and wider. May you find the Irish–EU relationship as fascinating as we do!

Michael Holmes and Kathryn Simpson
Lille and Manchester 2021

Abbreviations and Irish terms

The following terms and abbreviations appear throughout the book. Other abbreviations are explained on a chapter-by-chapter basis.

1998 Agreement	Throughout the book the term 1998 Agreement is used to refer to the current Northern Ireland peace accord. The official title of the document is simply The Agreement; it is also known as the Belfast Agreement or the Good Friday Agreement.
CAP	Common Agricultural Policy
CFSP	Common Foreign and Security Policy
CSDP	Common Security and Defence Policy
CTA	Common Travel Area
ECB	European Central Bank
ECJ	European Court of Justice
EEA	European Economic Area
EEC	European Economic Community
EP	European Parliament
EPC	European Political Cooperation
ERDF	European Research Development Fund
ESM	European Single Market
FDI	foreign direct investment
G20	international forum of the governments and central bank governors from 19 countries and the EU
IMF	International Monetary Fund
JHA	Justice and Home Affairs
MEP	Member of the European Parliament
MLA	Member of the Legislative Assembly (Northern Ireland)
OECD	Organisation for Economic Cooperation & Development
OFMDFM	Office of the First Minister and Deputy First Minister
PM	Prime Minister

| TSCG | Treaty on Stability, Coordination and Governance in the Economic and Monetary Union (also referred to as European Fiscal Treaty) |
| Troika | Term used to refer to the decision group formed by the European Commission, the European Central Bank and the International Monetary Fund. |

Irish terms

It is common practice in Ireland to use Irish-language terms for certain political offices. For the benefit of readers who are not familiar with these terms, those which feature regularly in the book are indicated below. Any others are explained on a chapter-by-chapter basis.

Bunreacht na hÉireann	Constitution of Ireland
Dáil Éireann	Lower house of parliament
Óglaigh na hÉireann	Irish Armed Forces
Oireachtas	Irish parliament (both houses)
RTÉ	Raidió Teilifís Éireann – Ireland's national broadcaster
Seanad Éireann	Senate (upper house of parliament)
Tánaiste	Deputy Prime Minister
Taoiseach	Prime Minister
Teachta Dála	Member of Dáil Éireann

1

Ireland and the EU: crisis and change

Kathryn Simpson and Michael Holmes

Interesting times

It used to seem simple. European integration was good for Ireland, and Ireland was a good European, that was the mainstream consensus. In the run-up to the 2009 European election, several European and Irish leaders described Ireland as being 'at the heart of Europe'.[1] However, that pro-European consensus was already under strain. On 12 June 2008, 53% of Irish voters had rejected the Treaty of Lisbon in a referendum (Holmes 2008). This meant that the 2009 EP election was already something of a litmus test for the Irish–European relationship. And though no one could have foreseen it, it took place on the cusp of a dramatic transformation of Ireland's and Europe's circumstances.

The EU has gone through a series of crises 'unprecedented not only in the large number of specific crises it has contained but also in the severities of these crises' (Dinan et al. 2017: 360). Furthermore, these crises have not been self-contained but have fed into each other. The global financial crisis that erupted in 2008 had a specific impact on the Eurozone countries. This was followed by a succession of foreign policy challenges in the near neighbourhood of the EU, stemming both from the consequences of the Arab Spring uprisings in the Middle East and North Africa in the early 2010s and from the Ukrainian Revolution of 2014. The destabilisation triggered by the Arab Spring movements contributed strongly to the Mediterranean migration crisis from 2015. This in turn contributed to the rise of populist parties in many EU countries, which played into the Brexit referendum in the UK in 2016. And these inter-linked crises created an overarching crisis of EU governance, to the extent that analysts began to talk about 'European disintegration' (Vollaard 2018; Webber 2019).

This book examines how Ireland's relationship with the EU was affected by this succession of crises – or perhaps it is better to say relationships, since the book looks both at the Republic of Ireland and Northern Ireland. The various crises were not of equal significance in Ireland. The financial crisis was a huge issue for the Republic but less so for Northern Ireland; Brexit had a major impact in both polities; the migration and populism issues were less controversial; and the foreign policy challenges had a minimal impact. This opening chapter will provide a summary of the main features of each of the main crises to be considered, from both the EU and the Irish perspectives.

Financial crisis: from global to European to Irish

The global financial sector began showing signs of serious stress in 2007, with the bailout of Northern Rock bank in the UK and problems in BNP-Paribas. This tipped over into a full-fledged crisis in September 2008, with a dizzying sequence of bank failures. The problems originated in the United States, where deregulation and the development of high reward but high-risk trading strategies had gone the furthest. But in a highly internationalised financial system, the contagion spread rapidly. In the EU it encountered an additional twist. The constraints of Eurozone membership meant that economies that were running into difficulties were unable to avail themselves of some traditional remedies such as devaluation. In addition, European Central Bank (ECB) rules made it far more difficult to attempt the kinds of interventionist, reflationary strategies adopted in, for example, the United States.

Irish banks had borrowed very heavily on international markets, lured by a construction boom in the country during the late 1990s to 2007. As the global financial markets began to retrench, and as economic activity shrank, the Irish banks were particularly vulnerable. On 25 September 2008, the Irish government admitted that the country had fallen into recession for the first time since 1983. Five days later, they announced a €440 billion bank guarantee scheme, which drew the government into a spiral of funding to try to prop up those banks. Eventually, this led to the EU–ECB–IMF rescue package for the Irish economy on 21 November 2010. This was tied to stringent austerity conditions, which had already begun to be introduced by the Irish government as the public finances became increasingly stretched by the bank guarantee scheme. Although the state exited the bailout programme on 15 December 2013, many of the austerity measures remained in place.

Of course, Ireland was not the only EU member state experiencing a sharp financial crisis. Virtually every EU economy contracted between 2008 and 2009 (OECD 2020). Greece, Portugal, Spain and Cyprus joined Ireland in requiring a bailout from the Troika, while Italy was placed under similar strict austerity conditions to prevent it requiring a bailout. But the way in which successive Irish governments (initially a Fianna Fáil–Green coalition, succeeded by a Fine Gael–Labour one) adhered to demands for austerity and economic adjustment, and its apparent rapid recovery after swallowing this medicine, meant that there were suggestions that 'Europe's basket case was now Europe's poster child' (Roche et al. 2017: 2).

Crises of Europe's near neighbourhood

The EU also began to experience increasing instability in its near neighbourhood, with both a foreign policy crisis and a migration crisis in evidence. In Ukraine, the government of Viktor Yanukovych had negotiated an association agreement with the EU but delayed signing it out of concern for relations with Russia. After street protests, Yanukovych was overthrown in February 2014, leading to the annexation of Crimea by Russia and the development of an armed conflict in the Donbass region involving pro-Russian separatists. This led to a serious deterioration in EU–Russian relations, which went 'from courtship in 1999 to confrontation in 2015' (Maass 2017: 1). The EU imposed some sanctions, but there were also significant problems of coherency among member states, with some adopting quite a hostile anti-Russian stance and others being more conciliatory, due in large part to their trade links with Russia and in particular their dependency on access to Russian energy supplies (Thaler 2020).

The year after the Ukrainian crisis, EU policy coherence was again seriously challenged by events in the EU's near neighbourhood. The migration crisis can be traced back to the Arab Spring protest movement in several Middle East and North African countries in 2010–2012. The protests triggered repressive reactions in many countries and civil wars in a few. This triggered a wave of refugees and other migrants. Numbers attempting to cross the Mediterranean Sea into Europe began to grow from 2013, with more than 1 million people estimated to have tried to enter Europe in 2015 (IOM 2015), and at least 17,919 people are thought to have died in the attempt during 2014–2018 (IOM 2020: 32).

The EU responded with joint naval operations in the Mediterranean, such as Operation Mare Nostrum and Operation Triton in 2014, Operation Sofia in 2015 and Operation Themis in 2018. Whether these were to rescue migrants or dissuade them is open to some debate – Cusumano suggests that behind the humanitarian rhetoric was 'a form of organised hypocrisy' (2019: 3). Within the EU, different states responded in different ways. Greece and Italy were by far the most common points of entry into the EU, which created considerable burdens for them. Some EU member states, like Portugal, sought to respond with a generous and welcoming policy; others, such as Hungary, refused to accept refugees and actively tried to bar migrants even from transiting through their territory (VES 2016: 63). Agreements were concluded with Turkey (2016) and Libya (2017) to try to curb the flow of migrants.

Ireland did not have any strong preferences in relation to the EU's Russian policy. However, it was far more involved in the migration crisis. Irish naval patrol vessels participated in the joint EU operations and rescued over 10,000 migrants between 2015 and 2019 (Department of Defence 2019). In 2015, the Irish government committed to receiving 4,000 refugees, but by 2020 had still not achieved that target (Department of Justice 2020).

The Brexit crisis

A further shock awaited around the corner which had a far greater impact on Ireland. UK Prime Minister David Cameron hoped he could fend off the growing challenge from the right-wing Eurosceptic UK Independence Party by renegotiating the terms of UK membership of the EU and then winning a referendum to re-approve membership. The renegotiation was completed in February 2016, with Cameron declaring it gave the UK 'special status' in the EU (BBC 2016). On 23 June 2016, the referendum took place, and the UK voted to leave the EU (see Table 1.1). Cameron's gamble had failed.

Brexit was, of course, an existential issue for the EU. It was the first time a member state had left the EU,[2] and the Union had to expend time and energy on negotiating the terms of a new relationship with the UK as a non-member. It was also trying to do this while still dealing with the policy challenges, both economic and social, of earlier crises. A further destabilising factor was the surge of support for Eurosceptic parties in several other member states, such as AfD in Germany, Lega Nord in Italy and PiS in Poland (Rooduijn et al. 2019). This populist and Eurosceptic surge challenged the whole structure of EU governance, with growing concerns in some quarters about a perceived democratic deficit and accompanying demands for a restoration of some sovereignty back to the national level.

Table 1.1 Brexit referendum vote by region

	Leave	*Remain*
England	53.3%	46.7%
Northern Ireland	44.2%	55.8%
Scotland	38.0%	62.0%
Wales	52.5%	47.5%
UK overall	51.9%	48.1%

Source: Electoral Commission (2016).

Equally, Brexit was a huge issue for Ireland, which was often referred to as 'the country most affected by Brexit' (Emmanuel Macron, cited in *The Irish Times* 24 October 2017). In the Republic, there was a widespread consensus in favour of a Remain vote and subsequently strong support for maintaining Ireland's position in the EU. The Irish government identified four main challenges from Brexit (Department of Foreign Affairs 2017: 3):

- The potential damage Brexit could cause to the Northern Ireland peace process
- The potential for it to impede trade and economic activity
- The potential to inhibit freedom of movement and the Common Travel Area (CTA)
- The potential to weaken the EU and Ireland's influence therein.

The situation was also enormously sensitive for Northern Ireland, although here there was not the same degree of consensus. Nationalist parties called for a Remain vote while the Democratic Unionist Party (DUP) (the leading unionist party) campaigned for Leave. 'Northern Ireland is one of the most challenging aspects of Brexit because its relationship with both the UK and EU is so distinctive' (de Mars et al. 2018: 6).

Structure of the book

With so many potential strands to the narrative, the book does not attempt to present one single overarching argument about Ireland–EU relations. It proceeds as follows. In the following chapter, Ben Tonra examines Irish foreign policy and the EU. This includes discussion of the security debates around the EU's near neighbourhood and the EU's changing security outlook, arguing that 'hard choices are coming into view' for Ireland. It also assesses the impact of Brexit on Ireland's international stance, noting the former importance of the UK as a close partner for Ireland within the EU and analysing the subsequent attempts to shore up Ireland's foreign policy.

The focus then shifts onto the impact of the financial crisis. In Chapter 3, Patrick Gallagher, Fergal Rhatigan and Seán Ó Riain look at the economic relationship between Ireland and the EU over the decade from the financial crash to Brexit. They place this discussion in the context of the globalised nature of the Irish economy. They argue that perceptions shifted from growing unease about the impact of the EU on the Irish economy after the financial crash to a renewed enthusiasm for and commitment to the EU as the primary economic framework for Ireland following Brexit.

One of the detailed economic themes is developed further in Chapter 4, where Sheila Killian explores the impact of debates about control of taxation policy on the Irish–EU relationship. This is a debate which touches strongly on issues of economic nationalism, and again it particularly reflects Ireland's reputation as the 'state that is perhaps more closely allied than any other democracy with the interests of global transnational corporations' (O'Toole 2016). The chapter includes consideration of the controversial Apple case which brought the Irish government into conflict with the European Commission.

The following chapter moves on to an area of social policy which has a major impact on both political and economic issues. Aideen Elliott examines migration policy, looking first at Ireland's historical position as a country of emigration and then examining how the EU's approach to issues of migration and asylum has developed. It then explores in detail the EU's migration crisis and Ireland's contribution to the response, noting that Ireland has tended to associate itself with the more progressive group of member states in the EU on this issue.

Chapter 6 by Michael Holmes looks at Irish political parties and their policies on Europe. It notes that there has generally been a strong pro-EU consensus among Irish parties, but that there is also a strand of Euroscepticism, particularly evident during European referendums. The chapter argues that the financial crisis saw a strengthening of Eurosceptic stances, though noticeably on the left of the political spectrum and not on the right. However, the subsequent Brexit crisis actually led to a strengthening of the pro-EU consensus, albeit with a more critical and nationalist tone.

One of the interesting features of Irish politics during the financial crisis was the development of extra-parliamentary forms of action. In Chapter 7, Madelaine Moore and Silke Trommer examine these public protest movements, which included protests against water charges and other taxes, wider protests against austerity, and developing into protests on social issues such as marriage equality and abortion. They argue that while the protests undoubtedly helped create sharpened criticism of the EU, they also led to a more nuanced public understanding of the EU – critical of austerity but more appreciative of other social dimensions of the EU. In addition, the protests increasingly held domestic political elites to task for their actions at European level.

This suggests an evolution in Irish public opinion about the EU, and in Chapter 8 Kathryn Simpson examines this in more detail. She notes an apparent contradiction: that Ireland always registers among the most pro-EU countries in general opinion surveys, despite the fact that it has on several occasions voted against EU treaties. She explores how Irish public opinion developed during the financial crash and the Brexit crisis, and highlights how there was no discernible Irexit effect. Instead, although the Irish public continues to show levels of knowledge of the EU that are lower than the EU average, nonetheless their overall attitudes remain positive, and this was strengthened after Brexit.

One important factor in moulding public opinion is the media, and Anthony Cawley's chapter examines how the Irish media shapes attitudes and understanding about the EU. This starts with an examination of whether the media could or should have a role in creating a European public sphere. The chapter then analyses how the media in the Republic of Ireland reported the Brexit referendum. Cawley argues that their reporting was marked by a strongly Irish-focused perspective, and that a wider sense of Europe and Europeanness did not emerge.

In Chapter 10, Brigid Laffan and Jane O'Mahony look at the impact of Brexit on British–Irish relations, and particularly the border issue. They evaluate the Irish government's dual strategy of building a domestic consensus and establishing support at the European level. They also assess the implications for Ireland's EU membership beyond Brexit, arguing that it represents a huge challenge for the country, as it is losing a major trading partner and an ally on many issues in the EU, but also constitutes a decisive moment when Ireland committed itself to a European future.

Stephen Kinsella concentrates on the economic impact of Brexit on Ireland in Chapter 11, noting that there are potentially three 'economies' to consider: Northern Ireland, the Republic, but also the Republic's distinct multinational sector. He analyses the potential economic shock of Brexit in terms of the overall sectoral impact, in terms of its impact on the labour market, and in terms of one specific policy area, the energy sector. He concludes by highlighting the impact of Brexit on Irish economic diplomacy which saw the country reach out to new economic partners and allies in the EU.

The focus of the book then shifts more towards Northern Ireland. If Ireland was the EU member state most affected by Brexit, Northern Ireland was the part of the UK most affected by it. In Chapter 12, David Phinnemore and Lisa Whitten argue that 'Brexit has unsettled Northern Ireland', both in economic terms and in terms of its delicate political/constitutional balance. They look at the stances of the different parties on the EU and on Brexit, and they analyse in particular the border issue in the light of Brexit. Their chapter also goes into depth on the Protocol on Ireland and Northern Ireland, a key agreement between the EU and the UK intended to avoid a hard border, preserve the integrity of the EU single market and maintain Northern Ireland's place as a UK customs territory.

In Chapter 13, Jonathan Evershed analyses the specific constitutional issues that arise for Ireland and the UK after Brexit. He argues that Brexit created a crisis for the UK's improvised constitution, to the extent even of casting doubt on the continuing integrity of the UK, with renewed calls for independence in Scotland and for Irish unity. This in turn created a significant constitutional challenge for Ireland. While Ireland did not create the crisis, it was faced with its consequences.

One of the most important of those was the potential impact of Brexit on the peace process in Ireland, and James Pow examines this in Chapter 14. He starts by analysing the EU's contribution to the peace process, noting how joint membership of the EU helped create a framework of cooperation between the UK and Ireland. He then looks at how Brexit has disrupted three delicate balances on which the peace agreement was built: those between the communities in Northern Ireland, those with the Republic of Ireland and those with the UK.

Chapter 15, by Giada Lagana, examines in detail one aspect of the EU contribution to the peace process in Ireland. The Interreg programme offers special funding for cross-border regions within the EU and forms part of the overall framework of funding for Ireland – North and South – which has supported the peace process. She suggests that although the programme has been very successful in some other situations and still offers considerable opportunities in the Irish context, nonetheless the record to date shows only limited benefits, due mostly to the highly centralised nature of the UK and Irish states and to rivalry among agencies on both sides of the border.

Finally, in Chapter 16, Michael Holmes and Kathryn Simpson examine the possible future relationship of Ireland and the EU. For a long time, Ireland was seen as a pro-European country, one that had benefited from many EU policies and programmes. The analyses in this volume suggest that there is now a more questioning dimension to the relationship, but at the same time the broad outlook remains pro-European. In particular, Brexit has served to underline Ireland's commitment to, if not dependency on, the EU. However, there are several potential problems which could disrupt that commitment. Brexit has changed relations between the Republic and Northern Ireland, and between Ireland and Britain, in ways that are still far from known. The EU is also still changing, with emerging calls for deeper integration in some quarters. While Ireland is generally supportive of further integration, developments in areas such as defence cooperation and tax harmonisation would cause problems. Finally, the global situation is constantly evolving, and issues such as climate change, health security and deglobalisation could have a major impact on future Irish–EU relations.

Notes

1   See, for example, statements by European Commission President José Manuel Barroso (Barroso 2008), European Parliament President Jerzy Buzek (Buzek 2009), Labour Party leader Éamon Gilmore (Labour Party 2008), Fine Gael leader Enda Kenny (Fine Gael 2009) and Fianna Fáil leader Brian Cowen (Fianna Fáil 2009).

2 There are three other instances of territories leaving the EU or its precursor, the European Community: Algeria in 1962, Greenland in 1985 and Saint Barthélemy in 2012, but these had not been member states in their own right.

References

Barroso, J.M. (2008) 'At the heart of an open Europe: Ireland and the Treaty of Lisbon'. Speech to the National Forum on Europe, Dublin, 17 April. Available at: https://ec.europa.eu/commission/presscorner/detail/en/SPEECH_08_204 [accessed 10 February 2020].

BBC (2016) 'EU deal gives UK special status, says David Cameron'. BBC News, 20 February. Available at: www.bbc.com/news/uk-politics-35616768 [accessed 1 August 2020].

Buzek, J. (2009) 'Europe is back on track: the Lisbon Treaty good for Ireland – good for Europe'. European Parliament press release, 3 October. Available at: www.europarl.europa.eu/sides/getDoc.do?pubRef=-//EP//TEXT+IM-PRESS+20091003 IPR61802+0+DOC+XML+V0//EN&language=EN [accessed 10 February 2020].

Cusumano, E. (2019) 'Migrant rescue as organized hypocrisy: EU maritime missions offshore Libya between humanitarianism and border control'. *Conflict and Cooperation* 54(1): 3–24.

de Mars, S., C. Murray, A. O'Donoghue & B. Warwick (2018) *Bordering two unions: Northern Ireland and Brexit*. Bristol: Policy Press.

Department of Defence (2019) 'Over 10,000 people rescued in the Mediterranean by the Irish Naval Service'. Dublin: Department of Defence press release, 19 October. Available at: www.gov.ie/en/press-release/ff8436-over-10000-people-rescued-in-the-mediterranean-by-the-irish-naval-se/#:~:text=Paul%20Kehoe%2C%20 T.D.%2C%20today%20praised,humanitarian%20operation%20in%20May%20 2015 [accessed 1 August 2020].

Department of Foreign Affairs (2017) *Brexit: Ireland's priorities*. Dublin: Government Publications.

Department of Justice (2020) 'Irish refugee protection programme'. Dublin: Department of Justice and Equality. Available at: www.justice.ie/en/JELR/Pages/Irish_Refugee_Protection_Programme_(IRPP) [accessed 1 August 2020].

Dinan, D., N. Nugent & W.E. Paterson (eds) (2017) *The European Union in crisis*. Basingstoke: Palgrave Macmillan.

Electoral Commission (2016) *Results and turnout at the EU referendum*. Available at: www.electoralcommission.org.uk/who-we-are-and-what-we-do/elections-and-referendums/past-elections-and-referendums/eu-referendum/results-and-turn-out-eu-referendum [accessed 1 August 2020].

Fianna Fáil (2009) *Europe: we are better working together*, European election manifesto 2009. Dublin: Fianna Fáil. Available at: www.michaelpidgeon.com/manifestos/ [accessed 10 February 2020].

Fine Gael (2009) *Securing Ireland's future in Europe*. European Parliament manifesto 2009. Dublin: Fine Gael. Available at: www.michaelpidgeon.com/manifestos/ [accessed 10 February 2020].

Holmes, M. (2008) 'The referendum on the Treaty of Lisbon in the Republic of Ireland, 12 June 2008'. Sussex: EPERN Referendum Briefing Paper No. 16.

Available at: www.sussex.ac.uk/webteam/gateway/file.php?name=epern-ref-no16.
pdf&site=266 [accessed 14 June 2021].

IOM (2015) 'Irregular migrant, refugee arrivals in Europe top one million in 2015'.
Geneva: International Organisation for Migration press release, 22 December.
Available at: www.iom.int/news/irregular-migrant-refugee-arrivals-europe-top-
one-million-2015-iom [accessed 1 August 2020].

IOM (2020) *World migration report 2020*. Geneva: International Organisation for
Migration.

Labour Party (2008) 'Proud to be Irish: Yes to Europe'. *Labour Party blog*, 19 May.
Available at: www.labour.ie/news/blog/2008/05/19/proud-to-be-irish-yes-to-europe/
[accessed 10 February 2020].

Maass, A.-S. (2017) *EU–Russia relations, 1999–2015*. Abingdon and New York:
Routledge.

OECD (2020) 'Gross domestic product (GNP), 2008–2009'. Available at: https://
data.oecd.org/gdp/gross-domestic-product-gdp.htm [accessed 4 August 2020].

O'Toole, F. (2016) 'We should collect Apple's €13 billion and change Ireland'. *The
Irish Times*, 30 August. Available at: www.irishtimes.com/opinion/we-should-col-
lect-apple-s-13-billion-and-change-ireland-1.2773136 [accessed 1 August 2020].

Roche, W.K., P.J. O'Connell & A. Prothero (2017) 'Poster child or beautiful freak?
Austerity and recovery in Ireland' in W.K. Roche, P.J. O'Connell and A. Prothero
(eds) *Austerity and recovery in Ireland: Europe's poster child and the Great
Recession*, pp. 1–22. Oxford: Oxford University Press.

Rooduijn, M., S. Van Kessel, C. Froio, A. Pirro, S. De Lange, D. Halikiopoulou, P.
Lewis, C. Mudde & P. Taggart (2019) *The PopuList: an overview of populist, far
right, far left and Eurosceptic parties in Europe*. Available at: www.popu-list.org
[accessed 1 August 2020].

Thaler, P. (2020) *Shaping EU foreign policy towards Russia: improving coherence in
external relations*. Cheltenham: Edward Elgar Publishing.

VES (2016) *Improving the responses to the migration and refugee crisis in Europe*.
Lisbon: Vision Europe Summit.

Vollaard, H. (2018) *European disintegration: a search for explanations*. Basingstoke:
Palgrave Macmillan.

Webber, D. (2019) *European disintegration? The politics of crisis in the European
Union*. Basingstoke: Red Globe Macmillan.

2

The global island: Ireland in a changed Union

Ben Tonra

Introduction

At a moment when Europe faces serious security threats, grapples with the departure of the UK and deals with its own internal political challenges, Ireland faces a fundamental realignment of its foreign, security and defence policies. This chapter will assess the implications of Europe's challenges for Irish foreign, security and defence policy. It will evaluate whether Ireland's threat assessment differs from that of its European partners. It assesses the potential scope for deeper Irish engagement in collective European security and defence, and whether this can respect a long-standing tradition of non-membership of military alliances. Consideration will also be given to the larger reorientation of Irish foreign policy post-Brexit: an expansion in Ireland's global diplomatic footprint, new bilateral and multilateral relationships within the EU and, potentially, greater demands for solidarity in these new and reinforced European partnerships.

The 2016 decision of the UK electorate to withdraw from the EU posed especially significant and near existential challenges to the Irish state across the public policy spectrum, and none greater than in the area of foreign, security and defence policy. Moreover, Ireland's experience of the 2008 economic crash, associated new EU economic governance regimes and the political challenges to the very nature of the EU project, has given rise to a range of policy challenges facing the Irish state.

Brexit itself initiated something of a debate on Ireland's strategic position vis-à-vis the UK and EU26. While only a few commentators (Bassett 2017; Kinsella 2016; McGee 2016; Munchau 2016) suggested that Ireland should follow the UK out of the EU, Ireland's relationships with the other 26 EU member states became ever more significant. For some, the pervasive bilateral links between the UK and Ireland, and most especially concerns surrounding the border between Northern Ireland and Ireland, necessitated a special deal for Ireland from the EU. Such a special deal might encompass not only further differentiation on free movement of persons (already facil-itated by Ireland's non-Schengen[1] status) but also new exceptions made to EU customs and regulatory requirements for the freest possible movement of goods across the intra-Irish border. In the end it was judged that an approach built upon differentiation from the EU26 in an attempt to bridge the gulf between the UK and EU26 was both unrealistic and undesirable. Instead, the Irish Government, with substantial popular support (Smyth 2018), chose to strengthen its European commitment with support from the EU26 and to insist that the UK respect the principle of no return to the border of the past on the island of Ireland.

The roots of Irish foreign and defence policy in Europe

Ireland had joined the European Communities at the close of what has been termed a 'golden age' in Irish foreign policy (O'Driscoll 2012). Ireland joined the UN in 1955 as part of a Cold War package deal between East and West, and Irish diplomats had swiftly carved out a distinctive role that was firmly Western in values and orientation but without the political or diplo-matic baggage of military alignment to NATO (Dorr 2002). This somewhat anomalous status provided Irish ministers and diplomats with some room for manoeuvre on the world stage and led to distinctive Irish positions on decolonisation, apartheid, the representation of China on the UN Security Council and on disarmament. As an illustrative example, the 1958 "Irish resolution" on disarmament ultimately led to the negotiation of the Nuclear Non-Proliferation Treaty.

It is difficult to say whether this independent-minded diplomacy would have survived in a UN which was becoming substantially less Western and less Northern in its political complexion. It is, however, certainly true to say that Irish political leaders insisted that Irish neutrality would be no barrier to Ireland's full commitment to economic and political integration in Europe (Maher 1986). Domestically, however, the argument was made rather differently. While the Labour Party and others of the political Left warned of the foreign policy implications of European integration, and the dangers this might ultimately pose for Ireland's military neutrality, propo-nents of membership insisted that the treaties themselves included nothing that could constrain foreign policy and certainly nothing that impinged on military neutrality.

Over the course of subsequent decades and the development of closer foreign policy cooperation,[2] Ireland's position was problematic, both domes-tically and within Europe. Domestically, every development of EU foreign and security policy has been contested. It was the sole ground of success in a constitutional challenge to Ireland's ratification of the Single European Act in 1986. This then necessitated a referendum to ratify that treaty and established the political precondition that has since governed ratification of all subsequent EU treaty changes by the Irish state. In all subsequent Irish referendums on major EU treaty changes, the allegation that the EU was on the path to the creation of a "European army" has been a potent weapon for No campaigners and a near-toxic issue for Yes campaigners (Garry et al. 2005; O'Brennan 2009; O'Mahony 2009; Sinnott et al. 2009).

The success of the "European army" argument led directly to the introduction of specific EU treaty protocols and formal EU Council Decisions defining the parameters of Irish engagement in European defence cooperation (see European Council 2002). With the 2002 Nice Treaty referendum, Article 29.4.9 of the Irish Constitution was formally amended to provide that 'The State shall not adopt a decision taken by the European Council to establish a common defence pursuant to Article 1.2 of the Treaty referred to in subsection 7 of this section where that common defence would include the State' (Bunreacht na hÉireann 1937, as amended 2015). This represents a definitive constitutional barrier to Irish participation in an EU common defence which can only be surmounted by a further referendum decision.

Within Europe, Ireland's anomalous position has been visible but not especially germane to wider EU debates on foreign, security and defence cooperation, except in so far as it has contributed to delays to treaty change. It has, in fact, been largely obscured by deeper European debates between Atlanticists and Europeanists. In such a universe, Irish diplomats have striven mightily to ensure that formal texts and treaty provisions always make provision for Irish military neutrality, even when such references are opaque and complex. This has led to several circumlocutions with a very unique Irish stamp, such as the distinction made in the Single European Act between discussions of the political and economic aspects of security (which were allowed) and the discussion of security itself (which was not), and the EU's nascent common defence policy which 'shall not prejudice the specific character of the security and defence policy of certain member states' (CVCE 2012) and was designed, inter alia, to encompass Ireland's military neutrality.

While Ireland's position was anomalous throughout the Cold War, the accession of states such as Austria, Finland and Sweden in 1995 and later Cyprus and Malta in 2004 underpinned the variegated nature of EU member states' own foreign and defence policies. Within this broader universe, Irish policy makers worked hard to present Ireland as a constructive and active partner on a number of key issues such as development cooperation, international justice and human rights, and has worked to make a substantive contribution to CSDP missions and operations.

A very high political premium is also placed domestically on Ireland's contributions to international security through its aforementioned engagement with peacekeeping and other overseas military operations, including those of the EU through the CSDP. Over the last twenty years hundreds of Irish troops have served across thousands of individual deployments.[3] These contributions, which (under Irish legislation) must be formally validated by UN authorisation, are highly prized and a point of national pride (Murphy 2012). To that end, cooperation in EU defence is most often validated as either another pathway (alongside traditional UN operations) to making that contribution and/or a means by which the Irish military can develop the training and experience necessary to make its peacekeeping contributions more effective. While Irish military engagement with EU security and defence structures is rarely promoted publicly, positive public attention has been derived from high-profile Irish engagement with selected EU military operations, such as those commanded by Irish officers (for example, EUFOR Chad and EUTM Somalia) and those with well-defined humanitarian impetus such as Operation Sophia (see, for example, Tonra 2018).

Within larger debates on the development of European security and defence cooperation per se, most Irish public discourse continues to be driven by concerns surrounding the protection of neutrality. As noted, Ireland's benign geo-strategic position allows for a debate on defence almost entirely divorced from considerations of national territorial defence (Jesse 2006; Tonra 2012). There are also a number of foreign policy issues on which Ireland consciously maintains a distinctive position even occasionally at odds with its EU partners, such as on the Middle East, on human rights and with respect to nuclear disarmament. On the issue of Israel/Palestine, Irish governments have adopted a supportive position with respect to the establishment of a Palestinian state and the status of the Occupied Territories, insisting for example that goods produced in these latter areas and imported to the EU be clearly labelled as such. On nuclear disarmament, Ireland continues to work with non-EU partners in advocating outlawing nuclear weapons, even as most of Ireland's EU partners rely on nuclear weapons and its associated strategy for their own defence.

Irish security and defence policy has traditionally been driven by three interconnected policy goals: territorial defence, aid to the civil power and international security operations. With Ireland's benign contemporary geo-strategic location, territorial defence has not been a significant issue since the end of the Second World War. While territorial defence is described as 'a fundamental security requirement and responsibility' in the 2015 government White Paper on defence (Government of Ireland 2015), it also clearly acknowledges that the probability of a conventional military attack on Ireland's territory is low.

New European challenges and Irish responses

There is little doubt that Europe's security environment has worsened over the last fifteen years. When Javier Solana drafted the EU's first security strategy statement in 2003, he could confidently declare that 'Europe has never been so prosperous, so secure or so free' (Council of the European Union 2003). Today, such a statement would ring hollow. In her equivalent 2016 Global Strategy, Federica Mogherini acknowledged that 'our Union is under threat' (EEAS 2016), beset from the outside but also weakened from within by the rise of far-right and illiberal forces. The Russian Federation's invasion, occupation and annexation of parts of Ukraine violated Europe's post war security order. The EU now faces arcs of geopolitical instability to the east and to the south. These are products of economic, demographic and environmental dislocations, but they are also the immediate result of unresolved security disputes and civil conflicts. At a time of such existential threats, it is noteworthy too that the commitment of Europe's traditional anchor for security and defence – the United States – has also come into question.

An "America First" foreign policy under Donald Trump's presidency witnessed both confused messaging from Washington and substantive policy challenges on Iran, climate change, trade and even the relevance of NATO itself. This re-ignited debates in the United States on burden-sharing within NATO (the United States provides upwards of 70 to 75% of the alliance's military capacity – see NATO 2019) and on the strategic autonomy of the European side of the alliance. Some European member states such as Poland, Portugal and the Netherlands, prioritise cooperation with NATO. Others, such as France, Spain and Italy, increasingly talk about the need to focus on reducing dependence on the United States for its defence. To all of this must be added the withdrawal of the UK from the EU. While estimates vary, this has reduced the collective security and defence capacity of the EU by upwards of 20% in purely material terms, while arguably diminishing it even further in political and strategic terms (Giegerich & Mölling 2018).

From 2018, however, developments in EU defence accelerated rapidly. French President Emmanuel Macron called for 'a common intervention force, a common defence budget and a common doctrine for action' in Europe (Macron 2017). This led directly to the creation of the nine-member European Intervention Initiative, designed to develop a common European strategic culture through enhanced cooperation in intelligence, scenario-building and strategy development together with practical interaction in training and operations. Beginning with the Global Strategy and developed through the 2016 Implementation Plan on Security and Defence, the member states of the EU committed themselves to setting 'a new level of ambition for the EU's security and defence policy' (EEAS 2018). This encompassed shared defence planning and budgeting, a reinforced agenda for the European Defence Agency, a review of the EU Battlegroups and funding of EU military operations, the creation of a new Military Planning and Conduct Capability cell to undertake mission command and the launch of Permanent Structured Cooperation (PESCO) which by 2020 comprised forty-seven specific defence projects designed to strengthen EU cooperation and build defence capacities among subsets of member states which may then be shared more widely. Finally, the active engagement of the EU Commission in the defence industrial realm put billions of euros on the table to address industrial and strategic weaknesses.

All of the above gave rise to significant policy choices and issues for an Irish state which has been comfortable in terms of foreign policy cooperation, writ large, but ambivalent towards the principle of security and defence cooperation. For many years, as noted earlier, Ireland has sheltered its policy of non-membership of military alliances within the quiet corner of debates between Atlanticists (led by the UK) and Europeanists (led by France). Their brief armistice, secured at the 1999 Saint-Malo Anglo-French summit, allowed the EU to proceed down the road of an 'autonomous' defence capacity. Progress was slow and there were many serious reversals, but Ireland engaged in these debates, participated in significant military missions and even commanded one of the largest of such in Chad in 2008. However, that engagement was hesitant and was frequently contested in domestic political terms.

Irish attitudes to European foreign, security and defence cooperation might best be characterised alongside Churchill's famous dictum about the UK and Europe: 'we are with Europe, but not of it. We are linked, but not compromised. We are interested and associated, but not absorbed' (Urwin 2014: 74). There is no doubt that Ireland shares security interests with its EU partners: as a global centre for social media and data storage, dependent on critical IT and energy infrastructures, hosting the headquarters of some of the highest-profile multinational companies (MNCs), and having a history where terrorism has played a role. Despite this, there is a distance in geographic, strategic and psychological terms that generates negative Irish attitudes towards European foreign, security and defence policy. Such cooperation is still seen as a cost, even a penalty, of EU membership. It is a bill Ireland reluctantly pays in return for markets and the wider benefits of membership.

That position is now much harder to sustain for Irish policy makers. As the EU as a whole faces increasing geo-strategic uncertainty and a loss of confidence in its transatlantic alliance, how soon might it be before debates surrounding the EU's strategic "autonomy" become wrapped up in contemporary and very loose political talk of an "EU army"? In truth, such declarations amount to little or nothing in practical terms. There is no prospect of the creation of a federalised Europe of the sort that could raise and direct its own army. However, there is a wider debate about European ambitions to deepen defence cooperation and military integration. Brexit, and the UK's absence from these debates, makes these ambitions sharper. President Macron's European Intervention Initiative may be a surrogate for his own frustrations at the limited scale, scope and ambition of PESCO, but it certainly foreshadows debates of greater defence ambition. The UK's withdrawal from the EU leaves Ireland exposed on several fronts. Its hesitancy and ambivalence towards security and defence may no longer be sustainable – hard choices are coming into view.

Irish defence post-Brexit

Ireland's military capacity is modest with a total force complement set at approximately 9,000 personnel divided between three branches of the Permanent Defence Forces, the Army, Naval Service and Air Corps, and a small Reserve Defence Force of just over 1,500 personnel (Department of Defence 2015: 6). Ireland is at the bottom of the league in terms of defence spending, allocating just 0.34% of gross domestic product (GDP) to that end. This is the lowest defence spending of any of the EU27 member states and places Ireland at about 150th internationally (World Bank 2020). The paucity of defence spending is of course translated into an exceptionally limited military capacity. In the absence of any fighter, attack or transport aircraft, combat tanks, heavy artillery or any naval assets beyond some offshore patrol vessels, Ireland can be said to lack the minimum conventional combat capability necessary to provide for any territorial defence based on credible deterrence.

This level of capacity also precludes Ireland from exercising any meaningful air defence. To date this has been limited to the operation of a small ground-based air defence system to protect high-profile visits of foreign heads of state and dignitaries at national events and state visits. Uniquely in the EU, Ireland lacks the type of radar system necessary to track and identify aircraft in its airspace that do not use their transponders. Thus, in lieu of any meaningful national air defence capacity, Ireland has instead relied upon the strategic interests of NATO forces to defend their airspace. Ad hoc understandings with the UK's Royal Air Force were placed on a formal footing subsequent to the signature in January 2015 of a Memorandum of Understanding between the British and Irish governments on defence cooperation (Oireachtas 2015).

Over the course of thirty years of civil strife in Northern Ireland, the posture of the defence forces was centred on meeting the threat posed by paramilitary groups. Today the picture is starkly different. Following a wholesale restructuring of the defence forces in 2012, the army was reduced. But Brexit changes this. The direct threat is three-fold: organised crime and cross-border smuggling, a renewed paramilitary threat targeting any new border infra-structures, and what might be called the threat to constitutional security arising from a weakening of the peace process.

The very function of Brexit is to increase divergence between the UK and the EU. In whatever direction that divergence occurs, it creates opportunities for illicit profits. Long-established and deeply entrenched local criminal fam-ilies and gangs are ideally placed to quickly take advantage of new opportu-nities as they arise. If the incentive structure is strong enough, existing links between these "ordinary" criminals and paramilitaries and/or international criminal networks may also be strengthened. For the state's security services such developments cannot go unanswered. Ireland's legal obligations to enforce EU law, as well as the state's responsibility to protect the health and safety of its citizens and the integrity of its own tax base, will require those services to act. However, the moment civilian services are deployed, they become the object of potential threat from those criminal networks, entailing a policing and potential defence forces' response. The dangers for escalation are all too apparent.

The avoidance of what has been termed "border infrastructure" was the leitmotif of Irish Brexit debates. Such infrastructure – to varying degrees and in different compositions – is the norm for inter-state borders around the world. In the context of the Irish border, however, such infrastructure would have been immediately perceived by a significant minority as illegitimate. For those entrusted with law and security this posed a serious challenge with the chair of the Police Federation of Northern Ireland, Mark Lindsay, warn-ing that any plan to install customs posts or immigration controls on the island would be 'a propaganda gift' to by-then weakened and marginalised paramilitary groups and making the security services 'sitting ducks for the terrorists' (McDonald 2017).

The 1998 Agreement represents several decades of painstaking political and constitutional negotiations between two sovereign governments and the political parties representing two counterpoised national communities with the contribution of a wide swath of civil society actors across Northern Ireland (Department of Foreign Affairs 1998) The agreement itself is a care-fully balanced structure of three strands, each addressing a particular set of relationships: governance within Northern Ireland, an institutional struc-ture to address the North/South dimension of relationships, and then an East–West strand to address relationships between the governments in the British–Irish Council.

Two critical points here relate directly to Brexit. The first is that the agree-ment was constructed within the context of Ireland and the UK's membership of the EU. Only on this basis was it possible to assume that the demilitarisation of the border in Ireland – and the elimination of the associated security infrastructure (watch-towers, check points, road barriers security installations, etc.) could result in an "open" border on the island of Ireland. The preamble to the 1998 Agreement provided that it would 'develop still further the unique relationship between their peoples and the close co-operation between their countries as friendly neighbours and as partners in the European Union' (Department of Foreign Affairs 1998). Secondly, the Agreement was constructed on a key principle that:

> [t]he birth right of all the people of Northern Ireland to identify themselves and be accepted as Irish or British or both, as they may so choose and accordingly confirm[s] that their right to hold both British and Irish citizenship is accepted by both Governments and would not be affected by any future change in the status of Northern Ireland. (Department of Foreign Affairs 1998)

Brexit critically weakened both foundations. The basic premise of the Agreement was to establish a constitutional settlement which provided for equal recognition of two national communities within Northern Ireland whether Irish or British or both. That formulation was accompanied by an entire underpinning structure of human rights protections designed to copperfasten that principle in both law and practice. The associated human rights and equality provisions of the Agreement were designed to instil confidence from both national communities in the political institutions of the Agreement and thereby the associated constitutional settlement such that both could have confidence in the political process and understand that their legitimate national aspirations could be effectively pursued within the democratic political process. In that respect, EU law provided a critical framework sustaining those equality provisions, most especially in the realms of employment law and non-discrimination rights as enshrined in the EU Charter of Fundamental Rights.

A key element here was also that of citizenship. The Agreement acknowledges this, and the provision is of course central to addressing the core conflict over national identity which has been at the root of the centuries-old conflict on the island of Ireland and the continuing divisions in Northern Ireland itself.

Ireland's foreign policy reorientation

More broadly, beyond the bilateral issues of borders and security, Brexit has also forced a reconceptualisation of Ireland's overall foreign policy. While it would be wrong to describe Ireland as having relied upon the UK within the

EU, there is no doubt that in significant policy areas the two states shared comparable policy positions and priorities. In brief, this revolved around a preference for liberalised trade, limited economic regulation and tax sovereignty. Ireland here was not alone. In effect, the UK was at a core of a "liberal" economic coalition within the EU and while membership of that coalition ebbed and flowed according to issue and circumstance, the UK was at its fulcrum.

One study noted that not only was Ireland one of the UK's most assiduous correspondents on EU policy issues, but that the UK was, in turn, one of the "most responsive" to Irish Government approaches (ECFR 2018). This was based on a close correlation of shared interests across key economic and trade policy areas. Burnett (2018) also found that the UK was the only member state – large or small – that similarly placed Ireland among its top consultative partners. While Irish diplomats and officials placed much effort into contacting and garnering support from other like-minded states such as Germany and the Netherlands in many of the same issue areas, these partners were not similarly notable for their reciprocal interest in contacting their Irish counterparts for views or support.

Thus, Brexit required something of a reassessment of Irish diplomacy within the EU. In February 2018, for example, Ireland joined finance ministers from Denmark, Estonia, Finland, Latvia, Lithuania, the Netherlands and Sweden in signing a two-page declaration in which their 'shared views and values' (Valtiovarainministeriö 2018) towards a new European architecture on economic governance and the future of the single currency were outlined. This mini coalition soon came to be known as the New Hanseatic League.

This League was formed to fill the prospective vacuum to be left by the UK in promoting a more liberal, decentralised, free-trading conception of the EU and a counterweight to the more dirigiste tendencies of France and its allies. It quickly became something of a political shorthand to describe this collection of fiscally conservative northern European states. The irony of Ireland joining such a coalition so soon after its 2013 emergence from the Troika conditions is not lost, but it does reflect Ireland's policy priorities behind the deepening and extension of the European single market and the economic governance underpinning the single currency. It is also notable that at the group's core is a set of countries – most notably Sweden and Denmark – with powerful social democratic parties and a tradition of high taxation and public spending. The scope for extending the remit of this group has also been broached on the Irish side. Then Minister for Foreign Affairs Simon Coveney went so far as to suggest in 2018 that the same grouping might find common cause across key foreign policy issues such as the promotion of human rights, the Middle East peace process and relations with Africa (Coveney 2018a).

While this new diplomacy of the smaller member states captured some political attention at home and abroad, less visible but at least equally significant was Ireland's retooling of its relationships with the EU's big beasts, Germany and France. With Germany, the Berlin embassy was expanded and a new consulate was opened in Frankfurt in 2019 (Burnett 2018). Coveney declared that 'Germany is now an indispensable partner for Ireland' (Coveney 2018b) and German diplomatic support throughout the Brexit negotiations was critical and visible. Chancellor Angela Merkel stated that 'Ireland may rely on us and it is unconditional – that is a matter of fact' (Murray 2018). Ireland featured in Germany's own post-Brexit diplomatic review and was identified as one of the first EU member states with which to pursue stronger engagement through the "Like Minded Initiative" (Government of Germany 2018).

France is also a key Irish priority. In 2019, the Department of Foreign Affairs and Trade published a dedicated strategy towards France (DFAT 2019). This reviewed the scope and scale of bilateral relations and set out an ambitious programme to deepen and strengthen those ties. This encompassed a new focus on public diplomacy and more structured political contacts with both executive and legislative actors. It prioritised agreement and funding for an interconnector to link the Irish and continental electricity grid, which was ultimately secured later that same year. The Irish side also made a high-profile declaration of strengthened ties by formally joining the Organisation Internationale de la Francophonie as an observer member. The Minister of State for European Affairs, Helen McEntee, explained in 2018 that Irish accession was part of its wider foreign policy strategy to double the size of Ireland's global footprint by 2025 (DFAT 2018).

That doubling of Ireland's global footprint was initially made by Taoiseach Leo Varadkar in 2017 and came to fruition in 2018 as the "Global Ireland" programme (Government of Ireland 2018). The headline targets were a substantial expansion of Ireland's diplomatic network and a (renewed) pledge to achieve the UN target of donating 0.7% of gross national income to development projects within twelve years. The programme was framed as part of Ireland's response to Brexit, ensuring that 'Ireland is better positioned to build the alliances necessary to advance its interests and defend its positions in a post-Brexit EU, while also helping to secure our deep and positive relationship with the UK and its constituent parts into the future' (Government of Ireland 2018). This entailed the aforementioned strengthening of key bilateral and mini-lateral relationships within the EU, a reinforced focus on bilateral relations with the UK as well as a wider expansion of Ireland's global reach.

As regards the UK, the plan entailed additional resources to Ireland's embassy in London with an expansion of Irish government agencies in

London, Manchester and Glasgow and the reopening of its consulate in Cardiff. An additional consulate in the north of England was also proposed.

Globally, the plan entailed a significant diplomatic expansion with embassies opened in Wellington, Bogotá, Amman and Santiago de Chile, and new Consulates General in Los Angeles, Vancouver, Mumbai and Cardiff. This expansion, however, started from a low base. At the last review of the network in 2008 Ireland had just seventy-six overseas missions – compared with 121 Danish embassies and consulates and 151 Dutch equivalents. A campaign was also launched in July 2018 to secure a seat on the UN Security Council, which was successfully achieved in June 2020. This campaign was designed to place Ireland 'at the heart of UN decision-making on international peace, security and development' (IGNS 2018). Development was a key part of the overall Global Ireland programme. In 2019, the government published a new development aid strategy which repeated a commitment to delivering 0.7% of GNI to Official Development Assistance by 2030 (Irish Aid 2019). This target – long declared but not approached – had been abandoned in practice following the 2008 economic collapse. The government also underlined a commitment to join the African Development Bank.

A significant – if lesser profiled – aspect of the Global Ireland project was its economic and trade promotion. Herein the Irish state sought to better mobilise its agencies in pursuit of investment, trade and other economic opportunities. The Irish economy potentially faces major disruption to its substantial trading links to Great Britain (the economic and trading relationship with Northern Ireland being governed separately, see Kinsella, Chapter 11, this volume). Thus, the agency dedicated to attracting inward investment, IDA Ireland, opened a new office in Toronto and reconfigured its Frankfurt headquarters with a view to doubling growth in investments from non-US markets. Similarly, the trade promotion agency, Enterprise Ireland, opened new offices in Seattle and Manchester, hoping to double Eurozone exports by its client companies and thereby reducing the proportion of those client exports to the UK. Agencies for food export and tourism were also resourced to pursue new market opportunities, most especially in Africa, Asia and the Far East. To that end, the programme also promised a new Asia Pacific strategy to raise the state's profile and better pursue its interests in the wider Pacific region.

Conclusions

Brexit posed real and substantial challenges to the Irish state. It placed bilateral Ireland–UK relations and the 1998 Agreement under severe strain, it created new political dynamics within the EU at just the point when the EU itself was facing existential challenges from within and without, and it prompted a wider re-evaluation of Ireland's place in the global commons.

The most formidable challenges were to bilateral Ireland–UK relations, North–South relations on the island and inter-community relations within Northern Ireland. By the very nature and logic of Brexit, those challenges could only ever be mitigated and could never be eliminated. The negotiation of the Withdrawal Agreement and the deal on the EU–UK Trade and Cooperation Agreement sets out a future economic and trading relationship between the UK (in effect Great Britain) and the EU but leaves a difficult legacy and ongoing complications. While the direct defence/security implications of Brexit were mitigated by the terms of the Withdrawal Agreement, the political/diplomatic challenges were arguably heightened. Significant time, attention and political capital will have to be devoted in the coming years to the amelioration of these political tensions – most especially within Northern Ireland and on a North–South basis. This, of course, cannot even begin to factor in the future constitutional evolution which may yet flow from Brexit – on either of the neighbouring islands.

Of less immediate salience but perhaps an even greater longer-term challenge is that facing Irish foreign policy within Europe. Two aspects are of particular import: one structural and one tactical. The structural issue is the internal political dynamic occasioned by Brexit, linked with other internal political challenges to the wider political project of Europe. Ireland firmly nailed its colours to the mast in this respect with a deliberate and profound rededication of the state to its EU membership, based on unparalleled public support (see Simpson, Chapter 8, this volume). Ireland retooled its diplomatic infrastructure and reinforced key bilateral relationships within the EU. This structural shift, however, did not deal with a significant tactical challenge. The EU26 offered extraordinary support for Irish interests throughout the negotiations leading to the Brexit Withdrawal Agreement. While no explicit quid pro quo existed, there is no doubt that there may be an implied expectation that Ireland might show greater solidarity on issues where Ireland has been something of an outlier in the past. Whether this is on budgetary transfers, taxation issues, defence or regulation of the digital economy, Irish ministers, officials and diplomats will need to invest heavily in these strengthened relationships and move carefully in the construction of new policy coalitions absent the UK.

Finally, it would be wrong to ascribe the entirety of the changes that have been outlined above to the single variable of Brexit. Ireland has a long history of active and often principled global engagement. Certainly, Brexit upset the chess broad and rearranged the pieces with which Irish diplomats have traditionally played, but those very same diplomats can still rely on well-established strategies and principles which can be applied in this new context. As a small, globalised and open polity and economy there are fundamental principles which still underpin Ireland's global interests and values: reliance on the force of law over the law of force, dedication to multilateralism and the institutions of global governance, and a determination to sustain and defend universal human rights. What we can see from the reorientation of Irish foreign, security and defence policy discussed here gives witness to the fact that these continue to be the lodestars of Ireland's diplomatic firmament.

Notes

1 The 1985 Schengen Agreement and 1990 Schengen Convention created an open travel agreement among selected EU and other European states. Ireland did not join because of its pre-existing open travel agreement with the UK.
2 This began with the EPC in 1970, then the CFSP in 1993, and finally the CSDP, which dates back to 1999.
3 In international security operations in Europe (Kosovo), the Middle East (Iraq, Israel, Jordan, Kuwait, Lebanon and Syria), Africa (Central African Republic, Chad, Congo, Eritrea, Ethiopia, Ivory Coast, Liberia, Mali, Somalia and Uganda) and in the Asia-Pacific region (Afghanistan and East Timor).

References

Bassett, R. (2017) 'After Brexit: will Ireland be next to exit?' *Policy Exchange* 3 July. Available at: https://policyexchange.org.uk/publication/after-brexit-will-ireland-be-next-to-exit/ [accessed 16 June 2021].

Burnett, A. (2018) '"Our gallant allies in Europe" Irish diplomacy in a post-Brexit EU?' Dublin: Institute for International and European Affairs. Available at: www.iiea.com/wp-content/uploads/2019/06/Our-Gallant-Allies-in-Europe.pdf [accessed 7 June 2020].

Council of the European Union (2003) 'A secure Europe in a better world: European security strategy'. Council document 15895/03 PESC 787, 8 December. Available at: http://data.consilium.europa.eu/doc/document/ST-15895-2003-INIT/en/pdf [accessed 7 May 2020].

Coveney, S. (2018a) 'A shared agenda: sustaining the Good Friday Agreement in the context of Brexit'. Speech by Tánaiste and Minister for Foreign Affairs and Trade, Simon Coveney TD, Sophiahof, the Hague, 11 April. Available at: www.dfa.ie/news-and-media/speeches/speeches-archive/2018/april/tanaiste-speech-good-friday-agreement-brexit/ [accessed 7 July 2020].

Coveney, S. (2018b) 'Ireland, Germany and Europe: shaping the EU post-Brexit'. Berlin: Walter Hallstein-Institut für Europäisches Verfassungsrecht, 13 June 2018.

CVCE (2012) *EU Treaty – Article J4 (Maastricht, 7 February 1992)*. Luxembourg: Centre virtuel de la connaisance sur l'Europe. Available at: www.cvce.eu/content/

publication/2009/11/18/c2b77dcb-d037-4e25-8abe-38412430d481/publish-able_en.pdf [accessed 10 September 2020].

Department of Defence (2015) *White Paper on defence*. Available at: https://assets. gov.ie/21963/f1e7723dd1764a4281692f3f7cb96966.pdf [accessed 10 September 2020].

Department of Foreign Affairs (1998) *The Agreement (The Belfast Agreement/The Good Friday Agreement)*. Available at: www.dfa.ie/media/dfa/alldfawebsiteme-dia/ourrolesandpolicies/northernireland/good-friday-agreement.pdf [accessed 16 June 2021].

DFAT (2018) 'Ireland granted Observer Status at the Organisation Internationale de la Francophonie'. Available at: www.dfa.ie/news-and-media/press-releases/ press-release-archive/2018/october/ireland-granted-observer-status-at-the-organ-isation-internationale-de-la-francophonie.php [accessed 16 June 2021].

DFAT (2019) 'Global Ireland: Ireland's strategy for France 2019–2025 – "Together in spirit and action"'. Available at: www.dfa.ie/media/dfa/publications/Depart-ment-of-Foreign-Affairs-and-Trade---Global-Ireland---Ireland-Strategy-for-France-2019-2025.pdf [accessed 16 June 2021].

Dorr, N. (2002) 'Ireland at the United Nations' in B. Tonra & E. Ward (eds) *Ireland in international affairs: interests, institutions and identities*, pp. 104–128. Dublin: Institute of Public Administration.

ECFR (2018) *The EU coalition explorer*. London: European Council for Foreign Relations. Available at: www.ecfr.eu/eucoalitionexplorer [accessed 16 June 2021].

EEAS (2016) *Shared vision, common action: a stronger Europe, a global strategy for the European Union's foreign and security policy*. Available at: http://eeas. europa.eu/archives/docs/top_stories/pdf/eugs_review_web.pdf [accessed 7 June 2020].

EEAS (2018) 'Implementation plan on security and defence fact sheet'. Available at: https://eeas.europa.eu/sites/eeas/files/implementation_plan_on_security_and_ defence_02-03-2018.pdf [accessed 30 May 2020].

European Council (2002) 'Presidency Conclusions: Seville European Council 21 and 22 June 2002'. Available at: https://ec.europa.eu/commission/presscorner/detail/ en/DOC_02_13 [accessed 24 June 2020].

Garry, J., M. Marsh & R. Sinnott (2005) '"Second-order" versus "issue-voting" effects in EU referendums: evidence from the Irish Nice Treaty referendums'. *European Union Politics* 6(2): 201–221.

Giegerich, B. & C. Mölling (2018) *The United Kingdom's contribution to European security and defence*. London: International Institute for Strategic Studies, Febru-ary 2018.

Government of Germany (2018) 'Germany-Ireland joint plan of action strengthens cooperation'. Available at: www.auswaertiges-amt.de/en/aussenpolitik/laenderin-formationen/irland-node/deutsch-irischer-aktionsplan/2165914 [accessed 1 August 2020].

Government of Ireland (2015) *White Paper on Defence*. Available at: https:// assets.gov.ie/21963/f1e7723dd1764a4281692f3f7cb96966.pdf [accessed 14 June 2021].

Government of Ireland (2018) *Global Ireland: Ireland's global footprint to 2025*. Available at: https://merrionstreet.ie/MerrionStreet/en/ImageLibrary/20180612_ Global_Ireland.pdf [accessed 16 June 2021].

IGNS (2018) 'Taoiseach and Tánaiste launch Ireland's UN Security Council campaign'. *Irish Government News Service*, 2 July. Available at: https://merrionstreet.ie/en/

News-Room/News/Taoiseach_and_Tanaiste_travel_to_New_York_to_launch_Ire-
land%E2%80%99s_UN_Security_Council_campaign.html [accessed 20 September
2020].

Irish Aid (2019) *A better world: Ireland's policy for international development.*
Available at: www.irishaid.ie/media/irishaid/aboutus/abetterworldirelandspolicy-
forinternationaldevelopment/A-Better-World-Irelands-Policy-for-International-
Development.pdf [accessed 20 September 2020].

Jesse, N.G. (2006) 'Choosing to go it alone: Irish neutrality in theoretical and comparative perspective'. *International Political Science Review* 27(1): 7–28.

Kinsella, R. (2016) 'Why Ireland should consider Irexit'. *The Irish Times*, 20 August.
Available at: www.irishtimes.com/opinion/why-ireland-should-seriously-consider-
irexit-1.3202154 [accessed 12 June 2020].

Macron, E. (2017) 'Initiative for Europe'. Speech by M. Emmanuel Macron, President of the French Republic, 26 September. Available at: www.diplomatie.gouv.fr/
IMG/pdf/english_version_transcript_-_initiative_for_europe_-_speech_by_the_
president_of_the_french_republic_cle8de628.pdf [accessed 7 July 2020].

Maher, D.J. (1986) *The tortuous path: the course of Ireland's entry into the EEC,
1948–73.* Dublin: Institute of Public Administration.

McDonald, H. (2017) 'Brexit border "would make sitting ducks of Northern Ireland
police"'. *Guardian*, 15 January. Available at: www.theguardian.com/uk-
news/2017/jan/15/brexit-border-would-make-sitting-ducks-of-northern-ireland-
police [accessed 20 September 2020].

McGee, H. (2016) 'Eirexit: could Ireland follow Britain out of the EU?' *The Irish
Times*, 12 November. Available at: www.irishtimes.com/news/politics/eirexit-
could-ireland-follow-britain-out-of-the-eu-1.2864539 [accessed 12 July 2020].

Munchau, W. (2016) 'Ireland may have to consider leaving EU'. *The Irish Times*,
10 October. Available at: www.irishtimes.com/business/economy/wolfgang-
m%C3%BCnchau-ireland-may-have-to-consider-leaving-eu-1.2823535
[accessed 12 August 2020].

Murphy, R. (2012) 'International security and United Nations peacekeeping: the
Irish experience', in M. Kennedy, B. Tonra, J. Doyle & N. Dorr (eds) *Irish foreign
policy*, pp. 170–184. Dublin: Gill and Macmillan.

Murray, S. (2018) 'Merkel pledges "unconditional" support to Ireland in talks'. *Irish
Independent*, 21 March. Available at: www.independent.ie/business/brexit/
merkel-pledges-unconditional-support-to-ireland-in-talks-36726778.html
[accessed 12 May 2020].

NATO (2019) 'Defence expenditure of NATO countries, 2012–2019'. NATO press
release, 25 June. Available at: www.nato.int/nato_static_fl2014/assets/pdf/
pdf_2019_06/20190625_PR2019–069-EN.pdf [accessed 20 September 2020].

O'Brennan, J. (2009) 'Ireland says No (again): the 12 June 2008 referendum on the
Lisbon Treaty'. *Parliamentary Affairs* 62(2): 258–277.

O'Driscoll, M. (2012) 'Multilateralism: from "Plato's cave" to the European Community, 1945–73', in M. Kennedy, B. Tonra, J. Doyle & N. Dorr (eds) *Irish foreign
policy*, pp. 36–53, Dublin: Gill and Macmillan.

Oireachtas (2015) 'Memorandum of understanding between the Ministry of Defence of
the United Kingdom of Great Britain and Northern Ireland and the Department of
Defence Ireland on the enhancement of bilateral engagement on certain aspects
of defence and security cooperation'. Available at: https://ptfs-oireachtas.s3.
amazonaws.com/DriveH/AWData/Library3/DEFMemorandum_of_
Understanding_between_the_UK_and_Ireland_on_the_enhancement_of_bilateral_

engagement_on_certain_aspects_of_defence_and_security_co-operation 19012015_174233.pdf [accessed 20 September 2020].

O'Mahony, J (2009) 'Ireland's EU referendum experience'. *Irish Political Studies* 24(4): 429–446.

Sinnott, R., J.A. Elkink, K. O'Rourke & J. McBride (2009) *Attitudes and behaviour in the referendum on the Treaty of Lisbon.* Report for the Irish Department of Foreign Affairs, University College Dublin.

Smyth, P. (2018) 'More than 90% of Irish people want to stay in the EU, poll reveals'. *The Irish Times*, 8 May. Available at: www.irishtimes.com/news/politics/more-than-90-of-irish-people-want-to-stay-in-eu-poll-reveals-1.3488112 [accessed 7 June 2020].

Tonra, B. (2012) 'Security, defence and neutrality: the Irish dilemma', in M. Kennedy, B. Tonra, J. Doyle & N. Dorr (eds) *Irish foreign policy*, pp. 222–242. Dublin: Gill and Macmillan.

Tonra, B. (2018) *The (in)justices of peacekeeping: EUFOR Tchad/RCA.* GLOBUS Research Paper 3.

Urwin, D.W. (2014) *A political history of Western Europe since 1945.* Abingdon: Routledge.

Valtiovarainministeriö (2018) 'Finance ministers from Denmark, Estonia, Finland, Ireland, Latvia, Lithuania, the Netherlands and Sweden underline their shared views and values in the discussion on the architecture of the EMU'. Finnish Finance Ministry press release. Available at: https://vm.fi/documents/10623/6305483/Position+EMU+Denmark+Estonia+Finland+Ireland+Latvia+Lithuania+the+Netherlands+and+Sweden.pdf [accessed 20 September 2020].

World Bank (2020) 'Military expenditure (% of GDP)'. Available at: https://data.worldbank.org/indicator/MS.MIL.XPND.GD.ZS [accessed 20 September 2020].

3

A turbulent commitment: economic relations between Ireland and the EU between the crash and Brexit

*Patrick Gallagher, Fergal Rhatigan
and Seán Ó Riain*

Introduction

In 2010, Michel Barnier started his term as European Commissioner for Internal Market and Services, focusing in particular on the banking issues that had been at the core of Ireland's difficulties with Europe in the preceding years. Those difficult relationships continued through an era of austerity and the passing of the Fiscal Treaty in 2012 that committed member states to fiscally conservative policies. Meanwhile, Boris Johnson was in the middle of his term as elected Mayor of London, mixing policy with political novelty act in what remained a relatively marginal role in national and international politics.

In July 2019, Johnson was elected by the Conservative Party membership as the new Tory party leader and, therefore, Prime Minister of the UK. He immediately strengthened his public commitment to Brexit by 31 October 2019. Meanwhile, Barnier had become a popular figure in Ireland with regular photographs with Taoiseach Leo Varadkar and Tánaiste Simon Coveney designed to indicate that Ireland and the other EU member states stood united in the face of the threat of Brexit – and the return of a "hard border" on the island, a border that would divide the island of Ireland in parts inside and outside the EU.

How, in these nine short but tumultuous years, did Ireland's relationship with the EU shift so dramatically? How did the perception in 2010 that the EU was part of an existential threat to the viability of the Irish economy switch to a long-term commitment to integration with the EU, chosen in the face of the almost certainty of a diminished relationship with the UK and potential threats to peace on the island?

These questions are deeply intertwined with the economic ties between Ireland and three key pillars of the international economic order: the UK, a fading global power with deep ties to Ireland; the United States, a vital source of foreign investment; and the EU, with which Ireland has become ever more closely integrated. In addition, Ireland's relations with the United States and the UK were also deeply intertwined with its economic ties to Europe – primarily, in the case of the United States, as a destination market for mobile investment and, in the case of the UK, a new institutional context for historical compromises around trade and migration.

This chapter examines this process over the decade following the financial crash. It begins by outlining the multiple international ties that underpin Ireland's economy but that are often also sources of volatility. It then tells the story of the decade through the varying prominence of each of those sets of ties: the negotiation of the financial crisis and fiscal austerity with the EU from 2008 to 2012; the emergence of economic and employment growth through the middle of the decade, relying heavily on US investment seeking a base with the EU market; and the shock of the UK vote for Brexit in 2016, which intertwined political and economic dynamics more closely than ever and raised significant existential questions regarding Ireland's relationship to the EU.

The EU and Ireland's multiple interface periphery

Ireland occupies a distinctive place in the history of the European regional economy. If considered as a "European small open economy" it is distinctive in being the only such economy to miss out on the "Golden Age" of welfare capitalism in the decades after the Second World War (at least among the north-western European societies). If considered as a peripheral economy within Europe, it was the earliest such economy to join the EU, to be followed later by the Mediterranean and Eastern European societies. In both cases, the relationship with the UK was crucial, with Ireland entering the European Economic Community (EEC) with the UK in 1973 and having a long-standing colonial and peripheral relation with the British economy.

Ireland's economic relationship with the EU must therefore be considered in the context of this ambiguous history and complex relations. Indeed, over the past fifty years, Ireland has shifted from a "simple periphery" of the UK to a "multiple interface periphery" located between the UK, the United States and Europe (Ruane 2010). This multiplicity of connections allowed the Irish state and political economy some "strategic flexibility" and was a crucial element in the private and public investment during the 1990s boom. However, it also left Ireland vulnerable to additional levels of economic volatility (Ruane 2018).

At the national level, Ireland's engagement with the international economy was historically primarily through its relationship with Great Britain, both as colony and as a post-colonial economy dominated by unequal exchange with the UK. The historic conflict was with Britain, which was itself on the periphery of the European historical compromise and only weakly committed to the European project. Compared to the continental core, Ireland was a late developing but also liberal political economy. This too was linked to a history as part of the British Empire – the liberal political economies of the advanced capitalist world are largely those which fell under its influence.

However, the Irish economy was closely tied to a declining hegemonic global power. Where US and UK national wealth was almost the same entering the Second World War the United States exited the war with a much higher GDP per capita and the gap between the United States and the UK grew significantly over the following fifty years. Perhaps not surprisingly then, Ireland sought to turn outwards towards the international economy more broadly. This policy shift is typically dated to the late 1950s when Ireland apparently began its pursuit of "industrialisation by invitation", although in practice the politics of this shift were located well before in the 1940s (Ó Riain 2014). Over time, the Irish economy became increasingly Americanised. The first significant US investment came in 1971 when Digital Equipment Corporation set up a factory in Galway, but was firmly consolidated in the "Celtic Tiger" boom of the 1990s when US investment increased as UK and European industrial investment weakened. Of course, the US investment boom was intrinsically linked to Ireland's status as a platform within the EU single market.

Ireland's Europeanisation extended to significant migration flows and visitors for both business and tourism from the rest of Europe, which grew significantly faster than intra-European flows of capital. However, Ireland was the first of the EU members to enter the European project from outside the group of European countries whose most immediate concerns were around peace and coexistence. This in turn meant that Ireland had a different orientation to Europe, which was mediated more narrowly through a socio-economic lens (O'Brennan 2009). This meant that sectoral dynamics were highly significant, as Ireland sought to "catch up" in industrial development. Overall the entry of Ireland was a major challenge for the EU as it was the first country admitted to the EU with significantly worse structural development and lower national income per capita than elsewhere in the EU (Ó Riain 2014).

In the late 1980s, just as Ireland was introducing spending cuts at home, there was a major influx of EU funding. Even in the booming late 1990s EU funds accounted for over 15% of Irish public capital expenditure. It is important to remember also that the vast bulk of productive capital spending in the Irish economy during this period and later came from the public sector (White 2010). Ireland's relationship with Europe changed significantly in the 2000s. This was linked not only to domestic political shifts but equally to the changing character of the European economic project itself. The growing weight and power of finance in the global economy had significant effects in Europe where, overall, the public developmentalism within a trading union of the 1990s was marginalised by private financialisation in a monetary union.

Ireland's financial system mirrored industrial histories within the "multiple interface periphery". Historically linked to the UK financial system, closer ties developed over time with the United States, for instance through the development of the export platform International Financial Services Centre and the expansion of Irish banks into the United States. The dominant connection in recent decades, however, has been to Europe. Economic and Monetary Union created a single financial market across the EU, linked to the single currency of the euro. Together these created two major shifts that linked banks across Europe: massive increases in inter-bank lending and extensive movement by banks into markets in other European countries (Schoenmaker & Wagner 2013).

Europeanisation still primarily ran through Britain – UK funding of Irish banks made up 77% of total funding by 2008. The Irish system had strong ties to the liberal UK which shaped the actions and capabilities of the Irish banking sector. However, these financial interactions proved to be a conduit through which historical inequalities between the core and periphery in Europe were exacerbated (Bohle 2017). The peripheral economies offered significant profits for core banks (Clarke & Hardiman 2012) and were a source of moderately risky assets for inclusion in securitised products (Ó Riain 2014). Critically, lending from the core into the periphery scaled up the debts of peripheral economies well beyond the scale of the national economy, drove their economies towards consumption and away from the exports that could have helped pay for these debts, and exposed the core to the weakened peripheries that it had helped create (Gallagher 2019). These dynamics brought Ireland to a crisis of massive scale in 2008 that has deeply shaped a decade of Ireland's economic relations with Europe (Gallagher et al. forthcoming).

EU to the fore: financial and fiscal crises

The financial crisis of 2008 hit Ireland fast and hard. As funding to cover liabilities dried up for Irish banks, they turned to the state for help. In September 2008, the government issued a blanket guarantee covering the vast bulk of all the liabilities, including deposits, senior debt and sub-ordinated debt (Beblavý et al. 2014). The guarantee "firewalled" financial debt within the Irish banks, insulating the international lenders who had underpinned the boom of the previous five years. It also severely restricted the capacity of the state to pass any future losses onto the bond holders. Bank debt was now sovereign debt (Beblavý et al. 2014).

These two crises – financial and fiscal – were at the heart of Irish economic life after the crash and through the Great Recession that saw Ireland lose 15% of its employment between the start of 2008 and 2013. A financial crisis saw an immediate collapse of credit and investment, driving an economic crisis that showed up most immediately in the construction sector. As financial and economic activity crashed, employment and demand followed. The Irish state took on the massive costs of bank debts, aggravating a fiscal crisis that was already quickly emerging as tax revenues dipped with declining activity and nosedived as property transaction taxes collapsed (Ó Riain 2014).

While the specific role of the EU in the guarantee remains controversial, it is clear that the Commission and the ECB were determined to "firewall" the Irish crisis in Ireland, most likely because of a deep uncertainty as to the knock-on effects in the European banking system. In the absence of a banking union and a mechanism for covering bailouts, these uncertainties were fundamental (Gallagher et al. forthcoming). The politics of the Irish bailout was not simply a matter of the domestic politics of banking coordination (Grossman & Woll 2014), nor of the bargaining power of banks through the credible threat of exit (Culpepper & Reinke 2014), but also of inter-state politics within the EU, heightened by the transnational integration of banks (rather than their mobility across borders). The capacity of the Irish state to chart an alternative path was strongly limited by the terms of the guarantee and European anxiety about the spread of financial risks and debts across the Eurozone.

This was aggravated further by the response to this crisis and in particular the insistence on national austerity strategies as the appropriate policy response to the sovereign debt crises that spread rapidly through the European periphery. The primary strategy for tackling this crisis in Ireland and in Europe involved strategies of austerity and fiscal consolidation. The focus of this policy was firmly on reducing fiscal deficits and bringing the expansion of general government debt under control across Europe, and particularly in the periphery. The main goal of this policy, especially in Ireland since the bailout of 2011, was restoring creditworthiness – or in other words tackling countries' external legitimation crises in the financial markets. The dilemma here was that the fiscal contraction measures to achieve these twin goals were damaging to economic and employment growth, as well as undermining domestic political legitimacy. Where some analysts argued that fiscal contraction could in time produce economic expansion as investor confidence returned, most Irish commentators recognised that fiscal contraction was indeed contractionary such that growth predictions were revised downwards regularly through the course of the crisis. However, in practice, the resumption of growth was largely seen as following the restoration of stability to the public finances and external credit worthiness. The motors of growth were largely seen as market liberalisation combined with improved competitiveness and the restoration of investor confidence as stability was restored to public finances (Lane 2011).

This strategy has been turned into a long-term legal commitment through a project of institutionalisation of "fiscal prudence" in the years after the crash. Between the second referendum on the Lisbon Treaty in 2009 and the Fiscal Treaty referendum in 2012, Ireland submitted to direct governance by the EU–IMF funders of a government bailout in 2010 and saw a general election in 2011 which decimated the governing Fianna Fáil party.

The key element of the institutionalisation of fiscal conservatism (among other features) in Irish and European economic policy came in May 2012 when Irish voters, uniquely within the EU, were given the choice in a constitutional referendum whether to allow the government to sign the European Fiscal Treaty or not. A vote of 60% in favour of the Treaty was apparently a clear endorsement of the European response to the crisis. However, this assessment is complicated when we look at the reasons provided by those voting on each side of the poll. In particular, a large number of voters who voted yes did so despite, or indeed because of, assessments of the European situation which were largely negative. In particular, many voters voted yes because they did not believe that Ireland would gain access to crucial European resources (especially further bailout financing) if they did not ratify the Fiscal Treaty. Of the yes voters, 15% voted yes for positive reasons while 21% voted yes for primarily negative reasons, most of these to do with Europe (Ó Riain 2014).

On the face of it, Europe should have been the home of expansionary Keynesian interventions as these should have been politically and economically easier in countries with higher levels of social spending. Ironically, however, it was the countries of continental Europe, with their larger public sectors and "social economies", who were cheerleaders for austerity policies, while the "liberal", less free spending states of the UK and the United States were more willing to engage in sustained quantitative easing.

Indeed, the historical evidence – even before the monetarist era and economic globalisation – was that expansionary macro policies were followed primarily by left-leaning governments in liberal economies (Boix 2000). In the decade before the crisis, it was social and Christian democratic countries within the EU that ran the largest budget surpluses (Ó Riain 2014). While Ireland had run a surplus this was largely dependent on real estate transaction taxes and other sources of revenue that collapsed in the crash.

The post-crisis project of institutionalised fiscal conservatism was rooted therefore in a longer-standing, although submerged, tension within the EU. In social market countries, risk is internalised within the society itself through high levels of taxation and spending, linked to an underlying fiscal conservatism. The fiscal strength of the state insulates society relatively effectively from the vagaries of capitalist business cycle and crises – and ongoing state investment in social and economic activities is common (see, for example, the activities of the German state investment bank, KfW). However, in liberal political economies risk is externalised as the society tends to follow the ups and downs of the business cycle, of boom and bust, relying on external adjustments to escape from crisis. These countries therefore make greater use of measures such as currency devaluation and quantitative easing.

The Eurozone-level response emphasised the contractionary dimensions of both national models without taking on the counter-balancing expansionary measures. This approach demanded that the periphery become more responsible Europeans but has made the conditions impossible for it to do so: weakening social and productive investment, shrinking the state and promoting structural reforms that undermine the possibility of European style social contracts. Until the arrival of expanded quantitative easing in 2015 the EU had done little to reflate the European economy – and even this strategy favoured the financial sector over public investments or financing. This was a very different European environment to the policy programme that had been an important condition of the Celtic Tiger economy in Ireland in the 1990s, which had relied on direct public investment.

Within this broader politics of the European political economy, Ireland nonetheless occupied a distinctive position. It sat with Greece, Portugal and Spain as part of the periphery facing simultaneous financial and fiscal crises, but had a much better competitive position in export markets. The political commitment to European integration echoed that of the small open economies of continental Europe, but levels of public and private investment generally trailed those countries (despite their importance as a counter-balance to economic openness). Finally, while Ireland shared many liberal aspects of its political economy with the UK, it was much better placed to pursue an export strategy closer to the European model.

Importantly, Ireland's fiscal crisis was – despite its severity – still more manageable than much of the rest of the European periphery. Having taken on the costs of firewalling Europe's financial system, Ireland benefited from European level policies that helped it to manage this fiscal highwire act. Deeply controversial at the time, the bailout funds received from the EU ultimately turned out to be on comparatively favourable terms. Ireland's debt burden after the crisis of 2008 was serviced at low interest rates, significantly lower than in the recovery from the debt crisis of the 1980s. This itself was facilitated by a political fudge in early 2013 as a series of "promissory notes" of the Irish government (IOUs issued by the government for the dysfunctional Irish banks) were converted into government bonds – despite concerns across Europe that this was blurring the line between central bank monetary policy and government fiscal policy in unacceptable ways. The combination of this approach to debt-financing with ECB quantitative easing made the repayment of the bank debt which had landed on the Irish state somewhat easier. In this sense, Ireland seems to have "benefited" from a more benevolent EU policy than that operated in, for example, Greece – even if only after it had firewalled the European financial system from the spreading banking crisis of 2008. Nonetheless, by the mid-2010s, Ireland's employment and economic growth was recovering rapidly and the issues of debt and financing had receded in national and EU politics, even if still presenting a major economic risk.

United States to the fore: foreign investment, growth and the politics of tax

This leaves the question of where this growth came from. If Ireland was now finding it easier to manage its debt, the growth-inhibiting effects of austerity still remained (Roche et al. 2016). Even if, as McHale (2017) argues, a commitment to fiscal balancing of the budget was a critical element in restoring international confidence in the Irish economy, this in itself does not explain the remarkable growth since 2013, such that by the end of 2017 employment had recovered to pre-crash levels, without the same unsustainably large construction sector.

The obvious place to start looking for an answer was in foreign investment, an area where Ireland had a significant advantage over the other peripheral European countries (Ó Riain 2017; Brazys & Regan 2018). UN statistics indicate a steady trend towards increasing inward investment around the world since 1990 (and before) (UNCTAD 2018), and Ireland has gained an increasing share of that investment. At the height of the inward investment of the Celtic Tiger years between 1998 and 2002, Ireland attracted 2% of global inward investment and 4.4% of investment into the EU. However, even as the share of inward investment in global GNP increased in the 2010s, Ireland gained an increased share – taking 4.9% of world and 18.6% of EU inward investment between 2012 and 2016. Volatile and difficult to interpret as these statistics may be, the overall pattern is clear – Ireland's ability to attract an increasing share of world and EU inward investment was an even stronger contributor to growth after the Great Recession than in the celebrated growth years of the 1990s. Furthermore, employment grew significantly in foreign firms in Ireland during these years.

Access to the EU was clearly a key element in the attraction of foreign investment. However, Ireland's share of US investment in the EU also increased and a key element in this was also clearly the search for lower tax rates – and increasingly the ability to manage what counted as taxable income through profit shifting and various complex tax accounting schemes (Tørsløv et al. 2018). This is reflected in the notoriously unreliable character of Irish growth statistics, the most famous being the 26% growth in GDP in 2015, which led to the coining of the phrase "leprechaun economics" as a popular international label for the dubious character of Irish growth. While some of the growth effects of corporate tax-driven investment are exaggerated, the surge in foreign investment has played a key role in a surge in tax revenues – the additional corporation tax revenue in recent years has effectively kept Irish public finances in surplus.

Not surprisingly, the issue of corporate tax became increasingly prominent in EU politics with core economies such as France and Germany seeking to tip the balance back towards their revenue collection systems through a variety of initiatives. These related to digital taxes, the common consolidated tax base and moves towards qualified voting on taxation policy, opening up the possibility of EU decisions trumping national policies in relation to aspects of taxation. While little happened to concretely affect the practice of taxation, it was clear that political pressure was building. This reached a new level in 2016 when the EU Commission judged Ireland to have provided Apple with illegal state aid and ordered Apple to repay €13 billion plus interest in uncollected taxes. The Irish government appealed the ruling to the EU courts, an almost unique situation.

While foreign investment comes primarily from the United States, therefore, its political impact is quite significant within the EU and in particular in the politics of economic relations between Ireland and the EU. Nonetheless, it should be recognised that this politics is quite complex. The Irish corporate tax regulations become particularly beneficial to companies when they combine Irish legal frameworks with those in other EU countries such as the Netherlands and Malta to produce the "Dutch Sandwich" or "Single Malt" tax schemes.

It should also be noted that the growth story was somewhat broader than foreign direct investment (FDI). Irish-owned firms became increasingly important to employment growth, accounting for two-thirds of export-orientated employment between 2009 and 2015 (Barry and Bergin 2016). This growth was linked to an enterprise policy that has been pursued consistently for at least twenty years – with a range of supports provided mainly through Enterprise Ireland around organisational development, financing, research, marketing and exporting, and more (see Ó Riain 2004 for a detailed account). This project was supported in its early decades by EU Structural Funds and research funding.

Another sector significant in recent job growth is construction, despite the almost complete halt in domestic residential construction for almost a decade after the crisis. Construction investment in recent years has been primarily in non-residential building, with much of this driven by the growth in industry and ICT. This building activity has been heavily influenced by government action, led by the National Asset Management Agency (NAMA), a controversial agency that had a mandate after the crisis of 2008 to obtain the best return for the state on the distressed loans it took on from developers and banks. However, in practice, NAMA has played a very significant role in reshaping property development and the urban environment in a form of 'asset-price Keynesianism' (Byrne 2016; Byrne & Norris 2017). NAMA effectively remade the market, all the while denying it was playing any such role. Ironically perhaps, the strategy adopted in construction was based upon one long used in export-orientated sectors – using Ireland's many international ties to mobilise capital to take advantage of carefully constructed resources and opportunities. Construction is increasingly dominated by international players – initially by US investors, but since 2016 European investors have been equally important (Savills 2019).

Finally, tourism has also driven growth in employment in the accommodation and food sector, among others. Tourist spend in Ireland increased 77% from 2011 to 2018 and tourists from non-UK European countries accounted for over a third of this spend in every year, with the UK share declining while US tourists' share of spend in Ireland increasing rapidly to a third of the total by 2018. The multiple interface periphery strategy generated tourist visits that partly substituted for long stagnant domestic demand, led in this case by the United States but in interaction with the broader European economy.

UK to the fore: Brexit

There were long-term issues looming in the relationship between the Irish economic model and the EU – the institutionalisation of fiscal rules across the EU, the still incomplete project of banking union and financial safeguards, and the shifting politics of corporation tax. Each of these was significantly shaped by the politics of the post-crisis era but was also rooted in long-standing patterns of difference, compromise and conflict that made them predictable fault-lines.

However, another complexity in Ireland's relationship with the EU exploded in 2016 with the referendum decision in the UK to leave the EU. Ireland's colonial past with the UK, and its ongoing legacy, were now firmly on the EU agenda. This was a particularly potent issue given how Ireland's enthusiasm for integration with Europe was at odds with English reluctance. This resulted in a variety of fudges such as Ireland's decision to remain outside the Schengen Free Travel Area agreement in order to maintain open travel between Ireland and the UK after the UK decided not to join Schengen. Nonetheless, the context of European integration had been a vital part of the increasingly close ties between the North and South of Ireland in the all-island economy that had developed in conjunction with the peace process from the 1990s.

When David Cameron made his reckless decision to hold a vaguely specified referendum on leaving the EU, it always had the potential to re-open these issues (O'Rourke 2018). This was poorly understood in the UK, although signalled by the Irish government before the referendum. While migration has perhaps surprisingly not emerged as an issue in the discussions about the Irish border and Brexit, the issue of the Irish border and arrangements around customs checks and single market integrity in the wake of Brexit has become a central controversy in the form of the Irish backstop.

Ireland was to become the frontline of post-Brexit UK–EU relations – Ruane's (2018) observation about the two separate sources of crisis in the North and South of Ireland was now overtaken by the dynamics of British–EU relations. The political dynamics in the North and economic dynamics of the South were now unavoidably intertwined in the decision to be made about the border between the EU and the UK, what it might consist of, and how it might relate to the island of Ireland. In a different type of EU–UK politics there might well be a variety of possibilities for managing these relationships – indeed that is the lesson of the Northern Ireland peace process and the institutional creativity that, for the most part, attended it. However, the English nationalism that is at the heart of the Brexit project (O'Toole 2018), and that was further fuelled by the political debate over Brexit (Delanty 2019), made the Irish backstop a critical, and explosive, issue.

While perhaps not as disastrous as some feared, the economic implications of Brexit for Ireland are very serious – at a minimum weakening future growth and possibly producing a recession depending on uncertain knock-on effects. About a third of small firm exports are to the UK. This drops to only 15% for those over fifty employees and 9% for those over 250 employees, many of whom are multinationals. It is these weaker Irish firms that are most exposed, and the regions and workforces that depend upon them.

Nonetheless, it is clear that despite these challenges, Ireland chose Europe. What might have become a matter of strategic game playing in an era of normal politics was turned by the virulent politics of Brexit into the need to make a somewhat existential choice as to whether Ireland would tie itself to the UK or the EU in the coming decades. Despite the significant costs, this proved to be a relatively easy choice. A variety of strategic factors mean that it was almost unimaginable that Ireland would detach itself significantly from the EU – including the importance of the EU to foreign investment, the legal and regulatory entanglement between Ireland and the EU, and the popular legitimacy of the EU in Ireland.

More fundamentally, the existential choice was made clearer by the political instability in the UK. This undermined any trust in a political process after Brexit that might tempt an Irish government into a political fudge around Brexit itself. The contribution of Brexit to hastening the economic weakening of the UK meant that Ireland was even less likely to tie itself to the British leg of the multiple interface periphery and would in future become ever more committed to the United States and Europe. The arrival of Boris Johnson as Prime Minister has only made this choice easier through his uncompromising rhetoric on the backstop (see Phinnemore & Whitten, Chapter 12, this volume), even though the prospects for economic damage loom larger than ever.

Ireland made similar choices in the past and indeed its engagement with Europe in recent decades and its pursuit of US investment were in part attempts to reduce that dependence on the UK. Now, largely against its will, Ireland is choosing more momentously an economic path that diverges further from that of the UK.

Where next for Ireland in the European economy?

Prior to Brexit, Ireland was proceeding cautiously on a number of fronts within the EU, in part under the cover of UK liberalism. It included the attraction of foreign investment as a pillar of the growth model, which benefited from the political cover of the UK, even as the UK was an active competitor for that investment. The politics of mobile investment and corporate taxation is likely to become significantly more difficult for the Irish government within the EU after Brexit.

However the Brexit process ends (in the short and long term), it will have major implications for Ireland's economic relations with the EU. We can think briefly about three scenarios. The limited deal that the UK left with – an as yet uncertain one, given the controversy over the Northern Ireland protocol – will mean that Ireland will become even more de-linked from the UK economy over time, especially as domestic firms seek new markets and supply chains. Secondly, Ireland will have a deep interdependence with the EU, having clearly separated from the UK to become part of the EU club without UK political "protection". Ireland can be expected to de-link from the UK within EU politics and will quietly pursue economic diversification in the face of the risk of instability in the UK. Thirdly, if a compromise is reached that involves a border between the UK and Northern Ireland, we might expect the consolidation of a dual economy with rural Ireland closely tied to Northern Ireland, but urban Ireland ever more closely integrated with the EU. Ireland would presumably have to pay a significant political price for EU support that produced this outcome, with increased pressure likely around corporate tax in particular.

Given that a relatively 'hard' Brexit was ultimately implemented, and that the level of trust between the UK and EU even as regular trading partners is low, Ireland will become increasingly detached from the UK and will seek new alliances with other EU states.

Barnes and Wren (2012) argue that Ireland and the UK faced the choice after the crisis of a return to the form of "privatised Keynesianism" that dominated in the 2000s (with demand stoked by loose financial markets) or the turn to a more European strategy of export-orientated competitiveness.

This chapter has suggested that such a choice involves a much deeper transformation – one that anchors a strategy of competitiveness in invest-ment in both organisations and society, in empowerment of employees, in curbing the dominance of finance and wrapping all this in a blanket of fiscal prudence. The European "social contract" is clearly at the heart of this mix of institutions and policies. Mathematically, the balancing of a budget is possible with either low tax and spend or high tax and spend. In practice, however, the comparative evidence suggests that a developed social model and high investment economy is crucial to the ability to sustain fiscal pru-dence. Ireland appears to already be pursuing a different place in Europe, linked to a network of small open member states, the New Hanseatic League. Nonetheless, it seems likely that Ireland is about to more fully inte-grate into the European economic model than at any stage in its history.

References

Barnes, L. & A. Wren (2012) 'The liberal model in the crisis: continuity and change in Great Britain and Ireland', in N.G. Bermeo & J. Pontusson (eds) *Coping with crisis: government reactions to the Great Recession*, pp. 287–324. New York: Russell Sage Foundation.

Barry, F. & A. Bergin (2016) 'Business', in W. Roche, P. O'Connell & A. Prothero (eds) *Austerity and recovery in Ireland: Europe's poster child and the Great Recession*, pp. 62–84. Oxford: Oxford University Press.

Beblavý, M., D. Cobham & L.U. Ódor (2014) *The Euro area and the financial crisis*. New York: Cambridge University Press.

Bohle, D. (2017) 'Mortgaging Europe's Periphery'. LSE 'Europe in Question' Discus-sion Paper Series, LEQS Paper No. 124/2017.

Boix, C. (2000) 'Partisan governments, the international economy, and macroeco-nomic policies in advanced nations, 1960–93'. *World Politics* 53(1): 38–73.

Brazys, S. & A. Regan, (2018) 'Celtic Phoenix or leprechaun economics? The politics of an FDI-led growth model in Europe'. *New Political Economy* 23(2): 223–238.

Byrne, M. (2016) '"Asset price urbanism" and financialization after the crisis: Ireland's National Asset Management Agency'. *International Journal of Urban and Regional Research* 40(1): 31–45.

Byrne, M. & M. Norris (2017) 'Pro-cyclical social housing and the crisis of Irish housing policy: marketization, social housing and the property boom and bust'. *Housing Policy Debate* 28(1): 50–63.

Clarke, B. & N. Hardiman (2012) *Crisis in the Irish banking system: banking systems in the crisis – the faces of liberal capitalism*. Abingdon: Routledge, 107–133.

Culpepper, P.D. & R. Reinke (2014) 'Structural power and bank bailouts in the United Kingdom and the United States'. *Politics & Society* 42(4): 427–454.

Delanty, G. (2019) 'Reflections on the sociological significance of Brexit'. British Sociological Association. Available at: www.britsoc.co.uk/about/latest-news/2019/march/reflections-on-the-sociological-significance-of-brexit/ [accessed 31 August 2019].

Gallagher, P. (2019) *Financialisation and the politics of growth in Denmark and Ireland*. PhD Thesis, Department of Sociology, National University of Ireland Maynooth.

Gallagher, P., M. Byrne, F. Rhatigan & S. Ó Riain (forthcoming) 'The politics of banking in Ireland', in D. Farrell & N. Hardiman (eds) *The handbook of Irish politics*. Oxford: Oxford University Press.

Grossman, E. & C. Woll (2014) 'Saving the banks: the political economy of bailouts'. *Comparative Political Studies* 47(4): 574–600.

Lane, P.R. (2011) 'The Irish crisis', IIIS Discussion Paper No. 356, IIIS: TCD.

McHale, J. (2017) 'Why austerity?' in E. Heffernan, J. McHale & N. Moore-Cherry (eds) *Debating austerity in Ireland: crisis, experience and recovery*, pp. 37–52. Dublin: Royal Irish Academy.

O'Brennan, J. (2009) 'Ireland says No again: the 12 June 2008 Referendum on the Lisbon Treaty'. *Parliamentary Affairs* 62(2): 258–277.

Ó Riain, S. (2004) *The politics of high tech growth*. New York: Cambridge University Press.

Ó Riain, S. (2014) *The rise and fall of Ireland's Celtic Tiger: liberalism, boom and bust*. Cambridge: Cambridge University Press.

Ó Riain, S. (2017) 'Ireland's recovery: explanation, potential and pitfalls', in E. Heffernan, J. McHale & N. Moore-Cherry (eds) *Debating austerity in Ireland: crisis, experience and recovery*, pp. 219–234. Dublin: Royal Irish Academy.

O'Rourke, K. (2018) *A short history of Brexit: from Brentry to Backstop*. London: Pelican Books.

O'Toole, F. (2018) *Heroic failure: Brexit and the politics of pain*. New York: Apollo Books.

Roche, W., P. O'Connell & A. Prothero (2016) 'Introduction', in W. Roche, P. O'Connell & A. Prothero (eds) *Austerity and recovery in Ireland: Europe's poster child and the Great Recession*, pp. 1–22. Oxford: Oxford University Press.

Ruane, J. (2010) 'Ireland's multiple interface-periphery development model: achievements and limits', in M. Bøss (ed.) *The nation-state in transformation: the governance, growth and cohesion of small states under globalisation*. Aarhus: Aarhus University Press.

Ruane, J. (2018) 'Modelling Ireland's crises: North, South, and North–South inter-sections', in N. Ó Dochartaigh, K. Hayward & E. Meehan (eds) *Dynamics of political change in Ireland*, pp. 93–109. Abingdon: Routledge.
Savills (2019) *Ireland investment report 2019*. Dublin: Savills Research.
Schoenmaker, D. & W. Wagner (2013) 'Cross-border banking in Europe and finan-cial stability'. *International Finance* 16: 1–22.
Tørsløv, T., L. Wier & G. Zucman (2018) 'The hidden profits of nations'. NBER Working Paper 24701. Available at: www.nber.org/papers/w24701 [accessed 3 November 2018].
UNCTAD (2018) *Investment report 2018*. Geneva: UN.
White, R. (2010) *Years of high income largely wasted*. Dublin: Davy Stockbrokers.

4

Sovereign or not sovereign: tax policy, Ireland and the EU

Sheila Killian

Introduction

This chapter addresses the issue of tax policy in the context of Ireland's relationship with the EU and, in turn, the EU's relationship with the wider world. Tax policy is an interesting prism through which to examine these relationships, particularly in the context of Ireland's increasing dependence on FDI and the way in which this drives the country's relationship with the United States as the source of this FDI, independent of the relationships between the United States and the EU. The chapter is organised as follows: initially, there is a discussion on tax policy, to set the context for the chapter and to identify some key international players. This is followed by a discussion on both tax competition and tax avoidance, in order to better understand the tensions between Ireland and the EU relating to Ireland's tax policy. Next, the genesis of Ireland's policy of tax competition is outlined, as well as how it developed in counterpoint to EU concerns up to the financial crisis. The next section focuses on the period since the crisis, considering how Ireland's tax policy persisted through the financial crisis, and describing the new climate of concern about tax avoidance, and how this has manifested itself through key EU proposals on taxation, the OECD Base-Erosion and Profit-Shifting (BEPS) process, and the EU's use of state aid rules to challenge Ireland's interactions with Apple. The final section explores some key future influences and the great unknown that is Brexit.

Introducing tax policy

Tax policy is different in several key ways from other aspects of fiscal policy. Changes in tax rules can be seen as political in nature, with the annual budget announced by the Minister for Finance amid a media fanfare of speculation and surprise. During the lead up to the budget announcement, there is a considerable level of more or less overt lobbying from key interest groups, and this is done quite openly in the form of pre-budget submissions as well as more privately. The rules in general change annually, and so those key elements that remain constant can come to characterise a nation's identity. In the case of Ireland, the commitment to the 12.5% corporation tax rate has become something of a national mantra with support over recent decades from across the parliament for maintaining the current policy (Killian 2013: 278). While other countries, including some EU countries, have low rates, the long-term commitment to this policy in Ireland has been distinctive. 'The country's corporation tax regime has remained amongst the most stable in Europe' (Barry & Bergin 2013: 22). This consistency alleviates risk for corporate tax planners considering long-term decisions such as the location of pivotal investments, and so it underpins the tax rate as a strategic part of Ireland's tax offering to multinational firms.

Within an EU context 'all tax decisions to be taken at the EU level are subject to unanimity' (Lampreave 2011: 4). While a considerable level of tax harmonisation has been achieved in the fields of sales taxes and value added taxes, this is not the case in direct taxes such as income tax and corporation tax. This affords a level of sovereignty to corporate tax policy in an EU context which, as outlined later, can lead to internal tensions within the EU. This is because, while tax policy lies within the gift of the national government, its impact is international in two key ways. Countries negotiate bilateral tax treaties to determine how transactions or entities that cross borders are to be taxed in each individual jurisdiction. The general aim of tax treaties is the avoidance of double taxation. However, as discussed in the next section, a consequence of how they are deployed can in some cases be the reduction or complete avoidance of taxation. While treaties are intended, at least by the OECD, to impact on levels of FDI, the evidence on this is at best mixed (Blonigen & Davies 2004; Davies 2004; Kumas & Millimet 2018). Certainly their impact on developing countries is an issue of some debate (Beer & Loeprick 2018; Janský & Šedivý 2018), and their continued renegotiation speaks to the effect they have, if not on absolute levels of FDI, then on the ease with which profits, royalties, dividends and interest can move across borders (Arel-Bundock 2017).

Secondly, nationally set tax rules are international in their impact because transactions are international, and multinational firms with a presence in more than one country are well positioned to take advantage of small differences in regulation or interpretation. This may arise because the complex network of tax treaties has 'inadvertently created opportunities for treaty shopping by multinational companies' (Arel-Bundock 2017: 349), or because transactions which take the form, for instance, of interest are seen as something else, such as dividends, in another jurisdiction (Nessy & Rahayu 2019). These so-called "hybrid mismatch arrangements" are the target of much of both the EU's and the OECD's work on international tax reform (Brown & Stewart 2017; Domingo 2019; Neugebauer & Lesage 2018). These issues are discussed in more detail in the next section.

Tax competition and tax avoidance

Ireland uses its low corporation tax rate of 12.5% as a headline element to attract FDI. The tax benefits of locating in Ireland often derive from other elements of Ireland's tax policy, notably the regulations on taxation of intellectual property, R&D expenditure and royalties as well as the way in which the country's corporate tax regime interacts with legislation in other countries. Nevertheless, the low rate itself has significant benefits for companies which avail themselves of it.

One way in which multinational firms take advantage of the rate is through transfer pricing. Most large multinational firms are in fact groups of companies, with subsidiaries or branches in a number of different countries. As well as conducting transactions with the rest of the world, they also have internal transactions, lending from one company within a group to another, for instance, buying and selling goods and services, transferring intellectual property and paying royalties or management charges from one company to another. These internal transactions need to be priced, and this "transfer price" at which goods or services are transferred from one company to another has significant tax implications. As an example, imagine there is an Irish company manufacturing a product which will be sold to a French sister company for distribution in that country. If the cost to the Irish company per unit is, say, €100 and the ultimate onwards price at which the French company will sell the product is, say, €200, then the price at which the product is sold from the Irish firm to the French one should be somewhere between €100 and €200. The closer this is to €200, the less profit there will be in France, and the more there will be in Ireland. Conversely, if the price is close to €100, the Irish firm will make less profit and the French one will make more. Now imagine that the Irish firm is taxed at 12.5% while the French one is taxed at 33%. There is an obvious incentive to the group to set the transfer price in such a way as to shift profit into low-tax Ireland and out of higher-tax France. By 2003 it was apparent that 'one consequence of the role of low CT in the Irish success story is the extent to which the economy – or at least its statistical representation – has been distorted through "transfer pricing"' (Walsh 2003: 224). To counter this, the standard approach from taxing authorities and the OECD is to impose arm's-length pricing on group transfers. This means that the price at which the Irish firm sells to its French sister should be the same as that at which it would sell to an unrelated party. This arm's-length rule can be an effective way of policing transfer pricing as long as there are comparable transactions with non-group companies with which to benchmark internal transactions. It becomes extremely challenging, if not unfeasible, however, when what is transferred is something unique and perhaps proprietary, as in the case of royalty payments, transfers of intellectual property or management charges.

In this way, the low corporation tax rate itself provides a significant competitive advantage to companies with an Irish subsidiary, and in turn to Ireland as a country competing for FDI. Having a tax rate that is lower than that applied by other countries is not defined as harmful tax competition (Killian 2006). However, many commentators are concerned about the very positive impact of Ireland's rate on the level of FDI in the country. As Lampreave argues:

> Although a low tax rate, in itself, should not be regarded as unfair competition, the author believes that, in the case of Ireland, this could be considered to be a harmful measure. This is because it is understood that the key factor that attracted a large number of MNEs [multinational entities] to operate in Ireland was the low Irish general corporation tax rate. (2011: 2)

As well as attracting companies to locate in a particular country, a low tax rate may create a certain level of moral hazard for companies operating there to engage in arrangements that push the boundary from tax compliance towards tax avoidance. Such arrangements may mean there is more taxable income in Ireland, and, in the example above, less taxable income in France. For this reason, fellow member states of the EU are often concerned about Ireland's low tax rate. However, there are more complex arrangements which can create even greater concern internationally.

For example, still on the basis of the low rate, companies may deploy a more complex arrangement and "invert" the location of their global headquarters through a merger between, for example, a large US firm and a smaller Irish firm whereby the Irish firm becomes the HQ. Such an arrangement has had significant tax benefits in the past, and the extent to which the activity is driven by tax rather than commercial considerations is shown by the case of the Pfizer/Allergan inversion proposal. Briefly, in November 2015, Pfizer announced its intention to merge with Allergan, an Irish-resident pharma company best known for the manufacture of Botox, and in the process to move its HQ to Ireland. Contractor (2016: 11) estimated the potential tax gains from the Pfizer inversion would have amounted to €150 million, based on the disparity between the US tax rate and the Irish one. This proposed merger, with a value of US$160bn, was the largest inversion ever attempted, and attracted a considerable level of criticism in media and political circles (Young 2015). In April 2016, following the closing by the

Obama administration of the domestic US provisions that allowed inversions to proceed (Humer & Pierson 2016), the merger was abandoned, citing an 'adverse tax law change', and with compensation being paid by Pfizer to Allergan for costs incurred (Pfizer 2016).

Companies or groups of companies can also engage in aggressive tax planning to exploit the tax treaty network of the countries in which their subsidiaries or holding companies are resident. As noted above, tax treaties are bilateral agreements between countries outlining, inter alia, the rates of withholding taxes that will apply to payments of interest, dividends or royalties from one country to another. Lewis (2013) describes the case of a South African sugar firm's investment in neighbouring Zambia which was routed through Dublin and thereby avoided significant Zambian withholding taxes by utilising the network of tax treaties which had been negotiated by Ireland. This case illustrates the key concern about tax avoidance; while tax minimisation is the language of business, and tax competition the language of countries, the overall impact is not costless. In Zambia, one in four children living in rural poverty are stunted due to malnutrition. Tax arrangements that deplete the coffers of the Zambian government reduce the potential for this problem to be addressed.

Whether or not such transactions are primarily driven by tax, it seems evident that the tax implications are a key element of corporate pricing, investment and location decisions: 'executives consider tax angles concurrently with strategy, rather than as an afterthought' (Contractor 2016: 13). This means that Irish tax policy and its interaction with the legislation of the EU and other countries, notably the United States, will directly impact on the investment, transfer pricing and restructuring decisions of multinational firms. In turn, this affects the capacity of other countries, including EU countries, to collect tax revenue in two ways: firstly, because companies located in those jurisdictions may be transacting with a sister company in Ireland; and secondly, because multinational firms may be more likely to locate in Ireland than in these countries. This has created considerable disquiet internationally about Ireland's tax policy, particularly since Ireland's accession to the EEC in 1973.

Ireland's strategy and its consequences

The origins of Ireland's policy of tax competition go back more than sixty years. After Ireland became independent from Britain, the country initially followed a protectionist strategy for economic development, relying on state-owned and controlled industry in areas such as shipping and steel to generate employment and economic growth (MacSharry & White 2000). This policy was abruptly reversed following the publication of the Whitaker Report in 1958. This marked a change in approach 'characterised by a belief in technocracy and a new individualistic meritocracy' (Crotty 2000: 217). It also involved 'a new belief in the economic value of openness and the pursuit of an exogenous-led development model … [which] placed the nature of inward investment high on the political agenda' (Collins & Grimes 2008: 443).

A key part of the strategy to attract this investment was tax policy. Export Sales Relief (ESR), introduced in the mid-1950s, was privately but "explicitly linked" to the attraction of FDI (Barry 2011: 13). The scope of tax relief for export sales was gradually expanded in the years following its introduction. In its final form, it applied a 0% rate of tax to profits of an exporting firm in circumstances where the company's sales were made to non-Irish customers. The tax rate on the balance of domestically derived profits at this time was initially 50% and gradually declined. While ESR was available to both domestic and multinational firms, it was targeted at and largely taken up by newly established multinational firms. Ruane notes that 'since the Irish corporate tax rate, ignoring other deductions, was approximately 45% throughout the period considered, the IDA considered that ESR outweighed all other incentives offered to induce foreign industry to locate in Ireland' (Ruane 1980: 78). Domestic firms were slower to adapt to the new incentives (Foster 1989), and O'Brien (1984) cites McAleese (1971) as finding that 'the substantial increase in exports that occurred in the late 1960s … was primarily due to the entry of new firms that were more export-oriented than established firms' (O'Brien 1984: 96).

The policy gradually began to be effective in attracting investment, with 350 foreign firms locating in Ireland during the 1960s and becoming leaders in the export sector (Burnham 2003: 538). This growth in exports did not immediately translate to a solution to economic stagnation. Barry (2003) examines Greece, Spain, Portugal and Ireland, the so-called "cohesion countries", comparing key economic indicators over the period of EU membership and notes that Ireland was slower to develop economically in the 1960–1973 period, a fact he attributes not to taxation but to issues in the labour market. Through the 1970s, however, ESR gained some traction, and this set the tone for the intertwining of Ireland's general economic policy and tax policies geared specifically for FDI, a pattern that would persist and become entrenched over the following decades. It also triggered the first sparks of tension between Ireland and the EEC over tax policy, and by 1980, ESR was attracting unwelcome attention from EU regulators: 'it is no secret that the EEC Commission was unhappy with Export Sales Relief' (McCarthy 1980: 367).

Soon after Ireland's entry to the EEC, the European Commission objected to the renewal of ESR on the basis that the distinction between a 0% tax on export profits and the 50% rate then applied to domestic profits was 'excessively discriminatory' (Burnham 2003: 540). Perhaps due to Ireland's relatively lacklustre economic performance, a compromise was granted which allowed ESR to continue for firms already availing of it up to the year 1990, while a new rate of 10% was introduced for profits deriving from goods manufactured in Ireland. The rate of 10% also applied to profits from key service activities in companies engaged in specific forms of trade in a special free trade zone around Shannon Airport in the west of the country, and in the International Financial Services Centre (IFSC) in Dublin (Killian 2013). Because the new 10% rate applied to all manufactured goods and not only to exports, it was not considered to be a discriminatory measure by the EEC. Manufacturing was not formally defined in legislation and so came to be determined by case law as an irreversible process leading to a commercially different product. Over time, this led to some surreal outcomes, such as when bananas that were imported to Ireland in an unripe state and then artificially ripened in ethylene chambers, were considered to be manufactured, and so profits on their sale were taxed at 10%. Other qualifying activities 'include[d] plant cloning, fish production, meat processing, design and planning services, ship repairing, certain qualifying shipping activities and newspaper production' (Svalborn 2001: 7).

As Ireland moved out of stagnation from the late 1980s onwards, manufacturing relief began to attract increasing levels of FDI to the country and, as a consequence, drew increased attention from European neighbours. In an analysis of data from the Irish Revenue Commissioners, Gillanders noted that 'an examination of the database of the names of companies in the top range shows a preponderance of manufacturing multinationals' (1988: 105). Towards the end of the 1990s, 'the EU began to increase pressure on Ireland to phase out the 10% corporate tax rate for manufacturing and selected services' (Burnham 2003: 55). At the time, the rate of tax for non-manufacturing services outside of the zones at Shannon or the IFSC was 40%, falling to 38% (Killian 2013: 377). When manufacturing relief expired, Ireland's response was not to raise the 10% rate to match the higher rate applicable to other forms of trading profit in the country, but rather to converge the rates at a new and universal low rate of 12.5% to apply to trading profits from 1 January 2003.

From the beginning, the importance of tax to Ireland's economic policy was often expressed in relation to the relative disadvantages of Ireland's peripheral, island location on the edge of Europe, and the lack of industrial tradition. Barry articulates this national view neatly: 'Moves towards corporation-tax harmonization could be particularly damaging to the periphery, as it would increase the importance of centrality and infrastructure – areas in which core countries clearly dominate – in the battle to attract

FDI inflows' (Barry 2003: 817). Much of the FDI attracted to Ireland by low taxes in recent years has been in the services sector. One study calculated that over the period from 2008 to 2012 inward FDI to Ireland from the United States amounted to approximately US$14bn in services, and just US$8.5bn in manufacturing (Heinemann et al. 2018: 93). This switch was initially driven by financial services (Purdue & Huang 2016) and more recently is largely made up of computer, data and information services (Brazys & Regan 2017). Because the services sector is more responsive to tax incentives than manufacturing (Davies et al. 2016), and is relatively mobile compared to manufacturing, there is always the possibility that the companies involved will relocate again to a jurisdiction that offers a more favourable tax position. This is seen as an implicit threat to Ireland's success from other countries in the region, both within and outside of the EU, and has led to Ireland's vigorous defence of, and commitment to, its competitive corporation tax policy.

The pattern that evolved in response to this narrative highlights how key changes in Irish tax policy – the phasing out of ESR and the introduction of manufacturing relief; the phasing out of manufacturing relief and the introduction of the 12.5% rate – came about largely in response to objections from the EU. In a report commissioned by the Irish Department of Finance, the language used is telling: 'ESR could not survive in an EU environment ... The 10% effective tax rate then fell foul of EU rules in 1998 and, in turn, was replaced by a general 12.5% tax rate' (Ernst & Young 2014: 5). This indicates that the changes were primarily driven by a desire to stay within the limits of acceptability of the EU while maintaining aggressive competition on corporate tax rates.

Irish tax policy following the financial crisis

Ireland's combative stance on maintaining a low rate of tax while remaining in good standing with the EU is a delicate balance. As internal tax competition across the EU became a concern throughout the late 1990s (Radaelli 1999), Ireland's tax regime was 'frequently considered a poster child of this development' (Schmidtke 2016: 74). Ireland's ability to maintain this trajectory was expected to come under some pressure during the financial crisis, with the onset of direct negotiations with EU institutions on the question of a bailout. However, despite the position of relative weakness Ireland occupied at the time, the commitment to the 12.5% rate was maintained. Dara Calleary, a junior minister in the government in 2010, speaking in parliament described it as 'an absolute red line in terms of any discussions that have taken place ... critical to supporting our economic recovery and employment growth and is a cornerstone of our industrial policy and an integral part of our international brand' (Oireachtas 2010). This reflects a consistency in the Irish attitude to tax policy over the decades, articulating tax sovereignty as a key element of the country's economic policy, and defined in terms of national agency in setting tax rates and tax bases.

Post-crisis, however, international concern about tax avoidance and its impact on competition between domestic and MNCs, as well as between countries, came to a head within the OECD. In an alignment with the G20, the OECD launched a global initiative to counter BEPS. This project was endorsed by the G20 and gradually gathered momentum and political buy-in from a wider group of countries. This led to far more media and public concern about tax avoidance, particularly by multinational firms, and so more public debate on the EU's own proposition to counter internal competition within the EU, the Common Consolidated Corporate Tax Base, or CCCTB.

The CCCTB as a proposal has evolved over time, but its essential proposition is that any company located in an EU country would have the tax that is collected in that country shared with other EU countries where it has employees, assets or sales. The details of this allocation have varied, but the proposal in essence is designed to counter a situation where a company is located in a low-tax jurisdiction, such as Ireland, while making significant sales, and therefore deriving profit, from other countries which do not have taxing rights. As noted earlier, however, unanimity among member states is required for such a measure to be brought into being, and Ireland is among the countries which has resisted. Ireland's most commonly offered defence is that the CCCTB, by factoring in the location of sales, favours the larger markets in bigger EU countries such as France or Germany over smaller, more peripheral countries such as Ireland.

While the OECD, through the broad adoption of the BEPS principles, has been seen 'to act as a kind of informal (lower case) world tax organisation' (Cockfield 2005: 136), the EU has also risen to prominence as an international agent of tax policy (Christensen 2018) despite the lack of momentum around the CCCTB proposals. As described in Barrera and Bustamante (2018), some of the most high-profile challenges from the EU to tax avoidance in recent years have as a point of origin the rules on state aid, rather than on taxes. To breach the EU rules on state aid, an advantage needs to have been conferred by the state on particular entities on a selective basis, distorting competition and impacting other EU states (European Commission 2019).

The most high-profile case taken under this heading centred on the relationship between Apple and the Irish government. Apple established two subsidiaries in Ireland, one of which conducted extensive manufacturing operations, and the second of which, Apples Sales International, was non-resident in Ireland by reason of being managed and controlled from overseas. Non-residence meant that Irish tax was limited to Irish-source income, and as described in Yang et al. (2016), the proportion of this income liable to Irish tax was set at an agreed ratio. The combination of this and the fact that the company was not in fact taxable in any other jurisdiction meant that the bulk of this company's income was not taxable worldwide. The case made by the EU was that this was an arrangement entered into with the Irish government, and that the tax terms extended to Apple were favourable and unique. Both Apple and Ireland contested this view, but nonetheless, in 2016, the country was required to collect taxes from Apple amounting to US$14.5 billion plus interest. This tactic, challenging tax outcomes using EU state aid rules, bypassed the need for member state unanimity on tax rules. It was a move described by tax practitioners as 'dumbfounding' (Yoder 2016: 3) and marked a significant shift in the narrative on tax relations between the EU and the United States (Wang 2018). In September 2019, Margaret Vestager, who had led the charge in this case, was appointed to 'an unprecedented second term as the EU's competition commissioner' (Rankin 2019: 1). This represents a strong indication of an energy and determination within the EU to tackle tax avoidance and an ambition to be seen as a major player in this field internationally.

Conclusion and possible futures

Tax policy and the way in which it has developed in Ireland illustrate the complexity of the Ireland–EU relationship. Ireland has always sought to compete for FDI, using its corporation tax rules as a key plank of economic policy. Membership of the EU is also an important element of Ireland's attractiveness for FDI. However, Ireland's tax policy, in pushing the envelope of competition, has repeatedly met with the disapproval of the EU and, on occasion, the threat of sanction. An interesting aspect of Ireland's responses to these potential barriers is the way in which they have led to new innovations in its tax competition including the 10% manufacturing rate, the 12.5% blanket rate of corporation tax for trading profits, and most recently the knowledge box (Ireland's set of tax incentives for intellectual property). The efforts of the EU to curb internal tax competition appear in large part to have transformed rather than eradicated it. As long as unanimity is maintained for tax policy changes across the EU, tax policy will remain a key outlier as a sovereign element of policy despite European integration.

At the time of writing, Ireland's tax policy has aligned with the EU BEPS process, but the new momentum within the EU brings uncertainty and promises that EU challenges to Irish policy may move beyond the potentially stymied CCCTB proposals. Meanwhile the prospect of Brexit raises its own challenges, not only for Ireland but also for the EU as a whole. The impact of Brexit on Irish tax policy remains a significant source of uncertainty. Writing prior to the referendum, there was some optimism, with Purdue and Huang (2015) predicting a potential upside for FDI into Ireland in the financial services sector, for example, in the event that the firms based in the City of London lost free access to the EU. As the potential departure date nears, the focus has switched to more problematic areas, including VAT and Customs along the border between Ireland and Northern Ireland, and most recently, the risk of a potential fall-off in corporation tax receipts due to a decline in economic activity[1] and labour market conditions (Conefrey et al. 2019).

The tax policy of the UK in the immediate aftermath of Brexit is also both unknown and significant. If freed from the shackles of EU scrutiny, the UK might pursue a more aggressive policy of tax competition, particularly if any negotiated withdrawal agreement retains free access to the market and movement of goods for companies located in the UK. This kind of tax competition would impact across the EU but might be more keenly felt in Ireland since the two locations are broadly similar in terms of access, education, language and other factors that are key to FDI decisions. It would also have a disproportionate impact on Ireland given the country's current policy of courting multinational investment. Davies et al. (2016: 19), for instance, estimate that a 1% reduction in UK corporate tax rates could decrease the likelihood of FDI locating in Ireland by more than 4%. How the EU response will play out in the new geography of the EU is unclear, but already key players such as Chartered Accountants Ireland are flagging Ireland's engagement with the New Hanseatic League of countries as a potential alliance on tax issues, which would be important following the departure of the UK (Keegan 2018).

All of these factors, together with some uncertainty around US foreign fiscal policy during the Trump presidency, has led to more widespread comment on Ireland's dependence on corporation tax as a source of revenue, and recommendations from bodies such as the Fiscal Council not to rely on what could become more unstable levels of corporate tax income (IFAC 2019). This could become an interesting long-term impact of Brexit, if it indirectly led to measures that seek to make Ireland's position less focused on FDI. Aggressive tax competition from a UK which has exited the EU would also pose challenges to the EU as a whole. It remains unclear how the EU might respond to such an external threat, but it does raise the intriguing possibility of the EU allying with Ireland on tax policy to address a common competitor, particularly if Brexit were to catalyse a moderation of Ireland's own tax competition ambitions.

Note

1   For more on the economic impact of Brexit, see Kinsella, Chapter 11, this volume.

References

Arel-Bundock, V. (2017) 'The unintended consequences of bilateralism: treaty shopping and international tax policy'. *International Organization* 71(2): 349–371.

Barrera, R. & J. Bustamante (2018) 'The rotten apple: tax avoidance in Ireland'. *The International Trade Journal* 32(1): 150–161.

Barry, F. (2003) 'Economic integration and convergence processes in the EU cohesion countries'. *Journal of Common Market Studies* 41(5): 897–921.

Barry, F. (2011) 'Foreign investment and the politics of export profits tax relief 1956'. *Irish Economic and Social History* 38: 54–73.

Barry, F. & A. Bergin (2013) 'Offshoring, inward investment and export performance in Ireland'. *The Oxford handbook of offshoring and global employment.* Oxford: Oxford University Press.

Beer, S. & J. Loeprick (2018) *The cost and benefits of tax treaties with investment hubs: findings from sub-Saharan Africa.* Washington: The World Bank.

Blonigen, B.A. & R.B. Davies (2004) 'The effects of bilateral tax treaties on US FDI activity'. *International Tax and Public Finance* 11(5): 601–622.

Brazys, S. & A. Regan (2017) 'The politics of capitalist diversity in Europe: explaining Ireland's divergent recovery from the euro crisis'. *Perspectives on Politics* 15(2): 411–427.

Brown, B. & T. Stewart (2017) 'New Zealand's BEPS proposals go beyond OECD's recommendations'. *International Tax Review* 28: 41.

Burnham, J.B. (2003) 'Why Ireland boomed'. *The Independent Review* 7(4): 537–556.

Christensen, R.C. (2018) 'The rise of the EU in international tax policy'. Available at: https://doi.org/10.31235/osf.io/tn329 [accessed 11 April 2019].

Cockfield, A.J. (2005) 'The rise of the OECD as informal world tax organization through national responses to e-commerce tax challenges'. *Yale Journal of Law & Technology* 8: 136.

Collins, P. & S. Grimes (2008) 'Ireland's foreign-owned technology sector: evolving towards sustainability?' *Growth and Change* 39(3): 436–463.

Conefrey, T., R. Hickey & G. Walsh (2019) 'Debt and uncertainty: managing risks to the public finances'. *Central Bank of Ireland Economic Letter* 11.

Contractor, F.J. (2016) Tax avoidance by multinational companies: methods, policies, and ethics. *Rutgers Business Review* 1(1). Available at: SSRN: https://ssrn.com/abstract=3005385.

Crotty, W. (2000) 'Ireland: economics and the reinventing of a nation'. *Policy Studies Journal* 28(4): 799–814.

Davies, R.B. (2004) 'Tax treaties and foreign direct investment: potential versus performance'. *International Tax and Public Finance* 11(6): 775–802.

Davies, R.B., I. Siedschlag & Z. Studnicka (2016) 'Corporate taxation and Foreign Direct Investment in EU countries: policy implications for Ireland'. *ESRI Quarterly Economic Commentary*, 14 June.

Domingo, M.S. (2019) 'Hybrid mismatch.com: neutralizing the tax effects of hybrid mismatch arrangements'. *North East Journal of Legal Studies* 38(1): 1.

Ernst & Young (2014) *The historical development and international context of the Irish corporate tax system.* Report commissioned by the Irish Department of Finance as part of Budget 2015. Dublin: Ernst & Young.

European Commission (2019) 'State aid control'. Available at: http://ec.europa.eu/competition/state_aid/overview/index_en.html [accessed 11 April 2019].

Foster, R.F. (1989) *Modern Ireland, 1600–1972.* New York: Penguin.

Gillanders, N. (1988) 'Corporation tax statistics from the records of the Revenue Commissioners'. *Journal of the Statistical and Social Inquiry Society of Ireland* XXVI(5): 93–134.

Heinemann, F., M. Olbert, O. Pfeiffer, T. Schwab, C. Spengel & K. Stutzenberger (2018) 'Implications of the US tax reform for transatlantic FDI'. *Intereconomics* 53(2): 87–93.

Humer, C. & R. Pierson (2016) 'Obama's inversion curbs kill Pfizer's $160 billion Allergan deal'. *Reuters Business News,* 5 April 2016.

IFAC (2019) *Irish Fiscal Advisory Council: Fiscal Assessment Report, June 2019.* Available at: www.fiscalcouncil.ie [accessed 1 November 2019].

Janský, P. & M. Šedivý (2018) 'Estimating the revenue costs of tax treaties in developing countries'. *The World Economy* 42(6): 1828–1849.

Keegan, B. (2018) *The New Hanseatic League.* Chartered Accountants Ireland press release, December. Available at: www.charteredaccountants.ie [accessed 1 November 2019].

Killian, S. (2006) 'Where's the harm in tax competition? Lessons from US multinationals in Ireland'. *Critical Perspectives on Accounting* 17(8): 1067–1087.

Killian, S. (2013) 'Crossed lines: two cases of tax policy incoherence'. *eJournal of Tax Research* 11(3): 375–385.

Kumas, A. & D.L. Millimet (2018) 'Reassessing the effects of bilateral tax treaties on US FDI activity'. *Journal of Economics and Finance* 42(3): 451–470.

Lampreave, P. (2011) 'Fiscal competitiveness versus harmful tax competition in the European Union'. *Bulletin for International Taxation, Amsterdam* 65(6): 17.

Lewis, M. (2013) 'Sweet nothings: the human cost of a British sugar giant avoiding taxes in southern Africa'. Report For *Action Aid UK,* Somerset, February.

MacSharry, R. & P. White (2000) *The making of the Celtic Tiger.* Dublin: Mercier.

McAleese, D. (1971) *Effective tariffs and the structure of industrial protection in Ireland.* Dublin: Economic and Social Research Institute.

McCarthy, J. (1980) 'Ireland: 10% tax rate for manufacturing companies'. *Intertax* 8(10): 367–369.

Nessy, E. & N. Rahayu (2019) 'Avoiding tax using hybrid mismatch arrangement schemes in Indonesia'. *Asia Pacific Business and Economics Conference* (APBEC 2018). Paris: Atlantis Press.

Neugebauer, J. & T. Lesage (2018) 'Implementation in Luxembourg of the EU Anti-Tax Avoidance Directive'. *International Tax Journal,* November.

O'Brien, M.H. (1984) 'Tax reform in Ireland'. *Fiscal Studies* 5(4): 30–43.

Oireachtas (2010) 'Online repository of Dáil Eireann debates'. Available at: http://debates.oireachtas.ie/dail/2010/11/23/00019.asp [accessed 1 November 2019].

Pfizer (2016) 'Pfizer announces termination of proposed combination with Allergan'. Press release, 6 April. Available at: www.pfizer.com/news [accessed 1 November 2019].

Purdue, D. & H. Huang (2015) *Brexit and its impact on the Irish economy.* Dublin: National Treasury Management Agency.

Purdue, D. & H. Huang (2016) *Irish exports: the facts, the fiction and the risks.* Dublin: National Treasury Management Agency.

Radaelli, C.M. (1999) 'Harmful tax competition in the EU: policy narratives and advocacy coalitions'. *Journal of Common Market Studies* 37(4): 661–682.

Rankin, J. (2019) 'Margrethe Vestager gets second term in EU competition job'. *Guardian*, 10 September 2019.

Ruane, F. (1980) 'Optimal labour subsidies and industrial development in Ireland'. *The Economic and Social Review* 11(2): 77–98.

Schmidtke, H. (2016) 'The differentiated politicisation of European tax governance'. *West European Politics* 39(1): 64–83.

Scott, S. & F. Convery (1999) 'Cohesion countries: experience in countries on the European periphery' in K. Schlegelmilch (ed.) *Green budget reform in Europe*, pp. 41–50. Berlin & Heidelberg: Springer.

Svalborn, O. (2001) *Ireland and the evolution of tax competition*. Master thesis, Faculty of Law, University of Lund, Sweden.

Walsh, B.M. (2003) 'Taxation and foreign direct investment in Ireland', in H.G. Grubel (ed.) *Tax reform in Canada: our path to greater prosperity*. Vancouver: Fraser Institute.

Wang, B. (2018) 'After the European Commission ordered Apple to pay back taxes to Ireland: Ireland's future in the new global tax environment'. *Indiana Journal of Global Legal Studies* 25(1): 539–564.

Whitaker, T.K. (1958) *Economic development*. Dublin: Stationery Office.

Yang, J.G., A.S. Meziani & Y. Shen (2016) 'Understanding Apple's global tax strategy in Ireland'. *International Tax Journal* 42(6): 41–48.

Yoder, L.D. (2016) 'The disturbing EU state aid proceedings'. *International Tax Journal* 42: 3–5.

Young, T. (2015) 'Why Pfizer-Allergan inversion criticism is misplaced'. *International Financial Law Review*, December.

5

Ireland's migration and asylum policies in an EU context: from opt-outs to solidarity?

Aideen Elliott

Introduction

Death and suffering of migrants at Europe's borders 'has become one of the defining moral and political issues of our time' (Steinhilper & Gruijters 2018: 515). Since 2015 migration has been on the agenda of most meetings of the European Council and 'how Europe deals with … these multiple crises will shape the future of the Union and the continent' (Laffan 2016: 916). This chapter will discuss some of the aspects of EU migration policy that lead to such a crisis situation and the implications for Ireland both in terms of Irish migration policy and Ireland's place in the EU.

Migration policy is an area that has seen limited Europeanisation, as Ireland maintains opt-outs in order to protect the CTA with the UK. The following sections consider the extent to which Ireland's migration policies have been shaped by EU membership, and the role that Ireland played in the EU response to the migration policy crisis of 2015. Ireland's migration and asylum policies remain largely unaffected by the EU migration policy crisis but have undergone significant changes in their own right in the past few years. These changes were brought about by developments at the national level rather than the EU level, with social movements and the judiciary being instrumental in the introduction of both the International Protection Act (IPA) (2015) and the Right to Work for asylum seekers (2017).

Ireland has a long history of emigration with a lasting and significant impact on Irish culture. It only became a country of net immigration in 1996 and was the last EU member state to do so. Even during this period of net immigration, returning Irish migrants accounted for a significant proportion of arrivals: at its peak in 1999 the figure was almost 55% (Ruhs & Quinn 2009). Once the financial crisis hit Ireland in 2008, Ireland's period of net immigration came to a halt. Nearly half a million people left Ireland between April 2008 and April 2014 (Healy 2015).

In 2004, Ireland was one of just three member states, alongside the UK and Sweden, to decide to allow citizens from the ten accession states to move to and work in the country immediately upon their accession to the EU. This accounted for the increases in the number of migrants arriving between 2005 and 2007 (Central Statistics Office 2018). When Romania and Bulgaria joined the EU on 1 January 2007, Ireland and the UK again acted in tandem, this time both placing much tighter constraints on would-be migrants from these countries (Smith 2008). Ireland is one of just six member states that hosts more EU than non-EU migrants (Eurostat 2015: 11). Ireland's Department of Justice notes that 'in terms of numbers it's really a story of European migrants here', noting that 'Poles are by far the largest group but even after the Poles if you look down at [the] top 10 next nations only one of them is outside [the] EU' (interviews 3 and 5).

Of the non-EU nationals coming to Ireland the vast majority have been workers (about 280,000 work permits were issued from 1998 to 2008), followed by asylum seekers (74,000 applications made from 1998 to 2008), and students and dependants (Ruhs & Quinn 2009). The number of asylum seekers and refugees in Ireland is low when viewed in a global or even a European context. In 2015, Lebanon, a country of four million people, was hosting over one million refugees from Syria alone (UNHCR 2015). In the same year 1.32 million asylum applications were lodged in the entire EU. This represents an increase in the EU of 110% on 2014, when 627,000 applications were recorded. In 2015, Ireland received 3,276 applications for asylum, 0.2% of the EU total (Eurostat 2015).

Europeanisation of migration and asylum policies

The Lisbon Treaty of 2007 was heralded as a game changer for EU migration and asylum law. Firstly, the treaty was seen as the moment when EU migration and asylum law became a policy field in its own right, freeing itself from being presented as a "spillover" or "flanking measure" of the internal market (Hampshire 2016a: 542; Kostakopolou 2010: 154; Thym 2013: 717). Secondly, the treaty was expected to yield more cohesive and progressive migration and asylum policies and remedy past failings (Hampshire 2016a: 543; Kostakopolou 2010: 151; Moreno-Lax 2014: 148). The Lisbon Treaty developed a situation where 'today almost every aspect of migration – from outside and within the European Union – has a supranational dimension' (Hampshire 2016a: 537). It also maintained certain aspects of migration policy that are linked to state sovereignty. For instance, Article 79 secured the right of member states to determine how many third-country nationals it admits to its territory for the purpose of seeking work (Gsir 2013: 106; Kostakopolou 2010: 156).

However, these developments did not apply to Ireland due to the opt-outs it had negotiated.[1] Since the Amsterdam Treaty of 1999, Ireland has been party to a protocol ensuring that Ireland and the UK can maintain their CTA by opting out of any related measures. EU policy is less pronounced on labour migration than on asylum and international protection (interview 1). Ireland chose not to opt in to the Blue Card Directive (2009/50). A permit that aims to attract highly skilled workers to the EU by providing more favourable entrance and residency conditions, the Blue Card has not been a success and negotiations to reform the directive are currently stalled (Gsir 2013). Ireland has instead implemented a Critical Skills Permit, which is an example of how Ireland "mirrors" EU policies but in this case avoids some of their pitfalls (interview 4).

In choosing not to participate in EU labour migration schemes and instead basing its policy more on national interests than EU direction, Ireland is actually not deviating from the behaviour of most other member states. Regarding the specific issue of labour migration, member states have demonstrated a clear resistance to transferring to the EU the power to establish a general rule defining the conditions under which third-country nationals could come to the EU for economic purposes. Instead, member states have opted for a step-by-step approach whereby common EU rules would apply to specific categories of migrant workers, for instance the Seasonal Workers Directive 2014/36 and Intra-Corporate Transfer Directive 2014/66 (Pascouau 2015). The Commission has repeatedly met with opposition to its proposals in the realm of labour migration policy and in respect of the negotiations on the Blue Card Directive, some member states considered that due to the discrepancy between the needs of various labour markets of the member states, the political solution proposed violated the principle of subsidiarity (Acosta 2009: 20; Gsir 2013: 97).

Similarly, once the Commission opens negotiations on a Mobility Partnership (a scheme for managing legal movement from third countries) each member state will be able to choose whether to participate or not. Hampshire notes the importance of their respective history with the third country in question as well as their geographical location in determining member state participation in a Mobility Partnership. While this is not surprising, 'it clearly illustrates how national interests persist within a common European external migration policy' (Hampshire 2016b: 580). Papagianni describes the EU as often functioning 'as a mere framework for the development of bilateral agreements' (2013: 290).

The Common European Asylum System (CEAS) was to be accomplished in two steps, adopting minimum standards in key areas as a first step and a "common procedure" and "uniform status" in the long term. In the first phase of the CEAS, Ireland opted in to the Qualifications Directive (2004), which dealt with minimum standards for the qualification and status of persons as refugees or as persons who otherwise need international protection and the content of the protection granted, and the Asylum Procedures Directive (2005), which focused on minimum standards on procedures in member states for granting and withdrawing refugee status (as did the UK). Ireland did not opt in to the Reception Conditions Directive (2003), which set down minimum standards for the treatment of asylum seekers as regards education and welfare. The Directive provides that an asylum seeker has the right to access the labour market no later than nine months after they lodge their asylum application. It was on this point that Ireland diverged, having a complete ban on working for asylum seekers, arguing that their needs were catered for in the direct provision system.

The Dublin Regulation determines which member state is responsible for examining an asylum application and hosting the asylum seeker. The Dublin system[2] aims to eliminate secondary movement between member states, assuming that there would be no need for an asylum seeker to move between them as the conditions should not vary from one to another. In 2008, the Commission recognised that this first phase of the CEAS had not been entirely successful in achieving harmonisation of asylum policies because there remained unacceptably divergent results from one member state to another and 'this is creating secondary movements and goes against the principle of providing equal access to protection across the EU' (EU Commission, in Bauloz et al. 2015: 5).

Partly as an unsuccessful effort towards harmonisation, most of the regulations and directives that had been adopted in the first phase of the CEAS were recast in what is now commonly referred to as the second generation of CEAS instruments adopted between 2011 and 2013. At that time Ireland chose not to opt in to any of these instruments as they advanced from minimum to common standards. However, Ireland remains legally bound by the first phase instruments, and in 2017 Ireland decided to opt in to the Reception Conditions Directive.

A recent development in Ireland's migration and asylum policies was the introduction of the IPA in 2015, replacing the Refugee Act of 1996. One aim of the IPA was to reduce waiting times for asylum seekers. The long waiting time for asylum seekers to receive a decision on their application is one of the most criticised aspects of Ireland's asylum regime as the average stay is thirty-eight months, with some in the system for seven years or more. As Thornton (2016) notes, successive Ministers of Justice had attempted to speed up the system. To streamline the system and prevent lengthy delays the IPA replaced a system of separate applications for refugee status and subsidiary protection with a single application that examines both in the same process.

While the single application procedure was welcomed by many civil society organisations, a number of groups, in particular the Movement of Asylum Seekers in Ireland, protested against the introduction of the IPA. This was partly because of changes to refugees' entitlements to family reunification. The IPA narrowed the definition of which family members qualified for reunification. The Seanad attempted to address this issue and in 2017 a bill that would revert to the family reunification provisions laid out in the Refugee Act 1996 passed through all stages in the Seanad with cross-party support but was opposed by the government.[3]

A further recent reform was the decision to opt in to the Reception Conditions Directive. For a number of years many civil society organisations had been campaigning for the Irish government to grant asylum seekers the right to access the labour market, as prescribed by this directive. The Irish government's decision to opt in came about from a successful legal challenge to the absolute ban on asylum seekers working. In May 2017, the Supreme Court ruled unanimously that the ban was unconstitutional,[4] leading to an announcement that Ireland would opt in to the Reception Conditions Directive.

Both reforms brought Ireland closer in line with European norms. The IPA was however greatly influenced by domestic factors. In summer 2014, asylum seekers began protesting about the conditions in direct provision centres. Since its inception in 2000, the direct provision system has been criticised as a violation of human rights by, among others, asylum seekers, the UN, several human rights NGOs, politicians in Ireland, the Children's Ombudsman and solidarity activists. Asylum seekers and their supporters successfully pushed the government to address the situation, leading to the McMahon Report which detailed 173 recommendations to Ireland's asylum procedures. The report recommended 'the enactment of the International Protection Bill and the implementation of the single application procedure as a matter of urgency' (2015: 17). The Department of Justice acknowledged the McMahon Report and identified the Bill as 'a key pillar of reforming recommendations' (Department of Justice 2015b). The IPA brought Ireland closer into line with the procedures applied in other EU member states (Sheridan 2017: 16) and gave further effect to a range of instruments of the CEAS (IHREC 2015). We could say therefore that the impetus for this legislative reform came from domestic politics rather than from the EU but was ultimately influenced by the CEAS and European norms.

The EU's migration policy crisis

In 2015, the number of people fleeing to Europe increased significantly. According to the UNHCR, over one million refugees and migrants reached

Europe by sea in 2015, with almost 4,000 feared drowned, most fleeing conflict and persecution. Of those arriving in Europe, 84% came from the world's top ten refugee-producing countries (UNHCR 2015). Article 26 of the Schengen Border Code (which Ireland has opted into) obliges member states to fine any carriers who carry passengers who are not in possession of the necessary documents. There exists at present no legal way for a person fleeing to enter the EU in order to apply for asylum. Of those granted international protection, 90% arrived through irregular means (van Ballegooij & Navarra 2018: 9) and so it follows that those fleeing to Europe rely heavily on smugglers in order to reach protection.

For some the situation was clearly a humanitarian crisis. The erection of internal borders was also described as a crisis for the rules of the EU, with the European Commissioner for Migration, Dimitris Avramopoulos, saying that Europe was not experiencing a refugee crisis but a crisis in solidarity. Den Heijer et al. (2016) named it a policy crisis. It was also a trigger for an illiberal backlash in several EU states (see, for example, Dinas et al. 2019). In any case, it was clear the events of 2015 and the reactions of the member states were a pivotal point in European cooperation on migration.

Since 2005, the EU has sought to coordinate and strengthen border control efforts of its member states through Frontex (the European Border and Coast Guard). This also involved working with third countries,[5] participating in controlling access to EU borders (Wunderlich 2013). Forced migrants destined for Europe therefore turned to smugglers, who in turn began using lighter boats in order to avoid detection. This made the EU's border one of the deadliest in the world (Jones 2016). While deals with Turkey and Libya blocked many people in these countries (in dire conditions and with widespread human rights abuses), in the first ten weeks of 2019, 234 individuals died on the three main Mediterranean Sea routes (IOM 2019). The conditions in which migrants and refugees were kept in Europe also cost lives, and it is widely acknowledged that the conditions in particular in the camps on the Greek islands (still) do not meet basic humanitarian standards (Amnesty International 2018).

In the summer of 2015 some EU states began to close their borders. The Schengen area and two decades of open borders in the EU were therefore under threat. In May 2015 the European Commission adopted the European Agenda on Migration, setting out both immediate actions to address the crisis and longer-term pillars of EU migration policy, saying that 'Europe cannot stand by whilst lives are being lost' and calling for the targeting of groups that 'exploit vulnerable migrants' (European Commission 2015: 3). The budget for the Frontex joint operations Triton and Poseidon was tripled, and immediate actions were concentrated on operations at sea both to conduct search and rescue and to target criminal smuggling networks. The

relocation of asylum seekers from Greece, Italy and Hungary and the resettlement of refugees from regional host countries, together with support for
frontline member states and working with third countries to tackle the
sources of migration were also enacted.

EUNAVFOR MED, named Operation Sophia, was launched on 22 June
2015:

> [The mission's] core mandate is to undertake systematic efforts to identify,
> capture and dispose of vessels and enabling assets used or suspected of being
> used by migrant smugglers or traffickers, in order to contribute to wider EU
> efforts to disrupt the business model of human smuggling and trafficking net-
> works in the Southern Central Mediterranean and prevent the further loss of
> life at sea. (EEAS 2017)

Supporting tasks included training the Libyan coastguard and navy. Operation Sophia rescued over 45,000 people from the Mediterranean, but search
and rescue was not part of its mandate (Operation Sophia 2018).

In December 2015, the European Commission proposed the establishment of a European Border and Coast Guard to address the perceived difficulties of Frontex, namely a shortage of resources and a lack of cooperation
from member states. In October 2016, at Bulgaria's border with Turkey, the
new agency was officially launched, and changes included a significant
increase in the number of permanent staff and the agency purchasing its
own equipment and deploying them in border operations. But the EU policy
responses gave priority 'to security-driven (home affairs) and military concerns and interests of the EU and its member states', focusing on border
controls, return and readmission, and fighting against smuggling 'instead of
first ensuring full compliance with fundamental human rights standards and
principles' (Carrera et al. 2015: 2).

The most contentious of the Agenda's six actions was of course the relocation scheme. Hungary and Slovakia unsuccessfully brought court actions
against the scheme to the ECJ. The relocation scheme was a recognition that
those member states who were receiving the highest numbers of asylum
seekers could not be expected to host all, or even the vast majority, of the
refugees and migrants arriving in the EU. The Council took two decisions[6]
to operationalise an emergency relocation mechanism to relocate asylum
seekers from Greece, Italy and Hungary to other member states. The number of asylum seekers allocated to each state was calculated using a formula
that took into account the country's population, total GDP, average number
of asylum applications over the previous four years, and their unemployment rate. In addition, the quotas were supposed to be mandatory rather
than voluntary. Member states were granted €6,000 for each person received
and Italy, Greece and Hungary €500 for each person relocated to cover

transport costs. Only asylum seekers hailing from a country with a 75% recognition rate[7] across the EU qualified for relocation. This created a number of problems since a number of refugee-producing countries, for example Afghanistan, did not meet these criteria.

The level of opposition from member states to this scheme was evidence of the scarcity of solidarity between member states. The EU failed to find a way to work together on this issue and so decided to broaden their search for close partners, leading them to rely even more heavily on third countries. Agreements with third countries are of course nothing new and cooperation dates back decades,[8] but this approach was one of the few things upon which member states could agree.

Ireland's role in the EU response to crisis

As mentioned earlier, Ireland has an opt-out from all migration-related measures in order to protect the CTA with the UK. In 2015, Ireland decided to opt in to a number of the measures outlined in the EU Agenda on Migration, notably to relocate asylum seekers from Greece and Italy, to resettle refugees from Lebanon, and to send the Irish Defence Forces to participate in the Mediterranean operations. Ireland also contributed to the EU trust funds for Africa and Turkey and provided some personnel to the European Asylum Support Office. The Irish Naval Service also participated in search and rescue missions in the Mediterranean under Operation Pontus.[9] In 2017, the Irish government decided that the Naval Service would join Operation Sophia.

Since any operation that involves the Irish Defence Forces taking part in an international military operation must have in addition to UN sanction, the approval of the Cabinet and of the Dáil, the move was debated in the Dáil and there was some public debate in advance of the vote. There was a certain amount of public pride in the search and rescue work done by the Irish Navy, as evidenced in 2015 by Óglaigh na hÉireann receiving the 'People of the Year' award, for the work of the Naval Service. Moving to Operation Sophia was met with concern from opposition TDs and in public debate that the move entailed a switch from a humanitarian to a military mission. Ethical concerns were voiced, in particular that resources could be diverted from rescuing drowning people, and the risk that Irish efforts could result in refugees and migrants being sent to Libyan detention centres. In July 2017, government and Dáil approval was secured for the deployment of an Irish Naval Service vessel as part of Operation Sophia. Moreno-Lax (2018: 120) has argued that Operation Sophia actually entails a "rescue-without-protection" model because it aims to "spare" migrants from the urgent dangers of irregular voyages, but without any real opportunities for them to exercise their right to claim asylum in a safe country or, worryingly, to escape Libya where they are detained in inhumane conditions. Although the risks of violating the principle of non-refoulement are extremely high,[10] the operation escapes critique by framing their work as humanitarian.

The Council decisions to relocate asylum seekers from Italy and Greece who were in clear need of protection (defined in the decisions as being from a country with an average acceptance rate of at least 75% on their asylum applications) were not binding on Ireland. However, Frances Fitzgerald, then Minister for Justice, announced that Ireland would exercise its right to opt in to the relocation scheme, pointing to the 'humanitarian concerns' of Irish people and acknowledging the fact that Europe-wide solutions were necessary (Department of Justice 2015a). Indeed, Ireland agreed to accept more asylum seekers than it was obliged to do: 'the EU quota for Ireland was 2,900 refugees but we have greatly exceeded that target and have voluntarily agreed to bring in 4,000 refugees' (Joint Committee on Justice and Equality 2017: 21). Ireland could have pledged to take fewer people, but the feeling was that this would not have been in line with the spirit of the scheme (interview 5). In practice, although Ireland had pledged to relocate 623 asylum seekers from Italy, they did not relocate any because of a dispute over security checks.[11] Relocation from Greece was more successful and in March 2018 the Department of Justice announced that Ireland had successfully relocated a total of 1,022 asylum seekers.

Ireland was one of the member states that agreed to participate in ad hoc measures to resolve particular disputes. For instance, in June 2018, the MV Lifeline, a ship operated by a German NGO, rescued 234 migrants off the coast of Libya. The ship was refused permission to dock by Italy, Malta and Spain and was left sitting 30 km off the coast of Italy. In August 2018, the *Diciotti*, an Italian coast guard vessel, picked up 190 migrants from a smuggling boat. Italy's recently elected Lega government refused to allow them to disembark from the ship, demanding instead that other EU countries host them. In both cases, Ireland agreed to accept 10% of those on board, citing in the latter case a commitment to European solidarity and calling it 'the right thing to do' (*The Irish Times* 2018).

At a time when anti-migrant sentiment was causing problems for the EU, throwing obstacles before potential solutions to the migration policy crisis, and declarations by certain political leaders in Europe were pitting their country against European solutions, the Irish political class promoted a more "solution friendly" discourse. Frances Fitzgerald stated that 'at a time when anti-immigration and anti-refugee sentiment has, unfortunately, been part of mainstream rhetoric in the international political and media debate, it matters that Ireland and this House stand by our tradition of supporting refugees' (Department of Justice and Equality 2016). One representative of a member state noted that:

> Ireland didn't have any obligations and decided by itself to be part of it because they think they are part of a community and in a community in difficult circumstances you have to help each other but you have also to help these people who need protection. So Ireland was a great partner and not like others who were difficult in this. (interview 6)

However, supporting refugees did not translate into criticising or opposing any EU actions that harm refugees. While NGOs raised concerns about the conditions in Libya and about migrants being returned to detention centres, Irish political leaders did not publicly question the ongoing EU missions in Libya. Indeed, Taoiseach Leo Varadkar was critical of some NGOs conducting search and rescue missions in the Mediterranean, going so far as to suggest they could be creating a pull factor (Leahy & Raleigh 2018). This is very much in line with the dominant framing that came from Brussels, one that is committed to working with Libya and that is hostile to search and rescue missions being run by civil society actors.

Of course, the numbers that Ireland have welcomed are minuscule and Ireland's influence in the area of migration is not strong since Ireland is not a country with an external border nor a large non-EU population. On the other hand, in terms of both action and discourse Ireland has been in line with the EU. As one Irish civil servant noted, 'migration is a human tragedy [but] it's not directly impacting us … they're there, it's impacting us to the extent that there's a moral imperative on us to help more. But it's not a national interest. Brexit is a national interest' (interview 7).

The Irish government could volunteer to host asylum seekers without being constrained by a fear of the political cost at home. Anti-migrant sentiment certainly exists in Ireland and the form, development and impact of institutional and everyday racism in Ireland has been well documented by organisations like European Network Against Racism who manage ireport, a racist incident reporting system, and by scholars such as Lentin and McVeigh (2002) and Fanning (2012). However, Zaun notes that voters' positions become influential only if they are mobilised by political parties (2018: 47). Anti-migrant parties have not been gaining ground in mainstream politics in Ireland. Analyses of Eurobarometer results have found that attitudes towards migrants have actually remained stable across most member states, so the rise in support for far-right parties is rather accounted for by the importance that voters place on the issue of migration. The data demonstrates that in a number of EU member states, there has been significant volatility in the perceived salience of migration as a political topic across many EU member states (Dennison & Geddes 2017). However, in Ireland, migration is not "a doorstep issue" and is not high enough on the list of voter priorities to have dissuaded the Irish government from opting in to the relocation scheme (interview 2).

Conclusion

Migration policy has exposed deep differences among member states with respect to European solidarity, or as then European Council President Donald Tusk put it, a 'test of our Europeanness' (cited in Dinan et al. 2017: 122). Irish politicians have rhetorically emphasised solidarity with migrants and refugees but also solidarity with fellow EU member states, particularly those hosting far greater numbers of refugees than Ireland. Ireland's migration policy has also been concerned with accommodating the CTA with the UK. At home migration is not a "doorstep issue" and at an EU level it is not a "sacred cow" to use Brigid Laffan's term, unlike corporation tax or military neutrality (Laffan 2017).

EU membership has impacted on the make-up of Ireland's migrant population with the majority of migrants in Ireland being EU citizens. Europeanisation of Ireland's asylum and labour migration policies has been somewhat limited. Ireland's policies have moved closer to EU norms, but it appears that the motivation for policy change comes from domestic rather than EU level politics with social movements and the judiciary playing decisive roles in some of the major changes, namely the Right to Work for asylum seekers, reforms to the direct provision system and the IPA. Once the government decided to make changes to a migration policy area, they did look to EU norms, as shown in particular with the IPA.

Since 2015, migration has been high on the EU policy agenda and both "vertical" tensions between national governments and the EU institutions, and "horizontal" conflicts between member states, remain (Hampshire 2016a). Ireland has remained largely unaffected by the crisis, accepting numbers of refugees and migrants too low to have an impact. However, in this era of open questioning of whether democracy needs to be liberal, and discussion of "European values" in opting in to the Council decisions and embracing a relatively open rhetoric (if not practice), Ireland's politicians are placing Ireland squarely in the camp of open and "Europe-minded" states, playing a part in a union not just of economy but of the values and norms of the European project.

Notes

This work was supported by the Irish Research Council Government of Ireland Post-Graduate Scholarship (2016–2020). Data used in this chapter comes from interviews conducted with Irish civil servants in the Department of Justice and the

Department of Foreign Affairs in both Dublin and Brussels, as well as a year's field-work in Brussels consisting mainly of participant observation at migration-related events and extensive interviews with actors in each of the EU institutions and relevant agencies.

1 The opt-outs are in Articles 1 and 2 of Protocol No 21 on the position of the UK and Ireland in respect of the Area of Freedom, Security and Justice, annexed to the TEU and the TFEU.
2 The Dublin system was originally established by the Dublin Convention, signed in Dublin in 1990. In 2003, the Dublin Convention was replaced by the Dublin II Regulation. In 2013, the Dublin III Regulation was adopted, replacing the Dublin II Regulation. The Dublin III Regulation has been in force since 1 January 2014. These attempts to address weaknesses in the system are widely recognised as having left the problems intact and in May 2016, as part of its proposed reform of the CEAS, the Commission presented a draft proposal for the Dublin IV Regulation. No agreement was reached on Dublin IV.
3 The International Protection (Family Reunification) (Amendment) Bill 2017.
4 In the case N.H.V. v. Minister for Justice (see Refworld 2017).
5 These include Morocco, Senegal, Ukraine, Niger and Turkey.
6 Council Decision No. 2015/1523 (14 September 2015) and Council Decision No. 2015/1601 (22 September 2015).
7 The recognition rate measures the 'proportion of refugee claims accepted' (UNHCR 2009: 38).
8 Particularly between Libya and Italy, and Morocco and Spain.
9 Operation Pontus was a bilateral Italian programme running in parallel with, but separate to, Operation Sophia.
10 Non-refoulement is the practice of not forcing refugees or asylum seekers to return to a country in which they are liable to be subjected to persecution.
11 The Italian authorities did not permit security checks on their territory and although several other member states such as Portugal relocated asylum seekers from Italy without conducting their own security checks, Ireland did not.

References

Acosta, D. (2009) 'The good, the bad and the ugly in EU migration law: Is the European parliament becoming bad and ugly? (the adoption of directive 2008/15: The returns directive)'. *European Journal of Migration and Law* 11(1): 19–39.
Amnesty International (2018) '"I want to decide about my future": uprooted women in Greece speak out'. Available at: www.amnesty.org/en/documents/eur25/9071/2018/en/ [accessed 9 April 2020].
Bauloz, C., M. Ineli-Ciger, S. Singer & C. Bauloz (eds) (2015) *Seeking asylum in the European Union: selected protection issues raised by the second phase of the Common European Asylum System.* Leiden: Brill.
Carrera, S., S. Blockmans, D. Gros & E. Guild (2015) 'The EU's response to the refugee crisis: taking stock and setting policy priorities'. CEPS Essay, no. 20: 9.

Central Statistics Office (2018) *Population and Labour Force projections 2017–2051*. Available at: www.cso.ie/en/releasesandpublications/ep/p-plfp/population-andlabourforceprojections2017–2051/migrationassumptions/ [accessed 9 April 2020].

Den Heijer, M., J. Rijpma & T. Spijkerboer (2016) 'Coercion, prohibition and great expectations: the continuing failure of the Common European Asylum System'. *Common Market Law Review* 5(3): 607–642.

Dennison, J. & A. Geddes (2017) 'Are Europeans turning against asylum seekers and refugees?' Published by ECRE, 17 November. Available at: www.ecre.org/op-ed-are-europeans-turning-against-asylum-seekers-and-refugees/ [accessed 9 April 2020].

Department of Justice (2015a) *Ireland to accept up to 4,000 persons under Relocation and Resettlement programmes – Fitzgerald*. Available at: www.inis.gov.ie/en/INIS/Pages/Ireland%20to%20accept%20up%20to%204,000%20persons%20under%20Relocation%20and%20Resettlement%20programmes-%20Fitzgerald [accessed 9 April 2020].

Department of Justice (2015b) *Minister Fitzgerald publishes International Protection Bill 2015*. Available at: www.inis.gov.ie/en/INIS/Pages/Minister%20Fitzgerald%20publishes%20International%20Protection%20Bill%202015 [accessed 9 April 2020).

Department of Justice and Equality (2016) 'Speech by Minister for Justice and Equality: the EU migration and refugee crisis – Dáil Éireann'. Available at: www.justice.ie/en/JELR/Pages/SP16000093 [accessed 30 September 2020].

Dinan, D., N. Nugent & W.E. Paterson (2017) *The European Union in crisis*. Basingstoke: Palgrave Macmillan.

Dinas, E., K. Matakos, D. Xefteris & D. Hangartner (2019) 'Waking up the Golden Dawn: does exposure to the refugee crisis increase support for extreme right parties?' *Political analysis* 29(2): 244–254.

EEAS (2017) 'Factsheet on EUNAVFOR MED mission'. European External Action Service. Available at: https://eeas.europa.eu/sites/eeas/files/april_2017_-_factsheet_on_eunavfor_med_mission_english.pdf [accessed 30 September 2020].

European Commission (2015) 'Managing migration better in all aspects: a European Agenda on Migration'. European Commission press release, 15 May. Available at: https://ec.europa.eu/commission/presscorner/detail/en/IP_15_4956 [accessed 30 September 2020].

Eurostat (2015) 'Asylum in the EU member states: more than 410,000 first time asylum seekers registered in the third quarter of 2015, 1 out of 3 are from Syria'. *Eurostat News Release*. Available at: https://ec.europa.eu/eurostat/documents/2995521/7105334/3-10122015-AP-EN.pdf [accessed 9 April 2020].

Fanning, B. (2012) *Racism and social change in the Republic of Ireland*, 2nd edition. Manchester: Manchester University Press.

Gsir, S. (2013) 'EU labour immigration policy: discourses and mobility'. *Refugee Survey Quarterly* 32(4): 90–111.

Hampshire, J. (2016a) 'European migration governance since the Lisbon Treaty: introduction to the Special Issue'. *Journal of Ethnic and Migration Studies* 42(4): 537–553.

Hampshire, J. (2016b) 'Speaking with one voice? The European Union's global approach to migration and mobility and the limits of international migration cooperation'. *Journal of Ethnic and Migration Studies* 42(4): 571–586.

Healy T. (2015) 'Emigration has taken its toll'. *NERI Nevin Economic Research Institute blog*. Available at: www.nerinstitute.net/blog/monday-blog-emigration-has-taken-its-toll [accessed 9 April 2020].

Irish Human Rights and Equality Commission (2015) *IHREC Recommendations on the General Scheme of the International Protection Bill 2015*. Available at: www.ihrec.ie/download/pdf/ihrec_recs_general_scheme_internation_protection_bill_26_june_2015.pdf [accessed 9 April 2020].

IOM (2019) 'Mediterranean migrant arrivals reach 10,308 in 2019; deaths reach 234', International Organisation for Migration press release. Available at: www.iom.int/news/mediterranean-migrant-arrivals-reach-10308-2019-deaths-reach-234 [accessed 9 April 2020].

The Irish Times (2018) 'Ireland to take up to 25 migrants who were stuck on boat off Italy', 30 September 2020.

Joint Committee on Justice and Equality (2017) *Joint committee report on immigration, asylum and the refugee crisis*. Available at: www.justice.ie/en/JELR/Pages/SP17000309 [accessed 20 September 2020].

Jones, R. (2016) *Violent borders: refugees and the right to move*. London: Verso.

Kostakopoulou, D. (2010) 'An open and secure Europe? Fixity and fissures in the area of freedom, security and justice after Lisbon and Stockholm'. *European Security* 19(2): 151–167.

Laffan, B. (2016) 'Europe's union in crisis: tested and contested'. *West European Politics* 39(5): 915–932.

Laffan, B. (2017) 'Brexit may mean sacrifice of Ireland's sacred cows: a Macron presidency will bring renewed attention to Irish neutrality and our corporate tax regime'. *The Irish Times*, 16 May. Available at: www.irishtimes.com/opinion/ireland-may-have-to-sacrifice-sacred-cows-to-survive-brexit-1.3083791 [accessed 9 April 2020].

Leahy, P. & Raleigh, D. (2018) 'Naval Service does not send migrants back to camps in Libya, Government says: EU operation helps return of migrants to risk of rape, slavery and murder, charity says'. *The Irish Times*, 5 July. Available at: www.irishtimes.com/news/politics/naval-service-does-not-send-migrants-back-to-camps-in-libya-government-says-1.3555632 [accessed 9 April 2020].

Lentin, R. & McVeigh, R. (eds) (2002) *Racism and antiracism in Ireland*. Belfast: Beyond the Pale.

McMahon, B. (2015) *Working group to report to government on improvements to the protection process, including direct provision and supports to asylum seekers*. Dublin: Department of Justice and Euqality.

Moreno-Lax, V. (2014) 'Life after Lisbon: EU asylum policy as a factor of migration control', in D. Acosta Arcarazo & C. Murphy (eds) *EU security and justice law: after Lisbon and Stockholm*, 1st edition, pp. 146–167. Oxford: Hart Publishing.

Moreno-Lax, V. (2018) 'The EU humanitarian border and the securitization of human rights: the "Rescue-Through-Interdiction/Rescue-Without-Protection" paradigm'. *Journal of Common Market Studies* 56(1): 119–140.

Operation Sophia (2018) 'The Prime Minister of the Republic of Ireland visits EUNAVFOR MED Operation Sophia's headquarters'. Available at: www.operationsophia.eu/the-prime-minister-of-the-republic-of-ireland-visits-eunavfor-med-operation-sophias-headquarters/ [accessed 9 April 2020].

Papagianni, G. (2013) 'Forging an external EU migration policy: from externalisation of border management to a comprehensive policy?' *European Journal of Migration and Law* 15(3): 283–299.

Pascouau, Y. (2015) *EU labour migration policy by other means? The potential impact of EU economic governance reforms on labour migration policymaking.* Fieri Working Paper, European Policy Centre Policy Brief.

Refworld (2017) 'N.H.V v. Minister for Justice & Equality and ors, [2017] IESC 35'. Available at: www.refworld.org/cases,IRL_SC,5a623cca4.html [accessed 2 August 2020].

Ruhs, M. & E. Quinn (2009) *Ireland: from rapid immigration to recession.* Migration Policy Institute. Available at: www.migrationpolicy.org/article/ireland-rapid-immigration-recession [accessed 9 April 2020].

Sheridan, A. (2017) 'Returning rejected asylum seekers: practices and challenges in Ireland'. *European Migration Network, Economic and Social Research Institute (ESRI) Research Series.* Available at: https://emn.ie/files/p_201707030349252017_EMN%20Rejectedasylumseekers_online.pdf [accessed 30 September 2020].

Smith, J. (2008) 'Towards consensus? Centre-right parties and immigration policy in the UK and Ireland'. *Journal of European Public Policy* 15(3): 415–431.

Steinhilper, E. & R.J. Gruijters (2018) 'A contested crisis: policy narratives and empirical evidence on border deaths in the Mediterranean'. *Sociology* 52(3): 515–533.

Thornton, L. (2016) 'A view from outside the EU reception acquis: reception rights for asylum seekers in Ireland', in P. Minderhoud & K. Zwaan (eds) *The recast Reception Conditions Directive: central themes, problem issues, and implementation in selected member states*, pp. 49–76. Oisterwijk: Wolf Legal Publishers.

Thym, D. (2013) 'EU migration policy and its constitutional rationale: a cosmopolitan outlook'. *Common Market Law Review* 50(3): 709–736.

UNHCR (2009) *UNHCR statistical yearbook.* Geneva: UNHCR. Available at: www.unhcr.org/4ce531e09.pdf [accessed 30 September 2020].

UNHCR (2015) *Refugees from Syria: Lebanon.* Available at: https://data2.unhcr.org/en/documents/download/45826 [accessed 9 April 2020].

van Ballegooij, W. & C. Navarra (2018) 'Humanitarian visas: European added value assessment accompanying the European Parliament's Legislative Own-initiative Report'. *Research Paper, European Parliamentary Research Service.*

Wunderlich, D. (2013) 'Towards coherence of EU external migration policy? Implementing a complex policy'. *International Migration* 51(6): 26–40.

Zaun, N. (2018) 'States as gatekeepers in EU asylum politics: explaining the non-adoption of a refugee quota system'. *Journal of Common Market Studies* 56(1): 44–62.

Interviews

1 Department of Justice official, August 2017.
2 Department of Justice official, December 2017.
3 Department of Justice official, February 2018.
4 Department of Justice official, February 2018.
5 Department of Justice official, February 2018.
6 Member of the Permanent Representation to the EU of a member state, March 2018.
7 Department of Foreign Affairs official, February 2018.

6

Irish political parties and the EU: Euro-nationalism, not Euroscepticism

Michael Holmes

Introduction

The financial crisis triggered a 'continent-wide rise of Euroscepticism' (Torreblanca & Leonard 2013: 1), with the crisis having a significant impact on support for Eurosceptic parties (Hobolt & De Vries 2016). In some ways, Ireland is a perfect candidate to develop a strong Eurosceptic movement. Its political system is marked by a 'fundamental nationalist consensus' (Garvin 2005: 3), the financial crisis saw the imposition by the EU and IMF of a severe austerity programme and the loss of economic sovereignty, and it 'experienced dramatic increases in immigration flows' from the mid-1990s (Ruhs & Quinn 2009: 1). All these factors can be associated with the potential rise of Euroscepticism (see Taggart & Szczerbiak 2018).

Undoubtedly, 'the Eurozone crisis pushed Euroscepticism to the fore of the Irish party system and transformed the salience of these issues in the country's political debate' (Taggart & Szczerbiak 2018: 1210). And yet Irish party politics is also marked by the absence of a coherent and consistent Eurosceptic challenge. While the financial crisis did see some increased criticism of the EU, that subsequently diminished. If anything, Ireland emerged from the financial and Brexit crises with a stronger pro-EU consensus among its parties. Irish parties have found a way of expressing their nationalism through the EU rather than against it, so that Irish politics is marked more by this 'Euro-nationalism' than by Euroscepticism.

This chapter explores the changing – and unchanging – Irish party positions on European integration. It argues there are three reasons why Euroscepticism did not take off as it did elsewhere. First, most parties depicted the financial crisis as having been caused by domestic policy decisions, with the EU largely portrayed as a stern but necessary saviour. This was reinforced by the existence of a strong consensus that Ireland's best interests lay in accepting external prescriptions. Second, while there was a strong element of criticism of the EU in Sinn Féin, the main left-wing party in Ireland,[1] it was also trying to manoeuvre itself into being seen as a potential coalition partner and was aware that the EU issue was a potential deal-breaker on that front. Third, the Brexit crisis served to renew and significantly strengthen the pro-EU consensus in Ireland.

The next section will set out the positions of Irish parties on European integration prior to the financial crisis, demonstrating the deeply embedded pro-EU consensus in Irish politics. The following section will explore the development of party positions during the financial crisis, with a focus on the general elections of 2011 and 2016, the European election of 2014 and the referendums on the Treaty Lisbon in 2009 and the Fiscal Treaty (TSCG) in 2012. The subsequent section examines party policies on Brexit, looking at their positions during the UK referendum in 2016 and the subsequent debates around the UK's departure from the EU. Finally, the chapter will assess the overall patterns of development and will touch on possible future challenges to the Euro-nationalist consensus in Ireland.

Irish parties and European integration

The standard narrative about parties and European integration goes something like this: centre-right parties (especially Christian democrats and liberal democrats) are the founders of integration and are strongly supportive; centre-left parties (social democrats) joined in slightly later but have become equally committed supporters. This leaves the radical right and the radical left as the two areas where Euroscepticism tends to be found. In general, this model fits Ireland very nicely.[2] The country's two large centre-right parties, Fianna Fáil and Fine Gael, were unequivocally in favour of membership from the outset (Hayward & Fallon 2010; Reidy 2010). The smaller centre-left Labour Party was initially more hesitant but was quickly drawn to a pro-integration position (Holmes 2006, 2010). These three parties dominated Irish politics until the 1980s, but then the party system began to diversify. This brought some more critical EU voices into the Dáil, but their criticism was often limited. The Green Party was initially critical of the EU, but eventually became more supportive, as will be shown in this chapter (and see also Bolleyer & Panke 2010). The radical left[3] has generally been a stronghold of EU-critical perspectives, but even here there are signs of a shift to a more pro-EU stance (see Holmes 2019).

These patterns of Irish party stances on integration are evident from the positions adopted in the various EU-related referendums in Ireland (see Table 6.1).[4] The table highlights the consistent support of the two centre-right parties, joined slightly later by Labour. Perhaps the two notable features are the following. Firstly, there is evidence of centripetal pressures on some of the parties that are further to the left. This has been resisted by

Table 6.1 Irish parties and Ireland's European referendums – plus Brexit

	FG	FF	LP	GP	SF	AAA	PBPA
1972 – Membership	Yes	Yes	No		No		
1987 – Single European Act	Yes	Yes	split[a]		No		
1992 – Maastricht Treaty	Yes	Yes	Yes		No		
1998 – Treaty of Amsterdam	Yes	Yes	Yes		No		
2001 – Treaty of Nice (1)	Yes	Yes	Yes	No	No	No	
2002 – Treaty of Nice (2)	Yes	Yes	Yes	No	No	No	
2008 – Treaty of Lisbon (1)	Yes	Yes	Yes	split[b]	No	No	No
2009 – Treaty of Lisbon (2)	Yes	Yes	Yes	Yes	No	No	No
2012 – Fiscal Compact Treaty	Yes	Yes	Yes	split[b]	No	No	No
2016 – Brexit (UK)	(Yes)[c]	(Yes)[c]	(Yes)[c]	(Yes)[c]	Yes	No	No

Source: Author's elaboration from various sources.

Notes:
a. No official position agreed by the party.
b. Green Party rules required a two-thirds majority vote in a party conference to approve a Yes campaign. In both instances, this was missed by a handful of votes.
c. For the 2016 Brexit referendum, parentheses indicate that the party was not directly active in the UK.

some, but others have succumbed to it, and as this chapter will argue, that path became apparent for Sinn Féin during Brexit. The second feature is the absence of an anti-European right. This will be discussed in more detail through the chapter.

Why is there this strong pro-European position among Irish parties? Partly, it reflects a consensus about Irish economic policy since the late 1950s, seeking to develop an open, export-orientated state. There was strong agreement that membership of what was then called the European Community promised significant economic benefits. But it also reflected a feeling that a small state had few options in the international environment, and there was a strong perception that the Irish economy was already constrained by its dependence on the UK. Membership of the European project would reduce this dependence, rather than replace it with dependence on Europe. From this point of view, mainstream Irish nationalism was able to accept membership as a means of regaining rather than losing sovereignty.

Party responses to the economic crisis

The decision in September 2009 by the Fianna Fáil–Green Party coalition government to intervene to support Irish banks turned an escalating economic crisis into a political one as well. The political responses to the crisis revealed a growing ideological fault-line in Irish politics, one which had significant implications for how political parties engaged with European integration. This section examines how the parties responded to the crisis, looking at how they interpreted the cause of the crisis, how they responded in policy terms, what happened to them as a result and how this affected (if at all) their view of the EU.

In terms of the perceived causes of the crisis, it was evident that it had not been caused directly by the EU. Instead, it was seen as a result of a global crisis which triggered an Irish banking collapse. Fianna Fáil insisted that their attempt to prop up the banking system was absolutely necessary and the subsequent need to seek support from the EU was an inevitable consequence of the disaster. 'The aim of every action Fianna Fáil has taken in government over the last three years has been to return our country to the path of sustainable economic growth' (Fianna Fáil 2011: 2). But the Greens talked about Ireland being 'damaged by reckless financial policies, lax regulation and a failed political system' (Green Party 2011) – hardly a resounding endorsement from their partners in coalition.

This focus squarely on government failure rather than on the EU was strongly evident among the opposition parties. Fine Gael blamed Fianna Fáil for allowing 'structural faults within our own economy' (Fine Gael 2009: 13) to emerge, criticising their 'cosy culture of cronyism and low standards' (Fine Gael 2011: 2). Similarly, Labour focused on 'the mismanagement of the economy by Fianna Fáil' (Labour Party 2011: 13) as the cause of the crisis and condemning it as 'an act of economic treason' (Oireachtas 2010). Sinn Féin also blamed the government, arguing that 'Fianna Fáil and the Green Party have brought the country close to economic ruin' (Sinn Féin 2011: 18). However, they were equally critical of Fine Gael and the Labour Party, referring to an 'austerity agenda of Fine Gael, Labour, Fianna Fáil and the Troika' (Sinn Féin 2016a: 34).

Further differences emerge in terms of how the parties responded. There is something of an ideological split. For Fine Gael, the crisis was an opportunity for a move to the right, as they demanded that 'government must become smaller. Ireland's fiscal crisis means there is simply no other choice. Government has to deliver better value in order to reduce the deficit, avoid job-destroying tax increases and protect frontline services' (Fine Gael 2011: 6), and the party declared itself to be 'a pro-enterprise party' (Fine Gael 2016: 81). Parties to the left of the spectrum took a very different line, focusing on austerity and arguing the two centre-right parties were equally bad. Labour talked about a 'Fianna Fáil/Fine Gael austerity programme' (Labour Party 2011: 13); Sinn Féin criticised a 'savage budget [that] targeted working families and those on low and middle incomes' (Sinn Féin 2011: 3); and the United Left Alliance was particularly fierce about 'an unprecedented onslaught on living standards, spiralling mass unemployment and a dramatic rise in poverty' (ULA 2011: 3). However, the dearth of left-wing unity is also evident in their stances, with Sinn Féin saying that Fine Gael and Labour would do basically the same, while United Left expressed no faith in 'Labour and Sinn Fein, who also accept the capitalist market and refuse to rule out coalition with right wing parties' (ULA 2011: 3).

Indeed, Labour went into government in 2011 and soon found itself implementing the very policies it had railed against. However, it was not a good time to be in government for any party, and it proved disastrous for Labour. Both elections during the crisis decade produced sharp setbacks for the incumbents (see Table 6.2). In 2011, FF dropped almost 25% in its vote, losing fifty-seven seats, while the Greens lost all their seats. In 2016, it was the turn of Fine Gael and Labour to suffer the consequences of being in government, with Fine Gael dropping over 10% and Labour losing almost two-thirds of their support. The "two-and-a-half" party system that dominated Irish politics for many years no longer existed, and instead the party system became much more volatile and fragmented (Marsh et al. 2018: 1).

The votes went in various directions. Firstly, there was considerable volatility, with some parties doing well in one election but badly in another. Secondly, the left in general benefited, and within that broad family the radical left grew strongly. This is most evident in relation to Sinn Féin, but the People Before Profit Alliance (PBPA), the Anti-Austerity Alliance (AAA) and Independents 4 Change contributed to the change. Thirdly, there was an increase in votes for non-party candidates, with the number of independents in Dáil Éireann growing from five in 2007 to 19 in the 2016 and 2020 elections.[5] However, it is notable that a populist right-wing Eurosceptic movement was not among the beneficiaries of this electoral churn. Several such groupings emerged following the financial crisis, including Identity Ireland, the National Party and the Irish Freedom Party, but none of them won any representation, even at local council level.

The crisis undoubtedly caused some increased criticism of the EU, particularly on the left. United Left's ideological opposition is evident: 'we are opposed to the dictates of the EU and its neoliberal policies of curbing public spending and promoting austerity' (ULA 2011: 5). Reflecting their strong nationalist pedigree, Sinn Féin focused more on 'the sacrificing of our economic sovereignty to the IMF/EU' (Sinn Féin 2011: 15), though by the 2016 election it was saying it would seek to re-open negotiations with the EU about banking debt (Sinn Féin 2016a: 7). Labour called for renegotiation of the bailout conditions in 2011, with party leader Éamon Gilmore making a highly publicised declaration that Ireland faced a choice between 'Labour's way or Frankfurt's way' (Gilmore 2011). This proved something of an

Table 6.2 General and European election results, percentage votes and seats, 2007–2020

	FG	FF	Greens	Labour	Soc Dem	SF	OL[a]	Ind
2007 GE	27.3 (51)	41.6 (77)	4.7 (6)	10.1 (20)		6.9 (4)	1.1 (0)	5.8 (5)
2009 EP	29.1 (4)	24.1 (3)	1.9 (0)	13.9 (3)		11.2 (0)	2.8 (1)	11.5 (1)
2011 GE	36.1 (76)	17.5 (19)	1.8 (0)	19.5 (37)		9.9 (14)	2.4 (4)	12.6 (15)
2014 EP	22.3 (4)	22.3 (1)	4.9 (0)	5.3 (0)		19.5 (3)	3.2 (0)	19.8 (3)
2016 GE	25.5 (49)	24.3 (44)	2.7 (2)	6.6 (7)	3.0 (3)	13.9 (23)	5.5 (10)	15.7 (19)
2019 EP	29.6 (5[b])	16.6 (2[b])	11.4 (2)	3.1 (0)	1.2 (0)	11.7 (1)	9.7 (2)	15.7 (1)
2020 GE	20.9 (35)	22.2 (37)	7.1 (12)	4.4 (6)	2.9 (6)	24.5 (37)	3.0 (6)	12.2 (19)

Sources: Oireachtas (2007, 2011, 2016, 2020); European Parliament (2009, 2014, 2019); supplemented by Gallagher (2009, 2014, 2019).

Notes:

a. Other Left (including Socialist Party, AAA, PBP, ULA, RISE, I4C).

b. Includes an additional seat following redistribution after Brexit.

albatross around the neck of the party when it subsequently went into government with Fine Gael. Although the party insisted that it had successfully renegotiated the Troika terms and conditions (Labour Party 2014: 3), the public perception was that "Frankfurt's way" – the ECB demands accompanying the bailout – was fundamentally unchanged and punished Labour with huge losses in the 2014 European election and the 2016 general election.[6]

It is interesting to note that the centre-right parties also expressed some concern about the EU at this time, albeit couched in more fundamentally pro-integration language. Fine Gael accepted that 'the recent economic downturn demonstrates how important it is that we maintain close links to Europe. Membership of the Eurozone afforded us a protection' (Fine Gael 2009: 7), but also called for renegotiation of the terms: 'the current deal is bad for Ireland – and bad for Europe' (Fine Gael 2011: 5). Even Fianna Fáil, which had negotiated the bailout, stated that 'everyone now acknowledges that the structure of the Eurozone as a currency union was flawed and impeded countries who tried to combat the Eurozone crisis at the beginning', though it also called for 'a more ambitious fiscal union within the EU' (Fianna Fáil 2014: 6).

However, the two EU-related referendums during the period suggest a slight strengthening of the pro-EU consensus. The second Lisbon vote in 2009 and the vote on the European Fiscal Compact (TSCG) in 2012 provide a clear barometer of party stances on the EU. Fianna Fáil, Fine Gael and Labour called for a Yes in both votes. However, Éamon Ó Cuív resigned as deputy leader of Fianna Fáil and called for a No vote on the grounds that the treaty favoured bigger EU states at the expense of smaller ones (Sheahan & Kelly 2012). In the Lisbon re-run, the Greens for the first time endorsed support for a Yes campaign, which required a two-thirds majority at a party congress to be authorised. They very narrowly failed to reach that super-majority again for the TSCG and so did not adopt an official position. For the Lisbon campaign, opposition was split between the radical left, including Sinn Féin and the AAA/PBPA, and a range of extra-parliamentary right-wing groups. The latter had largely dissipated by the time of the TSCG referendum.

In overall terms, the financial crisis undoubtedly led to increased criticism of the EU. However, this was criticism rather than opposition, and it was couched in terms which made it quite easy to circumnavigate. The parties recognised that Ireland's overriding interest was in being part of an EU which creates an agreed, rules-based system and delivers a wide range of economic benefits for the country. Thus, even during the crisis, no parliamentary parties rejected the principle of participation in the EU. There is criticism of EU policies and procedures, but not the underlying principles. Perhaps the calls from the AAA and PBPA were the most trenchant, but even here there was support for European cooperation – just not necessarily this form of it. Sinn Féin also voiced strong criticisms, but these should be seen more in a context of their earlier outright rejection of the EU. Instead of calling for an Irish withdrawal, they called out the failings of the EU but still accepted that 'Ireland's place is in the European Union – but the European Union needs to change' (Sinn Féin 2014: 11).

Party responses to Brexit

The UK referendum on continued membership of the EU was a huge political issue on the neighbouring island. Ireland was clearly the EU member state that would be most directly impacted by a British decision to leave the Union. As Fianna Fáil put it, 'the costs of Brexit range from damaging to disastrous for the Irish economy' (Fianna Fáil 2019a: 17). This section looks at the stances of Irish parties on Brexit and how they engaged in the referendum, with a focus on the shift in policy of Sinn Féin. It also explores the responses in the post-referendum phase as Ireland sought to deal with the outcome of the vote.

Irish political parties were very active in the Brexit campaign. For those which are organised both in Northern Ireland and in the Republic – notably Sinn Féin, but also PBPA and the Green Party – this was fully to be expected. However, for other parties such as Fianna Fáil, Fine Gael and Labour, this posed an issue. There was a reluctance to be seen to be intervening in the internal affairs of another country,[7] even if those internal affairs would have a strong impact externally. Nonetheless, the issue was deemed so important for Ireland that both Fine Gael and Labour engaged in events in Britain, while Fianna Fáil campaigned in Northern Ireland. These interventions did arouse some opposition, particularly from Northern Irish unionists, but Irish politicians insisted that the issue was not just a matter for the UK electorate and that 'as a nation we cannot remain silent' (Fianna Fáil 2016a).

Most Irish parties were unequivocally in favour of Britain remaining in the EU. Labour stated 'respectfully, and with affection, your Irish friends ask that you stay' (Labour Party 2016a), while Fianna Fáil noted that 'this referendum is for Britain alone to decide' but then declared 'we do not believe that Brexit is in the best interests of the European Union and certainly not in the best interests of the island of Ireland' (Fianna Fáil 2016b). Similarly, Fine Gael declared that 'UK membership of the EU is beneficial for Ireland, the UK and the EU. We will advocate for continued UK membership of the EU' (Fine Gael 2016: 93).

There were some EU-critical stances on the radical left side, with the Socialist Party calling for a "Lexit" – 'an exit from the EU on a left basis'

(Gillespie 2016). But there was also a major shift on the radical left. Sinn Féin had called for a No vote in every other EU-related referendum in Ireland (and in the 1975 UK referendum). But they were unequivocal in their opposition to Brexit, with Martin McGuinness declaring 'Sinn Féin is campaigning vigorously against a Brexit and encouraging people to vote to Put Ireland First and vote to Remain' (Sinn Féin 2016b). Sinn Féin insisted that their campaign for a Remain vote 'should not be interpreted as a ringing endorsement of the current EU' (Sinn Féin 2016c) and criticised 'the democratic deficit at the heart of Europe, and the neoliberal tendencies within the bloc' (Sinn Féin 2016d). But party president Gerry Adams acknowledged that 'the EU has been a critical partner for peace in Ireland, providing substantial political and financial aid, which has led to greater economic and social progress on an all-island basis' (Sinn Féin 2017). Adams went on to say that 'Sinn Féin's approach to the European Union can best be described as a critical engagement' (Sinn Féin 2016e).

Sinn Féin also has a very strong interest in a different type of UK, one which does not include Northern Ireland. So, although it could be said that they "lost" the Brexit referendum, they quickly turned that into a step forward – a kind of pyrrhic defeat, perhaps. While the UK as a whole voted Leave, Northern Ireland voted Remain,[8] and Sinn Féin immediately argued that Irish people were being forced into something by an unjust union. They called for a referendum on Irish unity on the grounds that Northern Ireland was going to be dragged out of the EU against its will, with very damaging consequences for cross-border relations on the island of Ireland, particularly the peace process. They insisted that 'Brexit and the Good Friday Agreement are mutually incompatible' (RTÉ 2018). Again, it is worth noting how a perceived Irish national interest became a means for Sinn Féin's move to a more pro-EU position (Cochrane 2020). Outright opposition became selective criticism.

The degree of consensus among Irish parties on Brexit was remarkable. From Fine Gael and Fianna Fáil on the centre right, through the Greens and on to Labour and the Social Democrats on the centre left, and to Sinn Féin on the radical left, there was a strong consistency. They agreed that Brexit was bad, and specifically that it was bad for peace, bad for trade and bad for freedom of movement. They also agreed that the backstop was an essential safeguard.[9] Indeed, when a Fianna Fáil TD criticised the Fine Gael government[10] for creating a stand-off with the British government over the backstop, he was accused of a going on a 'bizarre ... solo run' by party colleagues and made to retract his statement (O'Connell 2019).

There was also mutual recognition of the consensus. The Labour Party leader had promised that 'my party will be supportive of the Government's efforts to work through this problem' (Labour Party 2016b), and said that 'all politicians wore the green jersey' (Clarke 2020). Fianna Fáil's Brexit spokesperson, Lisa Chambers, noted that 'elected representatives from all political parties and none have stood behind the Government and put our country's interests first. This is something of which we must be proud' (Fianna Fáil 2019b). This was acknowledged by the Fine Gael Foreign Minister, Simon Coveney, who agreed that 'the two main political parties have worked together on Brexit by and large, and in fact the other parties too, parties like Sinn Féin and the Labour Party and the Green Party and so on, by and large have supported me and the Taoiseach in what we have been trying to do' (RTÉ 2019). To have such widespread consensus on a policy area is highly unusual and indicates how Irish parties have a strong tendency to buy into the idea of an agreed Irish national interest.

Thus, Brexit also reinforced the broad pro-EU consensus among Irish parties. On the extremes, there was still some quite fierce criticism of the EU. On the far left, the Socialist Party labelled it 'the enemy of the 99%' (Gillespie 2016) and PBPA described it as 'a prison house for workers that fosters racism, xenophobia and austerity' (PBPA 2016). The post-referendum period also saw the launch of the far-right Irish Freedom Party, beginning with a conference calling for "Irexit" (Carswell 2018). However, the party failed to win any seats in the 2020 general election (for further analysis of Irexit, see Simpson, Chapter 8, this volume). In general, there was virtually no evidence of opposition to the EU among Irish parties in relation to Brexit. Indeed, there was hardly even any significant criticism of the Union. However, it is a vision of the EU as a bulwark for defending an Irish national interest – once again, the idea that the internationalism of the EU is a vehicle for advancing Irish interests is evident.

Of course, it was hard to see Brexit as anything other than the fault of the British government and the UK Conservatives were a ready-made scapegoat. Sinn Féin labelled them 'absolutely clueless' and 'more like an episode of "Yes Minister"' (Sinn Féin 2016f); Labour said, 'the Brexit campaign was won by deceit and untruths' and suggested that any eventual exit deal must be put to a second referendum (Labour Party 2016c); the Greens likened the UK to a 'pirate rogue state' (Green Party 2016). Only Fine Gael openly noted that with the departure of the UK 'Ireland has lost a natural ally' (Fine Gael 2019: 12). Brexit also had the effect of reminding Ireland of the benefits of EU membership, both in terms of the economic benefits of being part of the Union and the political advantage of having such a powerful partnership. Mostly, there was a strong desire to keep the EU working on Ireland's side. This was especially noticeable in parties with MEPs, who lobbied hard in Brussels. Again, there is a very strong sense of a shared Irish national interest with almost all parties wanting to be seen to be "wearing the green jersey".

Conclusion: Euro-nationalism, not Euroscepticism

The 2020 general election resulted in a three-party coalition government of Fianna Fáil, Fine Gael and the Greens. In some regards, this represented an historical transformation of Irish party politics. The two Civil War rivals who had formed the two poles of the Irish polity for almost 100 years found themselves in coalition and indeed they agreed to share the office of Taoiseach. Sinn Féin emerged as the largest single party in terms of votes, a further transformation of the Irish party landscape. And yet it is also worth noting that the two parties who were in power when the financial crisis struck Ireland – Fianna Fáil and the Greens – and the party that had been in power for much of the bailout period – Fine Gael – were all back in government. Is it a case of *plus ça change, plus c'est la même chose*? Or is there real political change taking place? And if so, where does that leave the Irish–EU relationship?

The period of the financial crisis and of Brexit should in certain respects have been the ideal opportunity for the emergence of a strong Eurosceptic movement in Ireland. Prior to the financial crisis, the boom years of the Celtic Tiger economy had seen the Republic become both a net contributor to the EU and more assertive of its own interests. The crisis then saw the Republic lose a great deal of its economic sovereignty, with very tough austerity policies being implemented at the behest of the Troika. And yet, if anything the already strong pro-EU consensus among Irish parties has become even stronger in this period. Partly, this is because of a perception that Ireland's economic success was at least in part due to EU support – so, perhaps eaten bread is not so soon forgotten after all. It was also clear that while the bailout conditions were harsh, nonetheless the crisis was not considered to be the EU's fault and it was now trying to support the economy with its bailout.

Notably, two parties which had previously been staunch critics of the EU, the Greens and Sinn Féin, came out in favour of deeper Irish commitment. In both cases, a further reason for the shift in policy can be discerned: the lure of participation in government. Both parties realised that one of the main obstacles to their being taken seriously as potential coalition partners was their opposition to the EU. While not totally abandoning earlier critiques, both sought to develop a more nuanced interpretation of the EU, which would give them greater leeway to engage in a government with some of the strongly pro-EU parties. Thus, these parties are not merely changing policy on the EU to seek electoral gain, they also show an appreciation of the benefits derived from the EU.

Finally, the various crises of this period did not reinforce each other. Notably, while the financial crisis did generate some more critical commentary about the EU, Brexit had the opposite effect of making parties aware of the benefits of membership and the perils of exit. Parties were also quite conscious of the strong public support for the EU in Ireland (see Simpson, Chapter 8, this volume). For most of them, outright Euroscepticism was only going to be a vote-loser. In the Dáil, only a small and fragmented radical left advocated any kind of Euroscepticism, and this stems from a strong left ideological stance. They were careful to avoid some of the other common tropes of Euroscepticism, particularly nationalist and anti-immigrant rhetoric. And despite the financial crisis, despite the inward migration to Ireland, despite the example of the large neighbouring island, the far right was minuscule and largely irrelevant. The various far-right parties failed to win any seats at national, European or local level during this period.

While undoubtedly there are economic and social benefits from membership, it is too simplistic to say, 'the EU is good for Ireland'. Membership also involves economic and social costs. But there is a widespread recognition that Ireland is a small state which has few options. It benefits from international rules and norms and needs international partnerships. But this chapter argues that the pro-EU consensus in Ireland is very much expressed from an Irish nationalist standpoint. The EU is approved of because it provides benefits and helps Ireland advance its interests. The Irish attitude to integration has always been "what's in it for us?", even if more and more politicians answer that by saying "quite a lot". This, then, is the "Euro-nationalism" evident in Irish parties. They see the EU in a positive light not out of any great commitment to ideals of European unity, but because it is a useful device for advancing their own nationally focused agendas.

However, it is perhaps worth ending on a note of caution. The idea of "Euro-nationalism" – using the EU as a vehicle for advancing national interests – depends to an extent on the EU continuing as a suitable vehicle. Depending on how the idea of an Irish interest is framed, that may not be the case in the near future. The various crises that have impacted on the EU since 2008 have led to many calls to strengthen the EU's capacities in several fields. Two of these would present a significant challenge to Irish parties if they were to develop. Firstly, virtually every party has consistently expressed support for Ireland's low corporation tax rate, so ideas for some form of consolidated corporate tax structure in the EU would be a deep challenge to them. Secondly, most parties have supported Irish neutrality, so suggestions that the EU needs a stronger defence capacity will cause further difficulties.

Overall, the financial crisis at one stage threatened to weaken the strong pro-EU consensus among Irish parliamentary parties, but not to destroy it entirely. However, the financial crisis also underlined Ireland's reliance on its European partnership. And when the Brexit crisis came along soon afterwards, that reliance was even more sharply evident and led to a significant strengthening of the consensus. However, the crises also created new faultlines which could in the future challenge that pro-EU consensus in Ireland.

Notes

1 Sinn Féin won the largest number of votes of any party in the 2020 election.
2 The categorisation of Irish parties – and especially Fianna Fáil and Fine Gael – is always open to debate. This chapter applies the classifications adopted by both Nordsieck (2020) and Volkens et al. (2020).
3 This includes the Workers' Party, Democratic Socialist Party, Democratic Left, the Socialist Party (also known as the Anti-Austerity Alliance), the People Before Profit Alliance (these latter two formed the short-lived United Left Alliance) and Sinn Féin.
4 Ireland has an unusually high incidence of EU-related referendums. The Irish constitution includes several clauses which are incompatible with EU membership, so each treaty requires a referendum to be approved.
5 The single-transferable-vote electoral system used in Ireland is propitious for independent candidates. See Weeks (2016).
6 Having won 19.4% of the vote in the 2011 general election – their second best-ever result – Labour collapsed to 5.3% in the 2014 European election and 6.6% in the 2016 general election. They lost all three of their seats in the European Parliament and dropped from 37 to just 7 seats in the Dáil (Holmes 2019).
7 Indeed, when Nigel Farage and UKIP intervened in the second Treaty of Lisbon referendum in the Republic, Irish parties had made exactly that criticism (Fitz-Gibbon 2009: 8).
8 See Chapter 1 for details.
9 The backstop was a commitment to prevent a hard border in Ireland after Brexit (see Phinnemore & Whitten, Chapter 12, this volume).
10 Though it might be worth noting that Fianna Fáil provided external support for the minority Fine Gael government between 2016 and 2020.

References

Bolleyer, N. & D. Panke (2010) 'The Irish Green Party and Europe: an unhappy marriage?', in K. Hayward & M.C. Murphy (eds) *The Europeanization of party politics in Ireland, North and South*, pp. 127–142. Abingdon: Routledge.
Carswell, S. (2018) 'Irexit conference: "I am hoping something comes of this"'. *The Irish Times*, 3 February. Available at: www.irishtimes.com/news/politics/irexit-conference-i-am-hoping-something-comes-of-this-1.3379392 [accessed 1 August 2020].
Clarke, V. (2020) '"All politicians wore the green jersey": Howlin says FG are arrogant for claiming success in Brexit negotiations'. *The Irish Examiner*, 30 January. Available at: www.irishexaminer.com/breakingnews/ireland/all-politicians-wore-the-green-jersey-howlin-says-fg-are-arrogant-for-claiming-success-in-brexit-negotiations-978952.html [accessed 1 August 2020].
Cochrane, F. (2020) *Breaking peace: Brexit and Northern Ireland*. Manchester: Manchester University Press.
European Parliament (2009, 2014, 2019) *European election results*. Brussels: European Parliament. Available at: europarl.europa.eu/election-results [accessed 25 June 2020].

Fianna Fáil (2011) *Real plan, better future: 2011 manifesto.* Dublin: Fianna Fáil.

Fianna Fáil (2014) *A Europe for us all: European election manifesto 2014.* Dublin: Fianna Fáil.

Fianna Fáil (2016a) 'Ireland entitled to advocate no to Brexit: Jim O'Callaghan'. Fianna Fáil press release, 27 January. Available at: www.fiannafail.ie/ireland-enti-tled-to-advocate-no-to-brexit-jim-ocallaghan/ [accessed 30 August 2020].

Fianna Fáil (2016b) 'Smith warns that Brexit could have serious implications for border counties'. Fianna Fáil press release, 1 June. Available at: www.fiannafail.ie/smith-warns-that-brexit-could-have-serious-implications-for-border-counties/ [accessed 30 August 2020].

Fianna Fáil (2019a) *Making Europe work for you: European Parliament elections manifesto 2019.* Dublin: Fianna Fáil.

Fianna Fáil (2019b) 'Speech by FF Brexit spokesperson Lisa Chambers at the Mac-gill Summer School 2019'. Fianna Fáil press release, 22 July. Available at: www.fiannafail.ie/speech-by-ff-brexit-spokesperson-lisa-chambers-at-the-macgill-sum-mer-school-2019/ [accessed 30 August 2020].

Fine Gael (2009) *Securing Ireland's future in Europe: Fine Gael's European election manifesto 2009*: Dublin: Fine Gael.

Fine Gael (2011) *Let's get Ireland working: Fine Gael manifesto.* Dublin: Fine Gael.

Fine Gael (2016) *Let's keep the recovery going: Fine Gael general election manifesto 2016.* Dublin: Fine Gael.

Fine Gael (2019) *Let's take Ireland forward together: European election manifesto 2019.* Dublin: Fine Gael.

FitzGibbon, J. (2009) 'The second referendum on the Treaty of Lisbon in the Repub-lic of Ireland, 2nd October 2009'. Sussex: EPERN Referendum Briefing Paper No. 17. Available at: www.sussex.ac.uk/webteam/gateway/file.php?name=epern-ref-no17.pdf&site=266 [accessed 1 August 2020].

Gallagher, M. (2009, 2014, 2019) *Ireland European Parliament election results.* Available at: tcd.ie/Political_Science/people/michael_gallagher/index.php [accessed 25 June 2020].

Garvin, T. (2005) *The evolution of Irish nationalist politics: Irish parties and Irish politics from the 18th century to modern times.* Dublin: Gill & Macmillan.

Gillespie, C. (2016) 'Ireland, Brexit and why the EU must be opposed'. Socialist Party blogpost, 28 June. Available at: https://socialistparty.ie/2016/06/ireland-brexit-and-why-the-eu-must-be-opposed/ [accessed 30 August 2020].

Gilmore, É. (2011) *Press conference, 3 February 2011.* Available at: www.youtube.com/watch?v=Kpr2zaXvb4M [accessed 1 August 2020].

Green Party (2011) *Renewing Ireland: Green Party manifesto 2011.* Dublin: Green Party.

Green Party (2016) 'European Greens to fight together against worst effects of Brexit'. Green Party press release, 16 October. Available at: www.greenparty.ie/european-greens-to-fight-together-against-worst-effects-of-brexit/ [accessed 30 August 2020].

Hayward, K. & J. Fallon (2010) 'Fianna Fáil: tenacious localism, tenuous European-isation', in K. Hayward & M.C. Murphy (eds) *The Europeanization of party politics in Ireland, North and South,* pp. 75–94. Abingdon: Routledge.

Hobolt, S.B. & C. De Vries (2016) 'Turning against the Union? The impact of the crisis on the Eurosceptic vote in the 2014 European Parliament elections'. *Electoral Studies* 44: 504–514.

Holmes, M. (2006) *The development of the Irish Labour Party's European policy: from opposition to support.* Lewiston and Lampeter: Edwin Mellen Press.

Holmes, M. (2010) 'The Irish Labour Party: the advantages, disadvantages and irrel-
evance of Europeanisation?', in K. Hayward & M.C. Murphy (eds) *The Europeanization of party politics in Ireland, North and South*, pp. 111–126. Abingdon:
Routledge.

Holmes, M. (2019) '"Frankfurt's way or Labour's way": The Irish Left and the crisis', in M. Holmes & K. Roder (eds) *The European Left and the financial crisis*,
pp. 68–85. Manchester: Manchester University Press.

Labour Party (2011) *One Ireland: jobs, reform, fairness. Labour manifesto 2011*.
Dublin: The Labour Party.

Labour Party (2014) *Working together for Ireland in Europe*. Dublin: The Labour
Party.

Labour Party (2016a) 'Brexit is likely to impact those who can least afford it: Brendan Howlin'. Labour Party blogpost, 16 June. Available at: www.labour.ie/news/
blog/2016/06/16/brexit-is-likely-to-impact-those-who-can-least-aff/ [accessed 30
August 2020].

Labour Party (2016b) 'EU must reject impulse to act swiftly and harshly against
Britain'. Labour Party press release, 27 June. Available at: www.labour.ie/
news/2016/06/27/eu-must-reject-impulse-to-act-swiftly-and-harshly/ [accessed
30 August 2020].

Labour Party (2016c) 'Address by Brendan Howlin to Labour Brexit seminar'.
Labour Party press release, 13 December. Available at: www.labour.ie/
news/2016/12/13/address-by-brendan-howlin-to-labour-brexit-seminar/
[accessed 30 August 2020].

Marsh, M., D.M. Farrell & T. Reidy (2018) *The post-crisis Irish voter: voting
behaviour in the Irish 2016 general election*. Manchester: Manchester University
Press.

Nordsieck, W. (2020) *Parties and elections in Europe*. Available at: www.parties-
and-elections.eu/index.html [accessed 1 August 2020].

O'Connell, H. (2019) 'Fianna Fáil's Dooley rebuked over his "bizarre" Brexit "solo
run"'. *Irish Independent*, 31 July. Available at: www.independent.ie/business/
brexit/fianna-fails-dooley-rebuked-over-his-bizarre-brexit-solo-run-38361509.
html [accessed 1 August 2020].

Oireachtas (2007, 2011, 2016, 2020) *Dáil general election results*. Dublin: Houses
of the Oireachtas. Available at: oireachtas.ie/en/elections [accessed 25 June 2020].

Oireachtas (2010) *Dáil Éireann debate, Wednesday 31 March 2010*. Available at:
www.oireachtas.ie/en/debates/debate/dail/2010-03-31/2/ [accessed 30 August
2020].

PBPA (2016) 'People Before Profit Alliance press statement on Brexit vote'. PBPA
press release, 24 June. Available at: www.peoplebeforeprofit.ie/2016/06/people-
before-profit-alliance-press-statement-on-brexit-vote/ [accessed 30 August 2020].

Reidy, T. (2010) 'Blissful Union? Fine Gael and the European Union', in K. Hayward
& M.C. Murphy (eds) *The Europeanization of party politics in Ireland, North
and South*, pp. 95–110. Abingdon: Routledge.

RTÉ (2018) 'Interview with Mary Lou McDonald'. *Today with Sean O'Rourke programme*, RTÉ Radio 1, 10 April. Available at: www.rte.ie/radio/radioplayer/
html5/#/radio1/10858857 (21:28) [accessed 30 August 2020].

RTÉ (2019) 'Interview with Simon Coveney'. *This Week programme*, RTÉ Radio 1,
19 May. Available at: www.rte.ie/radio/radioplayer/html5/#/radio1/21556944
(3:00–3:15) [accessed 20 May 2019].

Ruhs, M. & E. Quinn (2009) *Ireland: from rapid immigration to recession.* Washington: Migration Policy Institute. Available at: www.migrationpolicy.org/article/ireland-rapid-immigration-recession [accessed 24 January 2020].

Sheahan, F. & F. Kelly (2012) 'Ó Cuiv steps down as FF deputy leader over EU treaty'. *Irish Independent*, 29 February. Available at: www.independent.ie/irish-news/o-cuiv-steps-down-as-ff-deputy-leader-over-eu-treaty-26826949.html [accessed 1 August 2020].

Sinn Féin (2011) *There is a better way: Sinn Féin general election manifesto 2011.* Dublin: Sinn Féin.

Sinn Féin (2014) *Putting Ireland first: Sinn Féin EU manifesto 2014.* Dublin: Sinn Féin.

Sinn Féin (2016a) *For a fair recovery: Sinn Féin manifesto general election 2016.* Dublin: Sinn Féin.

Sinn Féin (2016b) 'Martin McGuinness' full speech at London Brexit event'. Sinn Féin press release, 16 June. Available at: www.sinnfein.ie/contents/40372 [accessed 30 August 2020].

Sinn Féin (2016c) 'EU needs to radically reform'. Sinn Féin press release, 24 June. Available at: www.sinnfein.ie/contents/40502 [accessed 30 August 2020].

Sinn Féin (2016d) 'Ní Riada calls for government consensus on Irish unity referendum'. Sinn Féin press release, 24 June. Available at: www.sinnfein.ie/ga/contents/40490 [accessed 30 August 2020].

Sinn Féin (2016e) 'Adams calls for "Yes to Remain" vote in Brexit referendum'. Sinn Féin press release, 9 June. Available at: www.sinnfein.ie/contents/40268 [accessed 30 August 2020].

Sinn Féin (2016f) 'British government Brexit approach like an episode of "Yes Minister": O'Dowd'. Sinn Féin press release, 15 November. Available at: www.sinnfein.ie/contents/42401 [accessed 30 August 2020].

Sinn Féin (2017) 'National interest must be to the fore following triggering of Article 50 – Adams'. Sinn Féin press release, 28 March. Available at: www.sinnfein.ie/contents/44028 [accessed 30 August 2020].

Taggart, P. & A. Szczerbiak (2018) 'Putting Brexit into perspective: the effect of the Eurozone and migration crises and Brexit on Euroscepticism in European states'. *Journal of European Public Policy* 25(8): 1194–1214.

Torreblanca, J.I. & M. Leonard (2013) *The continent-wide rise of Euroscepticism.* London: European Council on Foreign Relations. Available at: www.ecfr.eu/page/-/ECFR79_EUROSCEPTICISM_BRIEF_AW.pdf [accessed 24 January 2020].

Weeks, L. (2016) 'Independents and the election: the party crashers', in M. Gallagher and M. Marsh (eds) *How Ireland voted 2016: the election that nobody won*, pp. 207–226. Basingstoke: Palgrave Macmillan.

ULA (2011) *United Left Alliance: candidate pledge and programme for the 2011 general election.* Dublin: United Left Alliance.

Volkens, A., T. Burst, W. Krause, P. Lehmann, T. Matthieß, N. Merz, S. Regel, B. Weßels & L. Zehnter (2020) *The manifesto data collection: manifesto project.* Berlin: Wissenschaftszentrum Berlin für Sozialforschung (WZB). Available at: https://doi.org/10.25522/manifesto.mpds.2020a [accessed 30 August 2020].

7

Post-crash protest politics

Madelaine Moore and Silke Trommer

Introduction

Diverse and recurring forms of protest have marked the decade since the 2008 economic crash in Ireland. From household-centred contestations of housing taxes and water charges, to demonstrations and marches on issues such as austerity, asylum policy, homelessness, marriage equality and women's bodily autonomy, Irish citizens have aired their grievances through public protest and, often successfully, demanded change in Irish politics. These events stand in sharp contrast with suggestions that the Irish 'suffer[ed] austerity in silence' (Flinn 2011), or that Ireland has undergone a 'quiet revolution' (RTÉ 2018) during the era of austerity.

Despite the EU's prominent role in austerity politics and in the Irish bailout programme, the Irish remain consistently among the most Europhile in Europe (Simpson 2018).[1] According to the 2018 Eurobarometer report, 50% of Irish respondents trust the EU, while in other bailout states such as Italy, Greece and Portugal, 36%, 26% and 55%, respectively, of respondents trusted the EU (Kantar Public Brussels and European Commission 2018). Of Irish respondents 60% believe that their voice counts in the EU, making Ireland one of the highest-ranking EU member states in this regard (Kantar Public Brussels and European Commission 2018).[2]

In this chapter, we examine Irish public protest since 2008 in order to explore this seeming contradiction. We ask how Irish protesters' views of the EU evolved during the post-crash period 2008–2018. Instead of extrapolating from each protest taking place during this time as an isolated case, we understand the era of Irish austerity as one of heightened collective contestation. We do not claim that the same activists or grievances animated all protests taking place in this era. Building on the social movement literature (Gillan 2018; Koopmans 2004; McAdam et al. 2001), we treat the post-crash period 2008–2018 as consisting of interrelated waves of public protest. The focus on an Irish post-crash protest period allows us to analyse how ideas and activists travelled across protest activities, how protest movements learned from past actions and how future protest movements were shaped in these processes.

Methodologically, we use media analysis, document analysis, interviews and participant observation at protest events as data collection tools (see References for lists of interviewees and protests attended). Triangulation of data sources allow us to establish continuities and differences in how Irish protesters saw the EU over time. In particular, we examine what knowledge Irish protesters held of the EU, to what extent they identified with the EU and whether their views and knowledge of the EU shifted across time.

We argue that the period 2008–2018 saw a heightened engagement of Irish grass roots activists and protesters with European integration. As a result of these engagements, Irish protesters gradually acquired a more nuanced understanding of the workings of EU policy making than they previously held. They sharpened their critiques of the EU, but also began holding domestic elites to account for their actions and representational practices within EU political institutions and in negotiations with the EU. While Irish protesters have on balance remained in favour of European integration, they view austerity and neoliberalism as socially unjust, regressive and illegitimate policy agendas. This development presents a significant historical shift away from progressive Irish movements' traditionally positive attitudes towards the EU.

We begin our analysis by placing the post-crash public protest era within Ireland's socio-economic context of boom, bust and austerity. Following a brief review of the literature on post-crash protests in Ireland, we analyse Irish protesters' evolving views of the EU in detail. We conclude that the EU's association with austerity policies risked eroding Irish protesters' overall positive EU perceptions.

The socio-economic impact of Irish austerity

The socio-economic impact of the 2008 crash and of austerity was severe in Ireland. Table 7.1 displays the evolution of economic and social indicators during the period 2008–2018. The economic crisis was most profound in the period 2008–2015, when GDP growth was negative or low and unemployment soared, despite consistent negative net migration figures (see Elliott, Chapter 5, this volume). Household disposable income crashed during this period, while household indebtedness was consistently above 200% of net disposable income (OECD 2019). From 2015, the Irish economy performed a remarkable recovery, including the staggering one-off growth rate of 25% in 2015 (Country-economy.com 2019). By 2018, per capita GDP had nearly doubled compared to its 2009 level; growth figures were at around 6%, and after 2014 the unemployment rate and household indebtedness consistently dropped (OECD 2019).

Table 7.1 Irish socio-economic indicators, 2008–2018

Indicator [source]	2008	2009	2010	2011	2012	2013	2014	2015	2016	2017	2018
ECONOMY											
GDP (USD/capita) [*]	44,220	41,587	43,296	44,953	46,304	48,006	51,250	69,050	71,020	76,889	83,946
GDP growth (%) [~]	–4.4	–5.0	1.9	3.7	0.2	1.3	8.8	25.1	5.0	7.2	6.7
Unemployment rate (%) [*]	6.77	12.61	14.53	15.35	15.45	13.74	11.86	9.91	8.38	6.71	N/A
Low pay[a] [*]	20.5	21.5	20.5	24.2	21.8	23.3	25.1	24.0	22.5	N/A	N/A
Net migration (April–April) [+]	38,500	–7,800	–34,500	–34,100	–34,400	–33,100	–21,400	–11,600	16,200	19,800	34,000
HOUSEHOLDS											
Household disposable income growth (%) [*]	5.71	–0.32	–1.03	–5.78	0.77	–1.60	0.63	3.86	3.83	4.07	N/A
Household debt/disposable income (%) [*]	228.58	237.06	228.71	235.51	220.03	214.30	200.28	180.80	164.77	153.21	N/A
At risk of poverty rate (%) [+]	14.4	14.1	14.7	16	17.3	16.5	17.2	16.9	16.5	15.7	N/A
Deprivation rate (%) [+]	13.8	17.3	22.6	24.5	26.9	30.5	29.0	25.5	21.0	18.8	N/A
Consistent poverty rate (%) [+]	4.2	5.5	6.3	6.9	8.5	9.1	8.8	8.7	8.3	6.7	N/A
HOMELESSNESS & HEALTH											
Homelessness[b] [#]				3808			2,858	3,625	4,643	5,508	6,194
Homelessness[c] [+]									6,906		
Hospital beds (per 1000 inhabitants) [*]	4.85	2.83	2.73	2.62	2.54	2.56	2.57	2.92	2.90	N/A	N/A

Sources: OECD (2019) [*]; CSO (2019) [+]; Department of Housing Planning and Local Government (2019) [#]; Countryeconomy.com (2019) [~].

Notes:

a. Share of workers earning less than two-thirds of median earnings.

b. In emergency accommodation during Christmas.

c. In shelter or sleeping rough on census night.

Yet, social indicators do not replicate these positive trends. At-risk-of-poverty rates, deprivation rates and consistent poverty rates were above the 2008 level in 2018 (CSO 2019). Official statistics on homelessness in Ireland are not systematically compiled,[3] but existing figures point to an upward spiral with no recovery in sight. The collapse in the number of hospital beds per inhabitant witnessed during this decade was indicative of an escalating crisis in the healthcare sector (OECD 2019). Low pay rates remained relatively stable during the entire period (CSO 2019), lending credibility to arguments that there is a sizeable under-class in Ireland that is relatively isolated from general national economic trends.

Some scholarly works chime with a generalised narrative of Irish stoicism in the face of socio-economic crisis (Chabanet & Royall 2015; Layte & Lande 2018). For evidence, these observers point to the absence of significant militant street politics and/or large-scale marches and demonstrations in Ireland until 2014. However, the scholarship has since shown that these assessments lack in nuance and fulfil a political purpose of cementing a false image of Irish acceptance of austerity (see also Gaynor 2018 and Murphy 2016 on this point).

In analysing the varied protests of this period, scholars interpret at times short-lived and/or localised events as ongoing, diverse and resilient forms of civic organisation in opposition to Irish austerity and neoliberalism (Attuyer 2015; Cox 2017; Gaynor 2018; Murphy 2016). At times, such initiatives were successful, such as resistance to water charges (Trommer 2019). And at times, they have provided episodes through which activists and protesters have built networks and learned for future activisms and actions (Attuyer 2015; Kiersey 2014; Murphy 2016). Yet, this growing literature on Irish post-crash protest politics has not considered how Irish protesters during this period saw the EU, what visions of and for European integration were passed on from protest to protest, and how protesters helped shape EU–Ireland relations overall. We turn to this in the next section.

From "getting to know EU" to alternative Europes

The EU has, at times, played a divisive role in Irish grass roots activism. From the Irish women's and environmental movements emerging in the 1970s and 1980s, to the 1980s/1990s anti-drug movement, to water charges protests in the mid-1990s and bin charges protests in the early 2000s, grass roots activism and protest have long played a role in Irish public life (Connolly 2002; Cox 2017; Cullen 2003; Dukelow 2016; Leonard 2008). Pre-bailout, protest actions and boycotts targeting local government did not have a strong European dimension. On the other hand, Irish women's, LGBTIQ and environmental movements often looked towards European movements, and at times European institutions and policies, as a means of furthering their struggles (interview 6; Bellec & European Commission 2016). Traditionally, socially progressive Irish protesters have been Europhiles, while socially conservative Irish movements have been Eurosceptics. Conservative and religious movements have traditionally feared that European integration could give momentum to a liberal social agenda (Kennedy 2018).[4]

In the period following the double catastrophe of economic crisis and bailout, these long-held attitudes of Irish protesters towards European integration gradually shifted. In the immediate context of crash and austerity, anti-EU sentiments prevailed among Irish protesters. Anti-bailout protest actions targeted the EU and in particular the ECB. For example, in November 2010, at one of Ireland's largest anti-bailout protests with an estimated 100,000 people attending, one protester expressed his anger 'that the EU are telling us to cut euros off the minimum wage and boss Irish workers around while the people that caused this crisis get off scot-free' (quoted in Clark & McDonald 2010). At this time, protesters recalled that EU flags were being burned at anti-bailout protests in Ireland (interview 6). The Says No groups[5] and the Occupy Dame Street movement[6] that erupted following Occupy Wall Street (October 2011–March 2012) were also openly anti-EU and anti-IMF.

Rejection of the EU was often based on what protesters saw as the EU's neoliberal ideological underpinnings. Anti-bailout and anti-austerity protesters perceived the EU's neoliberal economic policy approach as responsible for the economic crisis, the bailout and for the heavy socio-economic cost of saving the economy (interviews 2, 4). As we shall show, these negative attitudes towards neoliberal Europe have carried over into water, housing and women's bodily autonomy protests, and are vibrant in Ireland.

At the same time, Irish protesters were aware that the "Brussels made me do this" line of defence of Irish political elites ignored the fact that the Irish government had unilaterally adopted austerity policies in 2008, two years prior to the EU–IMF bailout (Government of Ireland 2010). This knowledge ran counter to the idea that austerity was the result of EU–IMF interference alone. From 2010–2011, protesters thus equally targeted the then Fianna Fáil government, which they saw as responsible for a flawed policy response to the crisis and for failing to stand up to the Troika of the European Commission, ECB and IMF (interview 3). Protesters also criticised domestic media and policy circles for their "we all partied"[7] narrative and for presenting overpaid public sector workers and social benefit recipients as playing a key role in causing the crash (interview 5; Kollewe 2008; Mercille 2014).

The 2011 general election presented a watershed moment for Irish protesters. Opposition parties challenged austerity and the conditions of Ireland's bailout during the election campaign (BBC 2011). With their campaign rhetoric, opposition parties contributed to a generalised sense among protesters that Irish governments had some measure of agency in European politics and in negotiations with EU institutions. Perspectives began shifting from austerity as an EU–IMF imposition, to the Fianna Fáil government playing an active role in forging Brussels's austerity diktat, which was a continuity of the government's initial policy response to the crash. However, once in office, the Fine Gael–Labour government adopted three more austerity budgets. They also attempted to introduce consumption-based water billing that the previous government had agreed with the Troika under Ireland's bailout package (for a review of Irish water reforms, see Finn 2015).[8] In response, and as Ireland exited the bailout in 2013 (McDonald 2013), protest anger turned inwards, targeting the Labour Party, trade unions connected to Labour, the media, and domestic political and economic elites, with the EU playing a more subordinate role (Cox 2017; interviews 5, 13, 14).

During the Irish water charges protests that peaked in 2014, domestic politics became the key political terrain, with the EU and European politics perceived by protestors with some ambivalence. For many protesters, water charges were a prism for austerity, the unfairness of the bailout, corruption and the democratic deficit in Irish domestic politics (interviews 10, 13). The blockading of water meter installations, non-payment of bills and mass demonstrations of up to 200,000 people offered concrete actions which other policies in Ireland's austerity package had not afforded (Ogle 2016). Water charges protesters described the EU as 'a dysfunctional and corrupt institution … where the few get paid everything and the rest of us get to pay for that' (Interview 10). Yet they also reflected: 'Yes the troika is the problem, but these are the people that benefit from this, these people at home, they make money out of it' (interview 7).

Although the Irish government, media circles and domestic elites continued to portray water reforms as a bailout conditionality anchored in international loan agreements, EU law and institutions in certain instances played into the hands of water protesters. The so-called 'Irish exemption' in the European Water Directive in principle provided Ireland with the opportunity to abstain from water service privatisation and full cost recovery (European Commission 2008). Memories of the 1990s Dublin water boycotts and the fact that the Irish government had unilaterally proposed water reform as one loan conditionality in a letter to the IMF in 2010 (IMF 2010), also led protesters to see domestic elites as the key political agents driving the introduction of water charges.

Their views were further cemented when the European Commission's Directorate-General Eurostat ruled that the agency created to implement water reforms, Irish Water, was 'a non-market entity controlled by government' in 2015 (Eurostat 2015: 12). The ruling jeopardised the Irish government's public financing and fiscal consolidation plans and contributed in some degree to water reforms eventually being wound back in 2016 (for a full account, see Trommer 2019).

During this time, Irish protesters increasingly perceived distinct EU institutions as providing political opportunity for alternative policy outcomes. Water activists, for example, lobbied Irish MEPs to counter the privatisation agenda within water policy reviews (Right2Water Ireland 2015). Activists also campaigned for the implementation of the European Citizens Initiative on Right2Water that sought to keep European water services in public hands (interview 5). At the time of the Greek bailout referendum in 2015, Irish protesters carried Greek flags at protests (e.g. Right2Water Protest 20 June 2015), thus refuting the Irish government's prominent claim in European political circles that 'Ireland is not Greece'. Instead, Irish protesters questioned why the Irish government sided with pro-austerity member states in EU institutions in Europe's dealings with Greece. Protesters argued that the Irish government should align politically with those member states that favoured alternative approaches to the Eurozone crisis (interview 16).

Water protesters also forged transnational alliances with other water movements from across the EU, including the Italian Super Mario Brothers and the European Water Movement platform, and across the globe, including Detroit Water Warriors and Maude Barlow (Moloney 2015; interviews 1, 16).[9] The political platform Right2Change looked towards Syriza and Podemos as possible European models and allies for a revitalised left-wing European project (interviews 5, 16). Increasingly, Irish protesters argued that they were part of larger efforts to create a platform for European solidarity across anti-austerity campaigns in different member states (interviews 6, 16). They perceived Irish political elites as 'holding on to neoliberal Europe', rather than fashioning an alternative Europe centred on economic and social justice (interview 3).

The 2015 Marriage Equality Referendum and the 2018 Referendum on the 8th Amendment of the Irish Constitution present a second watershed moment in the evolution of Irish protesters' attitudes towards the EU. Following both referendums, Irish political elites and Irish and international media circles tapped into traditional perceptions of Ireland's closer relationship to Europe as a key driver of progressive social change in Ireland (Graham-Harrison 2018). The UK newspaper the *Guardian*, for example, described the 2018 abortion referendum as a 'remarkable political victory for [Taoiseach] Leo Varadkar' (Graham-Harrison 2018). LGBTIQ and women protesters rejected these accounts. Instead, they claimed that the successful referendums were the result of decades of grassroots activism carried out within a hostile domestic social climate and supported through activists' transnational links with movements in EU member states such as the UK, Poland and Italy, but also in the United States and Argentina (Monaghan 2018). In addition, protesters highlighted the importance of continuity and learning across Irish protest movements prior to and during the post-crash era. One activist recalled a 'ripple effect going on … a lot of people started with bin charges, then water charges, then marriage equality, then housing, now Repeal … The next one due back is housing' (interview 9). Repeal activists used similar grassroots organising tactics as the water campaign and many, especially young women, were active in both campaigns (interviews 7, 9).

Recalling that Taoiseach Leo Varadkar only began supporting the Yes campaign in the final month leading up to the 2018 referendum (Leahy 2018), protesters argued that Irish elites were attempting to instrumentalise the EU's image as a protector of social rights for their own political gain. Protesters explained that the demands of Repeal-the-8th and marriage equality movements sat well with an image of 'good European social democrats' (interview 12) at a time when 'Fianna Fáil and Fine Gael were reeling from water charges and … are in their weakest position ever' (interview 8). Protesters explained that by referencing Ireland's membership in a progressive social Europe, political elites took undue credit for the highly popular constitutional and legal changes. It also allowed them to silence the history of feminist and LGBTIQ struggles in Ireland in a similar fashion as Irish austerity protests had been silenced (Holborow 2018a).

Following the adoption of the Regulation of Termination of Pregnancy Act, the absence of publicly funded and adequate health infrastructure necessary to make abortion services accessible to all women living in Ireland prompted women's movements to join the austerity critiques expressed by anti-bailout, water and later housing movements (Abortion Rights Campaign 2018; Kennedy 2018). They highlighted that EU institutions and Irish political elites were jointly responsible for hollowing out the necessary material conditions for safe access to abortion through underfunding of public services, the continued control of maternity services by the Catholic Church and an out-of-control housing crisis that increased women's vulnerable position in society. They perceived Irish and European political elites' social liberalism as colliding with their economic neoliberalism (see also Holborow 2018b). As one interviewee pointed out, 'a socially progressive neoliberal … creates a veneer that this person cares about you. Not caring about what you do is not the same as caring about you' (interview 16). For these protesters, pursuing an austerity agenda was incompatible with a socially progressive agenda. This is a significant change in EU sentiments among Irish protest movements overall, where socially progressive movements traditionally looked favourably upon the EU. The effects of austerity and the pursuit of neoliberal policy agendas were hollowing out this support in the decade after the crisis.

A growing housing movement across Ireland building on the critiques of the anti-austerity, water and abortion rights protesters and demanding an end to austerity policies emerged in 2018. The housing movement largely targeted the domestic ruling elite and government policies that allowed for vulture funds to buy up property during the crisis,[10] the erosion of social housing and exorbitant rents (Carroll 2018; Harris 2018). Throughout 2018, groups such as Take Back the City used house occupations, blockaded evictions and set up local housing networks in order to demand affordable social housing (Thomas 2018). Many Take Back the City activists are young people, 'a lot of whom were probably politicised by Repeal' (Coulter quoted in Thomas 2018). Take Back the City groups made links with other European housing movements showing solidarity for housing protests in Berlin and Madrid in April 2019 (Take Back the City Dublin 2019). Activists also organised under the #RaisetheRoof campaign that brought together trade unions, women's groups, traveller rights groups and housing action groups holding regular protest actions throughout Ireland (Blaney 2019; Mandate 2019). This movement focused on the domestic political terrain, linking with the general anti-austerity movements and the momentum of Repeal, with the EU playing little role, except through solidarity actions with European protesters and attacks on European vulture funds. The housing movement echoed claims made by Repeal activists that socially progressive reforms mean very little when economic austerity leaves little means for these reforms to be actualised.

Conclusion

Our chapter shows that Irish protesters' perceptions of the EU shifted in the period 2008–2018. Campaigns to prevent public spending cuts or increased taxation have historically targeted domestic politics and showed no distinct European dimension in Ireland. Socially progressive campaigners, on the other hand, historically looked towards the EU as a source of legitimation and positive policy change. With the onset of the 2008 economic collapse and the era of Irish austerity, both of these positions became more nuanced. Significantly, Irish progressive movements became critical of the EU especially in regard to continued economic austerity.

Anti-austerity protesters initially saw EU institutions as clear targets of their anger; however, over time they learned about the intricacies of EU policy making and subsequently began laying a large proportion of blame on domestic elites. Protesters argued that Irish politicians held agency in European politics and could have pursued alternative policy agendas, working in tandem with other EU member states negatively affected by the EU's policy prescriptions for handling their public debt crises. The Right2Water campaign in particular sought to lobby Irish MEPs and pursued European institutional support. Marriage Equality and Repeal-the-8th protesters, on the other hand, became increasingly sceptical of the role that the EU was playing in helping them to advance their agendas. After successes in these referendums, they began pointing out that neoliberal policy agendas upheld by domestic and European political elites created practical obstacles to their newly won social rights.

Our chapter helps explain why Irish Eurobarometer data continually shows positive attitudes towards the EU, despite the bailout and austerity (see also Simpson and Loveless 2017). Our analysis shows that Irish protesters predominantly supported the European project and the idea of European integration, yet demanded that it be reformed. Critically, their dissatisfaction was levelled at the domestic ruling elite, with anger increasingly channelled at the domestic sphere over time. The majority of Irish protest movements also deepened their ties to movements across Europe and elsewhere during this period. They helped develop visions for alternative forms of European integration, thus forging European identities of their own.

Notes

1 For more analysis of Irish public opinion, see Simpson, Chapter 8, this volume.
2 These results have changed little in recent years, supporting Simpson's claim that the 'Republic of Ireland is often regarded as one of the most enthusiastic supporters of European integration' (Simpson 2018: 16). Despite rejecting the Nice Treaty in 2001 and Lisbon Treaty in 2008, the majority continued to support the EU and trusted in the institution throughout the crisis (Simpson 2018: 17).
3 For an account of how the Irish government defunded state agencies and critical civil society organisations compiling systematic data on poverty in the run-up to the 2008 crash and during austerity, see Gaynor (2018).
4 To counter such an agenda, these conservative movements had pushed for the 8th Amendment to the Irish Constitution. The 8th Amendment accorded a pregnant woman and her unborn baby an equal right to life. The 8th Amendment was included in the constitution after a successful referendum in 1983 and was transposed into national law through a legal framework that effectively made abortion illegal.
5 The Says No groups were community level groups that popped up across the country initially around the banking bailout and the housing tax, but later

evolved into the water charges protests and other issues of austerity. They are loosely organised by town or suburb and do not come under any one banner or organisation. The Says No groups continued throughout 2011 until the time of writing (2019), with Ireland Says No channelling most anger towards the Labour Party, perceived excessive government spending and corruption, and the growing housing crisis (see the Facebook page mostly run by activist Derek Byrne as an example (Ireland Says No 2018)).

6 Occupy Dame Street occurred between October 2011 and March 2012.

7 Then Finance Minister, Brian Lenihan, famously launched the Four-Year National Recovery Plan by stating on national television that 'I accept that there were failures in the political system … but let's be fair about it. We all partied' (Murray 2010). The narrative that it was everyone's responsibility for the crash was subsequently pushed by mainstream media.

8 Since the 1980s, water provisioning to most private households in Ireland had been financed through general taxation. Those outside of centralised water supplies (close to 20% of households) were serviced through public and private group water schemes which included metering and charges (Environmental Protection Agency 2012: i–ii).

9 These different groups were active against the effects of privatisation of water services, poor quality and accessibility. For example, the Super Mario Brothers were a group of Italian activists who, while wearing Super Mario masks, would reconnect people's water if they had been cut off due to an inability to pay their bills (RT International 2014). The European Water Movement is a solidarity platform that brings together many of the European water activists and supporting organisations. The Detroit Water Warriors fought against the poor quality and high costs of their water services ; and Maude Barlow is a Canadian water activist who co-founded the Blue Planet Project. Both Barlow and the Detroit Water Warriors visited Ireland during the water protests.

10 Vulture funds are forms of private equity firms that invest in debt. Following the crisis, Irish lenders sold off some of their non-performing loans, including mortgage arrears, to these firms at a discount, allowing the funds to restructure the loan so they could sell the loan at a profit or take possession of the property.

References

Abortion Rights Campaign (2018) 'Press release: ARC welcomes abortion legislation signed into law'. Available at: www.abortionrightscampaign.ie/2018/12/21/press-release-arc-welcomes-abortion-legislation-signed-into-law/ [accessed 10 January 2019].

Attuyer, K. (2015) 'When conflict strikes: contesting neoliberal urbanism outside participatory structures in inner-city Dublin'. *International Journal of Urban and Regional Research* 39(4): 807–823.

BBC (2011) 'New Irish leader in bailout vow'. *BBC News*, 27 February. Available at: www.bbc.com/news/world-europe-12590868 [accessed 20 January 2019].

Bellec, L. & European Commission (2016) *Ireland in the EU: joining the European Community*. Ireland: European Commission, 30 May. Available at: https://ec.europa.eu/ireland/about-us/ireland-in-eu_en [accessed 18 January 2019].

Blaney, Ferghal. 2019. 'Raise the Roof campaigners demanding urgent action on Irish housing'. *Irish Mirror*, 24 January 24. Available at: www.irishmirror.ie/news/irish-news/politics/raise-roof-campaigners-demanding-urgent-13903135 [accessed 15 May 2019].

Carroll, R. (2018) 'Dublin's homelessness crisis jars with narrative of Irish economic boom'. *Guardian*, 5 September. Available at: www.theguardian.com/cities/2018/sep/05/dublin-homelessness-crisis-jars-with-narrative-of-irish-economic-boom [accessed 15 May 2019].

Chabanet, Didier & Frédéric Royall (2015) 'The 2011 Indignés/Occupy movements in France and Ireland: an analysis of the causes of weak mobilisations'. *Modern & Contemporary France* 23(3): 327–49.

Clark, A. & H. McDonald (2010) 'Ireland bailout protest draws 100,000 to Dublin streets'. *Guardian*, 27 November. Available at: www.theguardian.com/business/2010/nov/27/ireland-bailout-dublin-protest [accessed 3 February 2019].

Connolly L. (2002) *The Irish Women's Movement: from revolution to devolution*. Basingstoke: Palgrave.

Countryeconomy.com (2019) 'Ireland GDP'. Available at: https://countryeconomy.com/gdp/ireland [accessed 27 May 2019].

Cox, L. (2017) 'The Irish water charges movement: theorising "the Social Movement in General"'. *Interface: A Journal for and About Social Movements* 9(1): 161–203.

CSO (2019) 'Statistics'. Available at: www.cso.ie/en/statistics/ [accessed 27 May 2019].

Cullen, B. (2003) *Community and drugs: a discussion of the context and consequences of community drug problems in Ireland, 1976–2001*. Dublin: University of Dublin Trinity College, Addiction Research Centre.

Department of Housing, Planning and Local Government (2019) 'Homelessness data'. Available at: www.housing.gov.ie/housing/homelessness/other/homelessness-data [accessed 27 May 2019].

Dukelow, F. (2016) 'Irish water services reform: past, present and future', in M. Murphy & F. Dukelow (eds) *The Irish welfare state in the twenty-first century: challenges and changes*, pp. 141–166. Basingstoke: Palgrave.

Environmental Protection Agency (2012) *The provision and quality of drinking water in Ireland*. Ireland: Office of Environmental Enforcement. Available at: www.epa.ie/pubs/reports/water/drinking/Drinking%20Water_web.pdf [accessed 18 September 2019].

European Commission (2008) 'Water note 5: economics in water policy – the value of Europe's waters'. *Water Information System for Europe*. Brussels: DG Environment European Commission.

Eurostat. Directorate D: Government Finance Statistics and Quality (2015) 'Sector classification of Irish Water', 24 July. Available at: http://ec.europa.eu/eurostat/documents/1015035/6761701/Advice-2015-IE-Classification-of-Irish-Water-UpdateIII.pdf [accessed 12 January 2017].

Finn, D. (2015) 'Water wars in Ireland'. *New Left Review* 95: 49–63.

Flinn, F. (2011) 'The Irish suffer austerity in silence'. *Bloomberg Businessweek*, 23 November. Available at: www.bloomberg.com/news/articles/2011–11–23/the-irish-suffer-austerity-in-silence [accessed 20 February 2019].

Gaynor, N. (2018) 'Governing austerity in Dublin: rationalisation, resilience and resistance'. *Journal of Urban Affairs*, https://doi.org/10.1080/07352166.2018.14 84256.

Gillan, K. (2018) 'Temporality in Social Movement Theory: vectors and events in the neoliberal timescape'. *Social Movement Studies* 19(5–6): 516–536.

Government of Ireland (2010) *National Recovery Plan 2011–2014*. Available at: http://budget.gov.ie/The%20National%20Recovery%20Plan%202011–2014. pdf [accessed 3 December 2018].

Graham-Harrison, E. (2018) 'Irish abortion vote is remarkable political victory for Leo Varadkar'. *Guardian*, 29 May. Available at: www.theguardian.com/ world/2018/may/29/irish-abortion-vote-remarkable-political-victory-leo-varad-kar [accessed 4 February 2019].

Harris, J. (2018) '30,000 empty homes and nowhere to live: inside Dublin's housing crisis'. *Guardian*, 29 November. Available at: www.theguardian.com/cities/2018/ nov/29/empty-dublin-housing-crisis-airbnb-homelessness-landlords [accessed 30 November 2018].

Holborow, M. (2018a) 'Ireland's abortion victory: women's lives, the liberal agenda and the radical left'. *International Socialism: A Quarterly Review of Socialist Theory* 160 (November). Available at: http://isj.org.uk/irelands-abortion-victory/ [accessed 5 November 2018].

Holborow, M. (2018b) 'Ireland: all changed, changed utterly'. *REBEL (blog)*, 28 May. Available at: www.rebelnews.ie/2018/05/28/ireland-all-changed-changed-utterly [accessed 5 November 2018].

IMF (2010) 'Ireland: Letter of Intent, Memorandum of Economic and Financial Pol-icies, and Technical Memorandum of Understanding'. Available at: www.imf.org/ external/np/loi/2010/irl/120310.pdf [accessed 21 June 2017].

Ireland Says No (2018) 'Ireland Says No: Home'. Facebook post, 2 March. Available at: www.facebook.com/IrelandSaysNo.DSN/ [accessed 4 February 2019].

Kantar Public Brussels and European Commission (2018) 'Standard Eurobarometer 90 autumn 2018: public opinion in the European Union first results'. *Public Opinion in the European Union*. Brussels: European Commission.

Kennedy, S. (2018) 'Ireland's fight for choice'. *Jacobin*, 25 March. Available at: http:// jacobinmag.com/2018/03/irelands-fight-for-choice [accessed 6 November 2018].

Kiersey, N. (2014) 'Occupy Dame Street as slow motion general strike? Justifying optimism in the wake of Ireland's failed multitudinal moment'. *Global Discourse* 4(2–3): 141–158.

Kollewe, J. (2008) 'Ireland falls into recession'. *Guardian*, 25 September. Available at: www.theguardian.com/business/2008/sep/25/recession.ireland [accessed 3 February 2019].

Koopmans, R. (2004) 'Protest in time and space: the evolution of waves of conten-tion', in H. Kriesi, D. Snow & S. Soule (eds) *The Blackwell companion to social movements*, pp. 19–46. Oxford: Blackwell Publishing.

Layte, R. & Landy, D. (2018) 'The fighting Irish? Explaining the temporal pattern of social protest during Ireland's fiscal crisis 2008–2014'. *Sociology* 52(6): 1270–1289.

Leahy, P. (2018) 'Leo Varadkar's shifting view on abortion will be key to campaign'. *The Irish Times*, 1 November. Available at: www.irishtimes.com/news/social-affairs/leo-varadkar-s-shifting-view-on-abortion-will-be-key-to-campaign-1.3351288 [accessed 6 November 2018].

Leonard, L. (2008) *The environmental movement in Ireland*. New York: Springer.

Mandate (2019) 'Cork members encouraged to attend Raise The Roof – Homes For All rally on March 11th'. *Mandate Trade Union Ireland (blog)*, 18 February. Available at: https://mandate.ie/2019/02/cork-members-encouraged-to-attend-raise-the-roof-homes-for-all-rally-on-march-11th/ [accessed 15 May 2019].

McAdam, D., S. Tarrow & C. Tilly (2001) *Dynamics of contention*. Cambridge: Cambridge University Press.

McDonald, H. (2013) 'Ireland becomes first country to exit Eurozone bailout programme'. *Guardian*, 13 December. Available at: www.theguardian.com/business/2013/dec/13/ireland-first-country-exit-eurozone-bailout [accessed 28 November 2018].

Mercille, J. (2014) 'The role of the media in fiscal consolidation programmes: the case of Ireland'. *Cambridge Journal of Economics* 38: 281–300.

Moloney, M. (2015) 'Right2Water goes to Brussels'. *An Phoblacht*. Available at: www.anphoblacht.com/contents/24792 [accessed 20 January 2019].

Monaghan, S. (2018) *March For Choice Dublin*. Speech. Dublin. Available at: www.youtube.com/watch?v=ZdyN7EPS-w0 [accessed 5 November 2018].

Murphy, M. (2016) 'Irish civil society: rearranging the deckchairs on the Titanic? A case study of fighting Irish social security retrenchment'. *Journal of Civil Society* 12(1): 17–32.

Murray, N. (2010) 'No, minister we didn't all "party" in the boom'. *Irish Examiner* 6 December. Available at: www.irishexaminer.com/ireland/politics/no-minister-we-didnt-all-party-in-the-boom-138578.html [accessed 20 September 2019].

OECD (2019) 'OECD data'. Available at: https://data.oecd.org/ [accessed 27 May 2019].

Ogle, B. (2016) *From bended knee to a new republic: how the fight for water is changing Ireland*. Dublin: The Liffey Press.

Right2Water Ireland (2015) 'Democracy denied in Europe yet again: Take action NOW!' *Right2Water Ireland (blog)*. 6 September. Available at: www.right2water.ie/blog/democracy-denied-europe-yet-again-take-action-now [accessed 15 May 2019].

RT International (2014) 'Super Mario to the rescue: mask-wearing plumbers restore water to Italian homes'. Available at: www.rt.com/news/210527-italy-plumbers-mario-water/ [accessed 20 September 2019].

RTÉ (2018) 'Result is culmination of quiet revolution: Varadkar'. *RTÉ News Online*, 26 May. Available at: www.rte.ie/news/eighth-amendment/2018/0526/966132-reaction/ [accessed 21 January 2019].

Simpson, K. (2018) 'The model EU citizen? Explaining Irish attitudes towards the EU'. *Political Insight* 9(1): 16–19.

Simpson, K. & M. Loveless (2017) 'Another chance? Concerns about inequality, support for the European Union and further European integration'. *Journal for European Public Policy* 24(7): 1069–1089.

Take Back the City Dublin (2019) 'Housing actions across Europe over the weekend, against rip-off rent, evictions and for public housing!' Facebook post, 8 April. Available at: www.facebook.com/TakeBackTheCityDublin/ [accessed 10 May 2019].

Thomas, C. (2018) 'Take Back the City protesters on why they've taken to the streets'. Thejournal.ie, 29 September. Available at: www.thejournal.ie/take-back-the-city-4255230-Sep2018/ [accessed 10 May 2019].

Trommer, S. (2019) 'Watering down austerity: scalar politics and disruptive resistance in Ireland'. *New Political Economy* 24(2): 218–234.

Interviews

1 Councillor (Sinn Féin) (male), Dublin, 3 December 2015.
2 Trade Union Organiser (Mandate) (male), Dublin, 4 December 2015.
3 Trade Union Organiser (Unite the Union) (male), Dublin, 10 December 2015.
4 Community activist (male), Dublin, 14 December 2015.
5 Trade Union Organiser (Mandate), Right2Water organiser (male) Dublin, 17 May 2018.
6 Politician TD (AAA) (male), Dublin, 17 May 2018.
7 Community activist (male), member of AAA, Dublin, 19 May 2018.
8 Councillor (PBP) (female), Dublin, 21 May 2018.
9 Walkinstown Says No activist (female), Dublin, 25 May 2018.
10 Community activist and member of Cork Says No to Water Meters (female), Cork, 26 May 2018.
11 Activist Academic (male), Dublin, 29 September 2018.
12 Dublin Says No activist (male), Dublin, 29 September 2018.
13 Dublin Says No activist (female) activist, Dublin, 29 September 2018.
14 Trade union organiser (Unite the Union)/Right2Water organiser (male), Dublin, 2 October 2018.

Protests attended

- Right2Water protest, Dublin, 20 June 2015.
- Save Moore Street protest, Dublin, 28 November 2015.
- National Demonstration on Homelessness and Housing, Dublin, 1 December 2015.
- Anti-water Charges protest, Dublin, 8 December 2015.
- Save Moore Street protest, Dublin, 18 February 2016.
- Dublin Bay North Repeal-the-8th leafleting and canvassing, Dublin, 22 May 2018.
- Cork Says No to Water Meters public stall, Cork, 25 May 2018.
- Repeal announcement, Dublin Castle, 26 May 2018.
- March for Choice, Dublin, 29 September 2018.

8

National interest and public interest: public opinion from the economic crisis to Brexit

Kathryn Simpson

Ireland and the EU

Since the 2008 economic crisis, trends in public opinion suggest that citizens of the EU are becoming more critical of the EU as individuals perceive themselves to be at heightened risk of economic insecurity (Simpson & Loveless 2017). Nevertheless, recent research has demonstrated that while individuals in Ireland were disappointed and angered by the performance of the EU during the economic crisis, overall they remain enthusiastic supporters of the EU (Simpson 2018a, 2018b, 2019). Brexit posed another period of instability – both economically and politically – for individuals in Ireland specifically for bilateral relations with the UK on economic and trading matters and the pursuit of Irish objectives as an EU member state. But Brexit also tended to reinforce a positive image of the EU among Irish people. This chapter examines Irish attitudes towards the EU.[1] It assesses the importance individuals place on both the economic crisis and the Brexit crisis and how this shaped Irish attitudes towards the EU. The results show that public opinion support for the EU in Ireland remains robust in spite of these two crises. While the EU continues to be regarded as an economic project in Ireland, evidence from this chapter demonstrates a shift towards more policy specific issues.

Ireland is often regarded as one of the most enthusiastic supporters of European integration since its accession to the EU in 1973 as they are often considered as "good Europeans" with a pro-integrationist attitude (Adshead & Tonge 2009; Gilland 2002; Kennedy & Sinnott 2006, 2007; Lyons 2008; Sinnott 1995, 2002, 2005). Yet, the reality of Irish public opinion is more nuanced: support for the EU in Ireland is not a single entity, but a complex set of opinions determined by a variety of factors. Research has shown that since the 1990s knowledge about the EU among the Irish public is low (Garry et al. 2005; Holmes 2005; Kennedy & Sinnott 2006, 2007; Laffan & O'Mahony 2008) with individuals in Ireland more likely to refer to the economic aspects of the EU, such as the freedom of movement, the euro and economic prosperity. This "knowledge deficit" is perhaps not surprising, as for the first twenty years of EU membership Ireland's self-perception of its status within the EU was that of a small, poor, peripheral member state. In their examination of the nuances of Irish public opinion towards the EU, Kennedy and Sinnott (2007) find that Irish individuals' knowledge of the EU does not affect the relationship between opinions about EU support and evaluations of domestic and European institutions. Therefore, the EU project in Ireland is not one which can be encapsulated by a single overarching judgement, but by many different facets.

The pro-EU tendency of the Irish began to be challenged in the 2000s when Ireland's economic boom led the Irish government into conflict with the EU over its management of the Irish economy. The Irish government was criticised for its refusal to dampen the successful Celtic Tiger economy and for its substantial tax concessions for foreign investors which were (and still are) regarded by the European Commission as breaking the spirit if not the law of the European Single Market (ESM). However, individuals in Ireland tend to focus on national or intergovernmental aspects of EU membership and representation rather than on the policy-making aspects of EU institutions which produce legislation that has an effect across all EU member states. Therefore, there remains a proportion of the population who oppose further sharing of sovereignty and are concerned about the impact Ireland's involvement in the EU is having on Irish identity, values and culture. The multifaceted nature of Irish public opinion towards the EU was borne out in the rejection of the Nice Treaty in May 2001 and the Lisbon Treaty in June 2008. These votes highlighted the potential emergence of a new popular scepticism towards the EU in so far as it concerns Irish interests and deeper European integration in Ireland (Simpson 2019).

Public opinion and the 2008 economic crisis

The 2008 economic crisis can be regarded as a decisive moment in Ireland's relationship with the EU as a result of the economic downturn and a widening of economic disparities experienced by individuals. However, despite this turning point Irish attitudes towards the EU have remained consistently positive (Simpson 2018a, 2018b, 2019). This can be seen in the variety of data sources pertaining to mass public opinion towards the EU in Ireland, in particular EU-related referendum results, large-N surveys[2] and opinion polls. When the Irish electorate voted No to the Lisbon Treaty in June 2008 both the domestic political and economic context played a vital role. The change in the *political context* from the first Lisbon Treaty referendum in

June 2008 to the second Lisbon Treaty referendum in October 2009 was a result of the Irish government's attempts to address concerns highlighted by the No campaign. These were issues in relation to military neutrality, the corporation tax rate, the belief that abortion services would be widely available, a weakening of workers' rights and a reduction in Irish influence at the EU level due to the loss of a permanent Irish EU Commissioner.[3]

However, it was perhaps the change in *economic context* from Lisbon 1 to Lisbon 2 which was most dramatic, as after the rejection of the first referendum on the Lisbon Treaty, the financial crisis impacted and Ireland plunged into recession. It was frequently expressed that as a result of the onset of the economic and financial crisis Ireland was safer as part of a larger economic community that could potentially offer Ireland protection, which Ireland did receive through a three-year Economic Adjustment Programme or bailout in December 2010 from the Troika (which it exited in December 2013).

Yet, perhaps the *economic context* was much more marked for the Fiscal Treaty referendum in 2012 than for any other EU-related referendum as a result of the ailing Irish economy and the Irish government's reliance on a multi-billion euro loan administered by the EU and the IMF. One of the advantages of the Fiscal Treaty is it addressed only one area: economic policy. This made it much less likely for debate over ratification by social and cultural issues that had become prominent in Lisbon 1. Ireland was supportive of the Fiscal Treaty – as a small EU member state suffering the effects of the Eurozone crisis and domestic banking failures, the Irish government regarded the Fiscal Treaty as a means to regain stability, growth and market confidence (Costello 2012), and the Irish electorate recognised this and voted to ratify the Fiscal Treaty in May 2012 by 60%.

Despite the emergence of a *potential* popular scepticism during 2001–2008 and the financial bailout received in 2010, Irish attitudes towards the EU continued to remain consistently positive. Analysis of Large-N survey data, most notably Standard Eurobarometer data from 1972–2019, shows that support for the EU in Ireland since 1987 in particular has been above the EU average and reached a record high of 83% in both 2017 and 2019 (see Figure 8.1) – with individuals in Ireland believing that membership of the EU is a "good thing" for Ireland.

The robustness of Ireland's support for the EU is reiterated further by Standard Eurobarometer data during 2009–2014 at the peak of the economic and financial crisis which demonstrates that the Irish electorate maintained that the EU was the best placed institution to take effective action against the economic and financial crisis (see Figure 8.2).

This vigour of support by individuals in Ireland for the EU is echoed when examining how individuals in Ireland perceive they have benefited

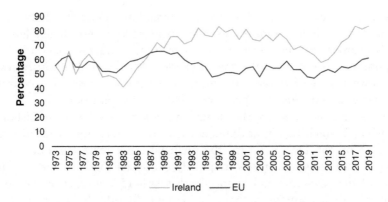

Figure 8.1 Support for the EU in Ireland, 1973–2019
Source: Standard Eurobarometer Data. N = 1,009.

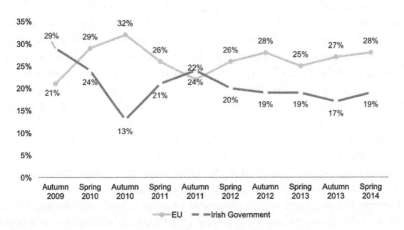

Figure 8.2 Effective action against the economic and financial crisis, 2009–2014.
Source: Standard Eurobarometer Data.

from EU membership. Support for the EU is once again above the EU average since 1984 in particular reaching an all-time high in 2018 of 91% – the highest across all 28 EU member states.

The individual-level responses in Figure 8.3 are notable as they highlight that individuals in Ireland regard the Irish state as much less effective in its action to manage the effects of the economic crisis since spring 2010. Additionally, what is robustly evident from all three analyses here is that despite the financial bailout from the Troika in 2010, individuals in Ireland continue to remain enthusiastic supporters of the EU (see Figures 8.1 and 8.2).

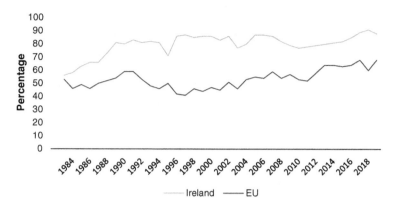

Figure 8.3 Benefited from EU membership, 1984–2019
Source: Standard Eurobarometer Data. N = 1,016.

They believe that membership of the EU is a good thing and that overall Ireland has benefited from membership of the EU.

Public opinion and the 2016 Brexit crisis

The vote by the UK to leave the EU on 23 June 2016 constituted a remarkable shock to UK politics. And this shock resonated just as much in Dublin. While the Irish government had put contingency plans in place, the 2016 EU referendum result in the UK placed Ireland in an unenviable and difficult position. The UK is not just Ireland's nearest neighbour, it is one of Ireland's 'largest trading partners, the main market for Irish agri-food produce, the geographic link to the continent (Ireland's land bridge) in getting goods to market and its most important ally within the European Council and the Council of Ministers' (O'Brennan 2019: 2; see also Murphy 2019). Brexit therefore represents a profound political and economic challenge to Ireland.

There is undoubtedly an awareness that Ireland has a special case in relation to Brexit. As one senior EU Commission official stated, 'Ireland is a good EU citizen … they went through the crisis and agony of the [bailout] programme and came out as a poster boy for resilience and toughing it out. So, what is at stake is absolutely enormous' (cited in Connelly 2017: 342). The weight of Ireland's concerns – trade and Northern Ireland – has allowed the Irish government to fuse the two issues in its negotiating strategy. As a senior Irish diplomat affirms, 'the logic of the peace process is based on a method to depoliticize the underlying constitutional problems, and to create a zone of peace and prosperity. That peace and prosperity is underlined by the free movement of goods and services' (cited in Connelly 2017: 342). As a consequence, Brexit negotiations demonstrated a remarkable 'reverse asymmetry' (O'Brennan 2019: 2) in UK–Irish relations as the historical dynamic of British power over Ireland yielded itself to the inside–outside asymmetrical logic of the Article 50 negotiations. Ireland's status as a privileged EU insider created a position where it could veto any withdrawal agreement that did not include a backstop[4] clause on the Irish border.

Public opinion support for the Irish government's negotiating strategy and management thus far of Brexit has been overwhelmingly positive. This is reflected in two opinion polls specifically – the *Sunday Business Post*/RED C Poll[5] in January 2019 and the Sky Data Poll[6] in February 2019 – which asked about attitudes towards Brexit in Ireland. The *Sunday Business Post*/Red C poll asked two specific questions relating to the backstop in particular. The findings are thought-provoking – 70% of respondents agreed that the Irish government should refuse to put up border infrastructure if there is a hard Brexit (24% disagree and 6% were unsure), and 64% disagreed that the Irish government should drop the backstop from the Brexit Withdrawal Agreement in order to help former Prime Minister Theresa May[7] get the deal through the House of Commons ahead of the UK's departure from the EU.[8] This is reiterated further in the Sky Data Poll where 79% of individuals in Ireland think that the Irish government should persist for a legal guarantee that there will be no hard border on the island of Ireland with just 7% of individuals in Ireland believing that the Irish government should prioritise a no deal Brexit.

Findings from the Sky Data Poll are also positive for the Irish government and for the EU – 60% of respondents believe the Irish government has done a good job in negotiating Brexit (17% think the Irish government has done a bad job and 23% unsure). In contrast, a vast majority – 84% of individuals in Ireland – think that the UK government had done a bad job in Brexit negotiations with just 6% believing it had done a good job. Finally, from an economic perspective, Irish respondents continue to align and display positive support for the EU. When asked to choose who to cut economic ties with, 81% of respondents said the UK while only 19% said the EU.

Relative to the rest of the EU, Ireland is especially vulnerable to the fallout from Brexit, both economically and politically. As a result, some argue that an Irish exit, or Irexit, from the EU would benefit the nation. The question of Irexit has developed primarily as an economic argument implying that Ireland will be left marginalised, peripheral and dependent post-Brexit. Irexit would allow for reintegration with the UK, thus reinstating close ties with one of its largest trading partners. From a political perspective, the formation of the Irish Freedom Party coined as a 'national movement of the

Irish people which has as its primary objective the re-establishment of the national independence and sovereignty of Ireland and the restoration of national democracy to be achieved through leaving the European Union' (Irish Freedom Party 2019), has politicised the Irexit debate. Primarily, the movement draws upon those individuals who feel aggrieved, display anti-establishment sentiments and who prescribe to the left-behind thesis (Goodwin & Heath 2016a, 2016b). However, there are also disconnects between the disparate elements in those attending events held by the Irish Freedom Party with many holding divergent views on immigration as well as the lack of leadership and direction of the group.

There are four fundamental economic and political problems with the Irexit thesis. Firstly, from an economic perspective, the stance on a possible Irexit omits the question of *how* Ireland developed economic independence and moved on from political domination by the UK when it joined the EU in 1973. Irish accession to the EU enabled the diversification in trade and investment, including the ESM, but also the attracting of FDI from the United States. Research also highlights that an economic realignment with the UK, moving away from the ESM, would 'substantially worsen the impacts of Brexit, with lower-skill and agricultural workers being dispro-portionately affected' (Davies & Francois 2018: 455). This emphasises that while the UK is indeed one of Ireland's most important trading partners, trade with the rest of the EU is much more important. Secondly, from a political perspective, the equal partnership between the UK and Ireland as EU member states facilitated negotiations on the issue of peace in Northern Ireland and in particular the 1998 Agreement (Murphy 2018, 2019; O'Brennan 2019). Thirdly, while populism may have ignited the two biggest politi-cal shocks of recent times (Brexit and the election of Trump as President of the United States), in Ireland there has been little proliferation of the far right (see Holmes, Chapter 6, this volume). This dispels, from a political and theoretical perspective, the basis and rationale for the Irexit movement. Finally, public opinion support for the EU in Ireland is *consistently positive* and there is little appetite among individuals in Ireland to leave the EU (Simpson 2018a, 2018b, 2019).

The first opinion poll since the UK officially exited the EU on 1 January 2020[9] found that 84% of individuals in Ireland believe that Ireland should remain a part of the EU. While this is the lowest level of support for the EU since the European Movement Ireland/Red C Poll began in 2013, the find-ings demonstrate that support for the EU in Ireland is overwhelmingly positive. The results also echo findings from the most recent Standard Euro-barometer data in 2019 when 83% of respondents noted that Ireland's membership of the EU was a "good thing" (see Figure 8.1) and that 88% of

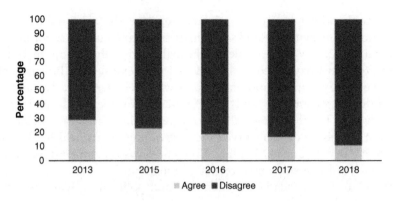

Figure 8.4 Brexit should lead to Irexit
Source: EMI/RED C Poll, 2013–2018. N = 1,000.

individuals believed that Ireland had benefited from being a member of the EU (Figure 8.3).

When considering the case for Irexit, opinion polling data is crucial. In the 2018 European Movement/Red C Poll there were two questions which examined Irexit. While there was understandable uncertainty about what changes and challenges Brexit would herald for Ireland, individuals were clear that leaving the EU is *not* in Ireland's interests. When asked "If the UK were to leave the EU, Ireland should leave too" only 11% of individuals in Ireland agreed. This demonstrates a dramatic decline from 2013 when support for Ireland leaving the EU in the event of Brexit was at 29% (Figure 8.4).[10]

The same poll also asks individuals whether "Ireland should remain a part of the EU". In 2018 and 2019 support for the EU in Ireland was at an all-time high with 92% and 93% of respondents agreeing with this statement, respectively. Again, this finding demonstrates consistent and positive support for the EU since 2013 with support for membership of the EU increasing year on year since 2013 (see Figure 8.5).

One of the most comprehensive opinion polls conducted on EU membership in Ireland since the 2016 Brexit vote in the UK complemented the findings of the 2018–2020 European Movement Ireland/Red C Poll findings. When asked whether Ireland should remain a member of the EU, 94% of respondents in the Ireland Thinks[11] poll agreed with this statement. In addition, the 2018 Standard Eurobarometer[12] individuals were asked "If a referendum was held tomorrow regarding Ireland's membership of the EU, how would you vote?" with 85% of individuals stating they would vote to remain in the EU – the highest of all twenty-seven EU member states and 19% above the EU average.

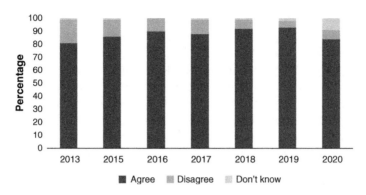

Figure 8.5 Ireland should remain part of the EU
Source: EMI/RED C Poll 2013–2020. N = 1,000.

The Irexit debate is a crude caricature of Ireland's political and economic situation which falls back on inherent clichés (i.e. Ireland is a small, peripheral member state, reliance on the UK, etc.), disregarding Ireland's success in Brexit negotiations (i.e. ensuring the UK cannot move forward to trade negotiations until the unique Irish issues have been fully addressed) and provides no indication of what Irexit and the future relationship with the EU would look like. But perhaps more importantly, it demonstrates a rudimentary understanding of Irish attitudes towards the EU. An Irexit is highly questionable.

Moving on from the crisis and embracing Brexit

The economic crisis and the Irish context highlight the heightened risk of economic adversity for individuals as a result of rising economic problems in both Ireland and the EU (Simpson 2018a; Simpson & Loveless 2017) with the focus on European integration now moving towards a more individualist egocentric perspective. European integration and governance have been centrally important in the economic transformation of Ireland, particularly through the alignment of state strategy with the action of economic and social interests. The 2008 economic crisis demonstrated that context, especially in the case of Ireland, is important and has directly influenced politics (Simpson 2018a).

In many ways, the outcome of the Brexit referendum was not surprising. Firstly, public opinion in the UK has consistently been the most Eurosceptic electorate in the EU since it joined the EU in 1973. Secondly, it is well established that referendums on European integration are highly unpredictable and that voters often reject proposals put to them by the government even when supported by a consensus among mainstream political parties and experts (Franklin et al. 1994, 1995; Hobolt 2009). On the one hand, the outcome of the EU referendum in the UK is a unique event since no other member state has decided to exit the EU. On the other, the sentiments that led to Brexit are by no means a uniquely British phenomenon with anti-immigration, anti-establishment and stark demographic divides between the winners and losers of the European integration process found in many states. Typically, Remain voters were likely to be younger, a graduate of a university and receiving a higher income, while Leave voters were likely to be older, with a lower level of educational attainment and earning a low income (Goodwin & Heath 2016a, 2016b).

The challenge of Brexit for the EU, and for the member states, is that many voters across Europe see the EU as part of the problem rather than the solution when it comes to protecting ordinary citizens from the challenges of an ever more integrated world. However, Ireland again somewhat bucks this trend as research shows that even during the economic crisis and financial bailouts received from the Troika, Ireland remained avid supporters of European integration (Simpson 2018a). Ireland is the EU member state which is most exposed to the economic effects of Brexit. All trade between the UK and Ireland is governed under the EU framework of the customs union and the ESM. Therefore, could Brexit determine a transformation in Irish public opinion? One which goes beyond the feeble Irexit debate and focuses on European integration in a more policy-orientated perspective?

Standard Eurobarometer data does not contain specific questions about Brexit. However, if the issue of Brexit permeates mass public opinion in Ireland, it would be expected to influence individual-level attitudes on the current economic situation in Ireland and in particular Ireland's future economic prospects. Standard Eurobarometer data asks respondents "What do you think are the two most important issues facing [Ireland]?" from 2007–2019 assessing issues such as crime, the economic situation, the cost of living, unemployment, housing, immigration, and health and social security. This Standard Eurobarometer data allows an examination of key issues facing Ireland during the economic and financial crisis and following the Brexit vote (see Figure 8.6).

Firstly, focusing on the financial crisis, between 2008 and 2015 the two most important issues individuals believed Ireland was facing were the economic situation and unemployment. The economic situation was regarded as the most important issue for Ireland in 2008 and the second most important issue in the period 2009–2014.[13] While the issue of unemployment was considered to be *the most important issue* facing Ireland during 2009–2014. These findings are consistent with previous research that identifies

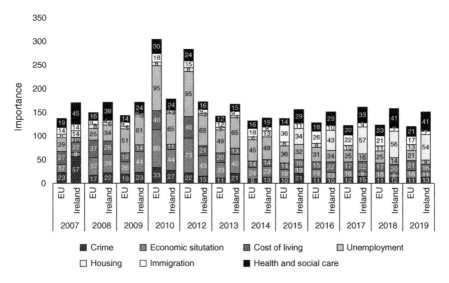

Figure 8.6 Most important issue for Ireland, 2007–2019
Source: Standard Eurobarometer Data. N = 1,000.

individuals experiencing economic adversity during the financial crisis as a result of rising economic problems in both Ireland and the EU. Secondly, during 2015–2019, a period which captures the context of pre, and (immediate) post, Brexit, individuals report more policy-orientated issues as the most important issues facing Ireland, most notably housing and health and social security. During 2015–2019, housing was regarded as *the most important issue* for Ireland while health and social security was viewed as the second most important issue.

However, perhaps the most notable shift in key issues since 2015 is the fact that individuals' economic perceptions and expectations have been overwhelmingly positive in Ireland. Since 2015, there has been a steady decline in individuals reporting that the economic situation is one of the most important issues in Ireland – from 13% in 2015 to 11% in 2019 – which is between five to seven percentage points *lower* than the EU average for the same period. The same pattern can be reported for the issue of unemployment. Since 2016, individuals have reported a decline in unemployment as the most important issue for Ireland – from 24% in 2016 to 9% in 2019 – and between seven and twelve percentage points *lower* than the EU average for the same period. The positive shift in public opinion towards the economy during a period of political and potential economic instability in light of Brexit highlights there are limited concerns for economic pessimism in Ireland.

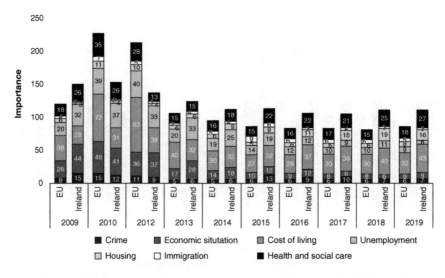

Figure 8.7 Most important issue for you personally (Ireland), 2009–2019
Source: Standard Eurobarometer Data. N = 1,000.

Standard Eurobarometer data can also examine what individuals believe to be the most important issues *they are facing at the moment* allowing an analysis at the individual level as well as the macro level. Figure 8.7 asks respondents "And personally, what are the two most important issues you are facing at the moment?" during 2009–2018[14] assessing the same issues such as crime (personal) economic situation, the cost of living, unemployment, housing, immigration, and health and social security. This Eurobarometer data allows an examination of key issues facing *individuals* in Ireland during the economic and financial crisis and following the Brexit vote. During 2009–2014, the two most important issues facing individuals in Ireland are the economic situation (the most important issue in 2009 and 2010, second most important issue in 2012), unemployment (the second most important issue in 2009 and 2010) and the cost of living (most important issue in 2012, 2013 and 2014). Again, these findings are consistent with the Eurobarometer data outlined in Figure 8.7 as well as previous research that identifies individuals experiencing economic adversity during the economic and financial crisis as a result of rising economic problems in both Ireland and the EU. Put simply, during the economic and financial crisis, economic pessimism at the individual level was widespread.

From 2015–2018 however, the two most important issues facing individuals are both economic and policy orientated. From 2015, the cost of living is reported as the most important issue individuals are facing in Ireland, with health and social care reported as the second most import- ant issue for individuals. What is noteworthy here is that both of these issues are far higher in Ireland than the EU average. This demonstrates that there is the possibility of a potential Brexit effect and sense of economic pessimism at the individual level not experienced at the macro level. However, it may be argued that for individuals in Ireland the ques- tion of whether and perhaps *how* Brexit will have an impact on Ireland at the macro level and individual level may not have a clear answer. There are indeed no specific Brexit questions from which to draw upon in Standard Eurobarometer data and Brexit is being contextualised in economic terms. Yet, what is clear is policy-orientated issues concerning health care, social care and principles of the welfare state are of great concern for individuals in Ireland.

What next for Ireland and the EU?

The Irish government's concerns about Brexit were first outlined in the 2014 *National Risk Assessment* (Department of the Taoiseach 2014: 17) and out- lined that a period of uncertainty regarding the UK's relationship with the EU would have an impact on Ireland in three areas. Firstly, in the pursuit of Ireland's objectives as an EU member state; secondly, regarding bilateral relations with the UK including the economic and trading relationship; and thirdly, issues in relation to Northern Ireland. The UK decision to leave the EU apportioned a considerable shock to Irish national interests. There are serious economic concerns about the potential detrimental effect of the UK being outside the ESM and customs union. The erection of barriers to trade between the UK and Ireland poses fundamental risks to the Irish economy while the effects of Brexit on the CTA are also problematic (Murphy 2018, 2019). However, when examining public opinion and the effect that Brexit will have on the macro level and individual level there does not appear to be a Brexit effect regarding the Irish economy – overall, attitudes towards the economy and individuals' personal economic situation are overwhelmingly positive. Perhaps a potential Brexit effect is still too early to determine for mass public opinion for two reasons. Firstly, there are no questions relating to Brexit specifically in the Standard Eurobarometer data over this time period; and secondly, the potential effects of Brexit are still in fact not known. This makes examining mass public opinion in relation to attitudes towards Brexit cumbersome.

However, it can be noted from both sets of opinion polling data that an Irexit is unlikely and that individuals in Ireland believe that EU membership is a good thing – this is a robust finding as it is also reflected in the analyses of Standard Eurobarometer also. One of the central components of the Irish government's approach to Brexit has been to engage with civil society and stakeholders, in particular creating an *All-Island Civic Dialogue* on Brexit as a participative and consultative exercise that aims to hear directly about the all-island implications of Brexit from a variety of stakeholders and across a wide range of sectors. The *All-Island Civic Dialogue* provides new opportunities for methods of public discussion among civil society actors which had not existed previously. Over time, these forums may conceivably elevate public knowledge of the EU and therefore impact on attitudes towards the EU.

Ireland, and perhaps more specifically Irish public opinion, has weathered the storm of the economic crisis (so far), the Brexit crisis and the debate around a potential Irexit. While an Irexit is unlikely, Ireland's relationship with the EU will not be without its challenges. Firstly, in the context of Brexit on issues such as the economic impact Ireland will experience as a consequence of the UK leaving the EU, as well as questions pertaining to the border between Northern Ireland and the Republic of Ireland. Secondly, in the context of the future relationship with the EU. While a knowledge deficit continues to exist among the mass public in Ireland with regards to the EU, the salience of EU membership and therefore support for the EU is consistently strong, robust and shows little sign of abating. Brexit has forced Ireland to think anew about its relationship with the UK and the EU, and instead of turning towards an historical periphery Ireland recognises that current challenges are global and do not respect borders. As a consequence, Ireland is best placed to meet these changes through continued cooperation and engagement subsequently influencing solutions as part of the EU. Brexit may indeed mean Brexit, but for Ireland remaining a member state of the EU is in its national interest – and public opinion recognises this.

Notes

1 The chapter uses a combination of survey data, Standard Eurobarometer data (2007–2019) and opinion polling data, RED C (2013–2020), Ireland Thinks (2018) and Sky Data (2019).
2 Large-N surveys look for patterns in a large number of cases. Generally speaking, large-N surveys have better external validity as they use a large number of cases and adopt a variable based approach. Large-N surveys are quantitative, aggregate and secondary data.
3 Guarantees on these issues were added as Protocols in the second referendum on the Lisbon Treaty.

4 The backstop was an insurance policy to avoid a hard border between Northern Ireland and the Republic of Ireland if a free trade deal between the UK and the EU was not reached by the end of the transition period of 2020 (UK in a Changing Europe 2019, and see also Phinnemore & Whitten, Chapter 12, this volume).

5 The *Sunday Business Post*/Red C Poll interviewed a random sample of 1,000 adults aged 18+ by telephone between 17–24 January 2019. Respondents were asked four questions and asked to respond either Agree, Disagree or Unsure.

6 The Sky Data Poll interviewed a nationally representative sample of Sky customers in the Republic of Ireland (N=1,611) online from 1–4 February 2019. Data are weighted to the profile of the population.

7 Prime Minister Theresa May stepped down as Leader of the Conservative Party on 7 June 2019 triggering a leadership contest within the Conservative Party and thus a new UK Prime Minister.

8 At the time of writing an extension to Article 50 until 31 October 2019 had been granted by the EU. Therefore, the UK did not leave the EU as scheduled on 29 March 2019 but on 31 January 2020.

9 The RED C Poll commissioned by the European Movement Ireland has been conducted annually since 2013 (apart from 2014) in order to ascertain the views of Irish people on a variety of issues related to Ireland–EU relations. The 2020 poll was conducted between 20–25 March 2020 among a representative sample of individuals in Ireland (N=1,000) aged 18+. A series of statements were read out and respondents were asked by Red C to Agree Strongly, Agree Slightly, Disagree Strongly or Disagree Slightly.

10 No European Movement Ireland/RED C Poll was conducted in 2014.

11 The Ireland Thinks poll was conducted between 15–24 August 2018 among a random sample of 942 individuals in Ireland aged 18+.

12 Standard Eurobarometer 90.1 was conducted between 8–26 September 2018 among all EU27 (N=27,601) aged 16+. For Ireland, N= 1,001.

13 Data is unavailable for the question *What do you think are the two most important issues facing [Ireland]?* as this question was not asked in any Standard Eurobarometer in 2011.

14 Please note that the data is unavailable for the question *And personally, what are the two most important issues you are facing at the moment]?* as this question was not asked in any Standard Eurobarometer in 2011.

References

Adshead, M. & J. Tonge (2009) *Politics in Ireland: convergence and divergence in a two-polity island*. Basingstoke: Palgrave Macmillan.

Connelly, T. (2017) *Brexit and Ireland: the dangers, the opportunities, and the inside story of the Irish response*. Dublin: Penguin Ireland.

Costello, T. (2012) 'The Fiscal Stability Treaty referendum 2012'. *Irish Political Studies* 29(3): 457–470.

Davies, R.B. & J. Francois (2018) 'Making the worst of a bad situation: a note on Irexit'. *The Economic and Social Review* 49(4): 455–462.

Department of the Taoiseach (2014) *National Risk Assessment 2014*. Dublin: Department of the Taoiseach. Available at: www.taoiseach.gov.ie/eng/Publications/Publications_2014/National_Risk_Assess,emt_report_2014.pdf [accessed 28 July 2020].

European Movement Ireland/Red C Poll 'Ireland and the EU 2013–2020'. Available at: www.europeanmovement.ie/programmes/ireland-and-the-eu-poll/ [accessed 28 July 2020].

Franklin, M., M. Marsh & L. McLaren (1994) 'Uncorking the bottle: popular opposition to European integration in the wake of Maastricht'. *Journal of Common Market Studies* 32(4): 455–472.

Franklin, M., C. Van der Eijk & M. Marsh (1995) 'Referendum outcomes and trust in government: public support for the EU in the wake of Maastricht'. *West European Politics* 18(3): 101–117.

Garry, J., M. Marsh & R. Sinnott (2005) 'Second-order versus issue-voting effects in EU referendums: evidence from the Nice Treaty referendums'. *European Union Politics* 6(2): 201–221.

Gilland, K. (2002) 'Ireland and European integration', in K. Goldmann & K. Gilland (eds) *Nationality versus Europeanisation: the view of the nation in four countries*, pp. 166–184. Stockholm: Dept. of Political Sciences, Stockholm University.

Goodwin, M.J. & O. Heath (2016a) 'The 2016 referendum, Brexit and the left-behind: an aggregate-level analysis of the result'. *Political Quarterly* 87(3): 323–332.

Goodwin, M.J. & O. Heath (2016b) 'Brexit vote explained: poverty, low skills and lack of opportunities'. *Joseph Rowntree Foundation*. Available at: www.jrf.org.uk/report/brexit-vote-explained-poverty-low-skills-and-lack-opportunities [accessed 20 September 2020].

Hobolt, S. (2009). *Europe in question: referendums on European integration*. Oxford: Oxford University Press.

Holmes, M. (2005) 'Irish approaches to European integration', in M. Holmes (ed.) *Ireland and the European Union: Nice, enlargement and the future of Europe*, pp. 1–14. Manchester: Manchester University Press.

Ireland Thinks (2018) 'Brexit poll'. Available at: www.irelandthinks.ie/blog [accessed 17 June 2020].

Irish Freedom Party (2019) 'Our manifesto'. Available at: www.irishfreedom.ie [accessed 20 September 2020].

Kennedy, R. & R. Sinnott (2006) 'Irish social and political cleavages', in J. Garry & D. Payne (eds) *Irish social and political attitudes*, pp. 78–94. Liverpool: Liverpool University Press.

Kennedy, R. & R. Sinnott (2007) 'Irish public opinion towards European integration'. *Irish Political Studies* 22(1): 61–81.

Laffan, B. & J. O'Mahony (2008) *Ireland and the European Union*. Basingstoke: Palgrave Macmillan.

Lyons, P. (2008) *Public opinion, politics and society in contemporary Ireland*. Dublin: Irish Academic Press.

Murphy, M.C. (2018) *Europe and Northern Ireland's future: negotiating Brexit's unique case*. Newcastle: Agenda Publishing.

Murphy, M.C. (2019) 'The Brexit crisis, Ireland and British–Irish relations: Europeanisation and/or de-Europeanisation'. *Irish Political Studies* 34(4): 530–550.

O'Brennan, J. (2019) 'Requiem for a shared interdependent past: Brexit & the deterioration in UK–Irish relations'. *Capital and Class* 43(1): 157–171.

Simpson, K. (2018a) 'What to do about inequality? Public opinion support for the European Union and further European integration in the Republic of Ireland'. *Irish Political Studies* 34(1): 69–91.

Simpson, K. (2018b) 'Ireland: the model EU citizen? Explaining Irish attitudes towards the European Union'. *Political Insight* 9(1): 16–19.

Simpson, K. (2019) 'European Union crises and Irish public opinion: continuity and change in patterns of support'. *Irish Political Studies* 34(4): 507–529.

Simpson, K. & M. Loveless (2017) 'Another chance? Concerns about inequality, support for the European Union and further European integration'. *Journal of European Public Policy* 24(7): 1069–1089.

Sinnott, R. (1995) *Knowledge of the European Union in Irish public opinion: sources and implications*. Occasional Paper No. 5. Dublin: Institute of European Affairs.

Sinnott, R. (2002) 'Cleavages, parties and referendums: relationships between representative and direct democracy in the Republic of Ireland'. *European Journal of Political Research* 41: 820–824.

Sinnott, R. (2005) 'Uphill task to win EU treaty poll here'. *The Irish Times*, 14 June 2005.

Sinnott, R., J. Elkink, K. O'Rourke & J. McBride (2010) *Attitudes and behaviour in the second referendum on the Treaty of Lisbon. Report prepared for the Department of Foreign Affairs*. Dublin: UCD Geary Institute.

Sky Data Poll (2019) Available at: https://interactive.news.sky.com/ROI_TABS_0219.pdf [accessed 28 July 2020].

Standard Eurobarometer Data. Available at: www.gesis.org/eurobarometer-data-service/survey-series/standard-special-eb/ [accessed 17 June 2020].

Sunday Business Post/Red C Poll (2019). Available at: www.businesspost.ie/politics/polling-data [accessed 28 July 2020].

UK in a Changing Europe (2019) *Brexit and the backstop: everything you need to know*. Available at: https://ukandeu.ac.uk/brexit-and-the-backstop-everything-you-need-to-know/ [accessed 17 April 2019].

9

'No time for diplomatic squeamishness': news media framing of Irish political interventions in the UK's EU referendum

Anthony Cawley

Introduction: framing Europe

The news media are key sources of information for citizens on political, economic and cultural institutions with which they have little direct contact or interaction. For a supranational entity such as the EU, national news media play a prominent role in explaining to citizens the Union's complex processes and interpreting their meaning and implications. However, reporting the EU has long been a "problem" for news media in member states, with a tendency for outlets to fall back on 'the reproduction of stereotypes, narrow national news values and basic suspicion of bureaucracy' (Kunelius 2008: 375). Such editorial approaches limit the scope for balanced reporting on the EU and encourage ideological distortions. The public's view of the EU is further obscured by journalists' predilection for conflict as a news value, with media outlets emphasising disagreements among member states or between the Union and individual countries over consensus in the framing of European issues.

In these regards, the news media have contributed to a broad knowledge deficit among citizens about the EU's purpose, functions and legitimacy, particularly as they relate to the Union's shared challenges, achievements and opportunities (Barbieri et al. 2019; Preston 2009a; Statham 2008). A holistic, transnational European perspective rarely features in national news agendas.

This chapter will offer an overview of how the Irish and UK news media covered the 2016 Brexit referendum. It will then focus on a distinctive sub-plot within the broader campaign narrative which gained traction in Ireland's print news media: coverage of Irish political inventions in the referendum to support Remain. During the campaign period, Irish government and opposition leaders visited Britain and appealed to Irish immigrants for a pro-EU vote.[1] The government's strategy was outside the norm of international relations and represented 'huge diplomatic risks' in seeking to sway a referendum result in another sovereign nation (Morrow & Byrne 2016: 30).

The research will identify the dominant political, economic and social frames through which the Irish print news media reported and interpreted the interventions. It will assess whether the referendum prompted inclusive news frames of shared EU values, interests and solidarity in the face of a Leave vote that would threaten the Union's cohesion. Finally, the chapter will consider whether the frames reflected a fresh potential for Irish news media to support a deeper, transnational perspective on European issues, in line with the concept of an EU public sphere.

National news media and an EU public sphere

Jürgen Habermas's concept of the public sphere has long been central to research on how mediated communication, in particular through the news media, could support citizens' awareness of and engagement with EU issues and politics, and foster attachment to a European identity (Kunelius 2008; Schlesinger & Kevin 2000; Tjernström 2008). With striking consistency, researchers have concluded that news media rarely reach beyond national concerns to a transnational EU perspective (Corcoran & Fahy 2009; Picard 2015; Preston 2009a, 2009b; Tjernström 2008). Arguments around a mediated European public sphere are often positioned in normative terms – as a journalistic ideal, or how news media *ought* to function in intertwining EU politics and citizens. The reality, however, is that national news media carry 'no obligation' to support EU interests or integration (Tjernström 2008: 517). Furthermore, the national perspective is seldom contested in a communication environment where 'European-wide news media effectively do not exist' (Picard 2015: 2).

Notwithstanding directives in areas such as audiovisual media, the EU hosts a significant divergence of media systems and news cultures across member states which serve audiences and frame the Union in different ways (Pfetsch et al. 2008; after Hallin & Mancini 2004). The EU's fragmented communication landscape compounds the difficulties that news media encounter in reconciling 'ideas of European homogeneity' (Tjernström 2008: 529) with political, economic, linguistic, social and cultural variance across the continent. The challenge reflects a problematic aspect of Habermas's original public sphere concept. It suggested a greater degree of cultural, social and political unity within the framework of nation states than tends to exist in reality – even more so if the concept is stretched to the supranational EU (Schlesinger & Kevin 2000).

Increased attention, therefore, has shifted to considering the potential for multiple, perhaps overlapping public spheres to support citizens' awareness of and dialogue on EU issues (Pfetsch 2018; Schlesinger & Kevin 2000; Tjernström 2008). In this more flexible conceptualisation, the news media retain a pivotal role as information intermediaries between the EU and citizens. However, the strongest evidence of an emergent sphere is at the level of specialist news media such as the *Financial Times*, which underpins a tightly bounded elite discourse on EU political, bureaucratic, policy and financial information (Hepp et al. 2016; Kunelius 2008; Picard 2015; Preston 2009a; Schlesinger & Kevin 2000; Statham 2008). As Corcoran and Fahy argue, this communicative space represents 'an elite micro-culture' in which the public 'plays little or no role' (2009: 109).

Within member states, the general news outlets with the largest audiences tend to rank EU issues low on their editorial priorities. The disinterest persists in part because journalists perceive EU subjects as being process-driven, intricate and requiring in-depth explanations, whereas national news cultures prioritise unambiguous, straightforward news stories (Preston 2009a; Statham 2008). Even when an EU issue registers on news agendas across member states, it tends not to be covered in a transnational or consistent manner, but rather is adapted to specific national concerns and interpretations (Corcoran & Fahy 2009; Pfetsch et al. 2008; Preston 2009a; Schlesinger & Kevin 2000). Studies have found a nationalisation rather than a Europeanisation of EU news. National news media have tended to report EU-wide projects or challenges such as single market integration, the euro crisis and Brexit with a strong orientation inward to member states' individual interests, while neglecting shared Union concerns (Barbieri et al. 2019; Picard 2015; Preston 2009a; Ridge-Newman et al. 2018; Statham 2008).

A by-product of the nationalisation process is that news media tend to provide shallow contextualisation of the roles, functions and legitimacy of EU institutions, a "communication deficit" that contributes to a knowledge and democratic deficit among EU citizens (Picard 2015; Preston 2009a; Statham 2008: 398). Dovetailing with this, journalists rarely identify with a broader European journalistic culture, except, perhaps, at the elite EU correspondent level (Preston 2009a; Statham 2008). This would seem to militate against what Schlesinger and Kevin (2000) argue would be a fundamental prerequisite to the news media supporting a coherent EU public sphere: a European news agenda providing a consistent basis for citizens to be informed about and engage with the Union.

Increasingly, notions of a deliberative and rational public sphere, bolstered by the news media, seem 'out of touch' with the reality of digital communicative spaces in the EU and across liberal democracies (Bennett &

Pfetsch 2018: 245). To a degree, this is because news media, even online, still rely on a traditional one-way model of communication, at odds with Habermas's ideal of citizen participation. Beyond news media, digital communication technologies and social media platforms have often served, counter-intuitively, to distort rather than enrich the public sphere. The EU greeted the emergence of the World Wide Web with optimistic rhetoric about seamless participatory communication among citizens across member states (Preston 2009a). However, as Preston has argued, even if online technologies compressed communication 'time-space' across the EU, they came to mirror traditional media forms in being adapted to, and somewhat constrained within, member states' varying socio-cultural contexts (Preston 2009a: 125). Fenton, too, criticised the simplistic assumption that digital media would empower the public sphere, calling it 'a techno-deterministic interpretation – better media equals better democracy' (Fenton 2018: 28). Such causal thinking was perceptible when Habermas linked the public sphere, supported by the news media, to the potential for citizens to embrace a constitutional patriotism: an allegiance to collective human rights, social justice and democratic principles that would transcend narrow nationalism and could bind a wider European identity (Corcoran & Fahy 2009; Habermas 2012; Kunelius 2008; Schlesinger & Kevin 2000).

Instead, digital communication technologies have contributed to a polarisation of political, economic and social views and have intensified intolerance of difference, as evidenced in the Brexit campaign (Pfetsch 2018). To a large extent, this has stemmed from the online proliferation of low quality, ideologically motivated and often false information, circulating within multiples of disconnected or 'dissonant' public spheres (Pfetsch 2018: 61). These fragmented spheres reflect that communication processes related to the EU are 'increasingly mediatised' (Hepp et al. 2016: 13), produced for and shaped by communications technologies and media platforms (Pfetsch 2018).

Furthermore, public spheres are fluid in the digital age, with citizens gathering information from a hybrid of online and social media sources as well as traditional media (Pfetsch 2018). In this criss-crossing information environment, audiences are less likely to trust mainstream news organisations, which further weakens 'traditional bases for validating information' (Bennett & Pfetsch 2018: 245–246). This meshes with a broader societal alienation from, and deepening crisis in, mainstream political institutions, including the EU, but also at the level of national, regional and local politics. Pointing to growing inequality, populism and the increasing unaccountability of political and economic elites, Fenton has questioned the continuing relevance of a public sphere concept that has depended on a 'liberal democratic frame that is now so undone' (2018: 28).

Referendum coverage in Ireland and the UK

The Irish news media have followed the trend across member states of reporting the EU primarily from a national perspective and of assuming a low audience interest in the Union unless an issue directly affects Ireland and/or its citizens (Preston 2009a). From a journalistic perspective, the UK's referendum blurred the lines between domestic, Anglo-Irish, EU and foreign news. The referendum outcome would have significant implications for Ireland both as an individual state and as a member of the EU, and for its historically close relationship with the UK. It is unsurprising, therefore, that the country's news media provided extensive coverage of the referendum campaign. With minor exceptions, the Irish news media supported Remain. Reportage and opinion focused on the 'profound implications' a Leave vote would bring for the all-island economy, the peace process and the border (McCann & Hainsworth 2016: 332).

The strength of the Irish news media's support for Remain was evident in its response to the Leave victory. *The Irish Times* (24 June 2016) described it as 'genuinely bewildering' and predicted that along with creating 'particularly acute' challenges for Ireland, Brexit would leave the UK 'poorer, more isolated and less influential'. The sentiment was echoed in the *Irish Independent* (24 June 2016), which warned that Ireland could expect trade, travel and financial disruptions as well as uncertainty around the border and the peace process. In a similar vein, RTÉ anticipated that the vote would have 'huge ramifications', highlighting that 'most commentators believe [Brexit's] negatives far outweigh the positives' for Ireland (RTÉ 24 June 2016).

The Irish news media's support for Remain reflected, in part, that it does not share with the British press a tradition of Euroscepticism. But it was at this juncture that a minor seam of pro-Leave sentiment surfaced in Irish coverage. A historically distinctive feature of the Irish newspaper market has been the robust circulation of UK newspapers. The "Irish" editions carry original news and commentary produced in newsrooms in Dublin, but derive much of their content and editorial ethos from their parent operations in, usually, London (Sweetman 2008). There are some notable differences between the Irish and UK editions of newspapers such as the *Daily Mail* and the *Sun*. In the UK, both titles are loyal to the Conservative Party. In Ireland, they temper support for any particular political party to mitigate 'the risk of alienating Irish readers' (Sweetman 2008: 576). Furthermore, the Irish editions regularly soften or change the editorial lines of their parent UK publications, especially on matters where the two countries' national interests diverge (Sweetman 2008).

This was visible in their reporting on the referendum campaign, which for the most part adopted an Irish perspective and was more balanced than the rigid pro-Brexit positions of their UK counterparts. For instance, the day after the referendum result, when its UK front page splashed the triumphant headline 'Take a bow, Britain!', the *Irish Daily Mail* (25 June 2016 (1)) reported that the Taoiseach was moving 'fast to bandage [the] wounds from Brexit'. Even still, the same edition carried pro-Leave arguments in its comment and analysis pieces, but crafted them for Irish audiences. One article asked, 'Will we be next to quit [the EU]?', and by way of an answer suggested it would be 'far from certain voters here [would] choose to stay' (*Irish Daily Mail* 25 June 2016 (3)). In a separate piece, the newspaper argued that if the EU didn't move quickly to protect Irish interests 'it will just be proving [the] UK's decision right' (*Irish Daily Mail* 25 June 2016 (2)).

Curiously, news coverage was less intensive in Northern Ireland, where the referendum was a domestic political event but the campaign was 'strangely low key' (Morrow & Byrne 2016: 30). Northern Ireland's news landscape is significantly different from that in the Republic, not least in the newspaper market where prominent titles still divide broadly across nationalist (*Irish News*) and unionist (*News Letter*, *Belfast Telegraph*) lines. For the most part, unionist political parties supported Leave and nationalist parties supported Remain. But this tension did not invigorate newspaper reporting on the referendum, which was 'muted' even when Prime Minister David Cameron campaigned in the region, and underpinned a 'feeling of [Northern Ireland] being marginal to big decisions' on the UK's future relationship with the EU (Baker 2018: 95). Northern Ireland's newspapers did point to the risk of a hard border, although the *News Letter* was more alarmed at a Leave vote's capacity to destabilise the UK's constitutional integrity (Baker 2018).

In parallel, Brexit's implications for Northern Ireland and the border were 'marginalised' in British press and broadcast coverage (Deacon et al. 2016: 34). The British news media were among the decisive factors in tilting the vote towards Leave. When measured by audience reach, British newspapers and their online platforms heavily favoured the Leave campaign (Deacon et al. 2016). Pro-Brexit titles included the *Sun*, the *Telegraph*, the *Daily Mail*, the *Express* and the *Times*, as well as their associated Sunday titles. Coverage was often couched in strong populist and nationalistic tones, as on the morning of the referendum when the *Express*'s front page (23 June 2016) issued a rallying cry to its readers: 'Your country needs you: Vote leave today'. The only national titles to support Remain were the *Guardian* and its sister title the *Observer*, the *Independent* and its Sunday edition,[2] as well as the daily and Sunday editions of the *Mirror*. On polling day, the *Daily Mirror* (23 June 2016) implored voters to think of their families and not 'take a leap into the dark' that risked their jobs, pay, pensions and the NHS.

British broadcast news outlets were under regulatory obligations to offer balanced coverage, but their attempts to be even-handed were problematic.

By 'artificially' upholding traditional notions of impartiality, journalists reported as fact numerous falsehoods and distorted claims from both sides, but particularly from Leave campaigners (Zelizer 2018: 148). In this environment, the news media struggled to provide the British public with 'the clarity that [was] so desperately needed' (Payne 2018: 109). Additionally, Eurosceptic right-wing newspapers led the 'normalising' of 'outrage' through demonising Remain campaigners (Payne 2018; Zelizer 2018: 148).

The 2016 referendum amplified a strain of Euroscepticism running through Britain's news media in general and tabloid press in particular. Rowinski (2016) highlights that Britain's Eurosceptic press have a long tradition of exaggerating differences with Europe and of framing the EU as the "other". Prior to the referendum, a multi-country study of press treatment of single market integration found more sympathetic coverage in France, Germany, Italy and Spain than in the UK, where the news media stressed 'all conflict lines that allow[ed] the importance of sovereignty to be highlighted' (Pfetsch et al. 2008: 484). A persistent narrative in British news media coverage of the referendum was that the EU was impinging on UK sovereignty.

Coverage of Irish political interventions in the UK's EU referendum

The Irish print news media's coverage of the interventions fell within journalism's practice of 'framing' news stories within a core set of ideas that make complex issues easily understandable for audiences. Journalists build news frames through source inclusion or exclusion, information interpretation and prioritisation, as well as language and image selection. In news discourse, frames define issues by amplifying certain ideological perspectives while downplaying or omitting alternatives (De Vreese 2005; Entman, 1993; Touri 2009). The perspectives encoded in news frames often originate in the "information subsidies" that governments and other institutional actors supply to journalists in the form of official statements and speeches and public relations content (Gandy 1982: 61). Frames also reflect journalism's indexing norm: the established news gathering routine through which journalists document (index) the views of authoritative official sources such as mainstream political leaders, and demote unofficial or critical perspectives (Bennett 1990).

This chapter's frames analysis focused on print media articles that carried reportage or editorial comment on an Irish political figure campaigning in the UK, commenting on the referendum while visiting the country for an official engagement, or appealing to Irish immigrants to vote Remain. On this definition, with the timeframe set to the official campaign period (15 April to

Table 9.1 Newspaper and article publication period

Newspaper	April (from 15th)	May	June (to 23rd)	Total
Irish Times	0	6	19	25
Irish Independent	0	4	23	27
Irish Examiner	0	1	6	7
Irish Sun	1	3	4	8
Irish Daily Mail	1	1	9	11
Irish Mirror	0	1	1	2
Overall	2	16	62	80

Source: Author.

23 June 2016), a search of the Newsstand database[3] returned a final sample of eighty articles: sixty-three news reports, sixteen opinion/analysis pieces and one feature. Table 9.1 breaks down the sample by newspaper and publication period.

Irish government officials signalled as early as April 2016 their intention to take an active role in the UK referendum campaign. But as Table 9.1 suggests, Irish political interventions, and news coverage thereof, intensified in June as polling day approached. That month, coverage of the interventions was interconnected with a number of significant events: Taoiseach Enda Kenny argued for a Remain vote in public comments at a British–Irish Council meeting in Scotland; British Prime Minister David Cameron withdrew from a scheduled Remain event with the Taoiseach; and Kenny cancelled his public engagements in Britain following the murder of MP Jo Cox.

Adopting a grounded theory approach, the author implemented a qualitative content analysis to identify the prominent and persistent news frames across the sample. Qualitative content analysis enables researchers to trace and interpret frames of discursive meaning across large samples of news texts (Schreier 2012). The coding phase returned the following as the primary frames through which the newspapers presented and defined Irish political interventions:

- Frame 1: The border/peace process
- Frame 2: The Irish economy
- Frame 3: British–Irish relations
- Frame 4: The EU
- Frame 5: Irish identity/European identity.

Frames 1 and 2 had the strongest presence in news coverage. Frame 3 had a moderate occurrence, with weaker showings for Frames 4 and 5.

Frame 1 looks at the border and the peace process. Central to each newspaper's coverage was the implications of a change to free movement and trade across the border. The newspapers did index the views of pro-Brexit politicians such as Conservative MP Theresa Villiers, who claimed that the 'border [would] stay as it is today' (*Irish Independent* 17 June 2016). Predominantly, however, the newspapers framed Brexit as negative for the border, with economic uncertainty tied to concerns for the peace process and security. The *Irish Independent* (10 June 2016 (2)) argued that impacts on North–South trade and the peace process 'would be inevitable'. The *Irish Sun* (13 June 2016) suggested that a hard border 'could raise tensions with unionists by reenergising demands for a united Ireland'.

In framing the border, the newspapers' primary source was the Taoiseach. The *Irish Daily Mail* (14 June 2016) indexed Kenny's view that the EU's role in supporting the peace process was 'quite often underestimated'. Likewise, the *Irish Examiner* (14 June 2016) carried Kenny's warning of a Leave vote's 'risks and challenges' to the peace process. Another prominent government source was the Minister for Foreign Affairs, Charlie Flanagan, who argued that Brexit would unsettle the 'invisible' border with the potential to create 'security issues between a non-EU UK and an EU Ireland' (*The Irish Times* 8 June 2016 (1)). Highlighted, also, was former Taoiseach Bertie Ahern's assessment that pro-Leave claims on the border did not 'stand up one inch' (*The Irish Times* 1 June 2016). In an editorial comment, *The Irish Times* (15 June 2016 (1)) predicted that the North–South relationship would be 'rewritten' following Brexit.

Frame 2 deals with the Irish economy. Coverage here centred on the impact that Brexit would have on the Republic's economy, with a prominent though weaker consideration of the all-island economy. The *Irish Daily Mail* (18 April 2016) highlighted that the government's decision to campaign in Britain had been 'prompted by fears over [Brexit's] likely effect on our economy'. Again, the primary news source was the Taoiseach. *The Irish Times* (21 June 2016) indexed Kenny's concern that any trade barriers between Ireland and the UK would 'add costs and be damaging'. Similarly, the *Irish Examiner* (16 June 2016) noted Kenny's assessment that a Leave victory would 'do serious damage to competitiveness'.

Brexit's anticipated impact on the economy was also filtered through the newspapers' comment pieces. *The Irish Times* (15 June 2016 (1)) highlighted the potential 'nightmare economic scenario of a split between our two largest export markets'. The *Irish Independent* (23 June 2016) flagged the 'prospect of new duties and tariffs' to disrupt trade. The newspapers did raise the issue of the government's contingency planning to protect the economy. But, as *The Irish Times* pointed out (15 June 2016 (1)), 'there's only so much contingency planning you can do when it's unclear what exactly Brexit means'.

Frame 3 focuses on the analysis of British–Irish relations. The newspapers' key concern was Brexit's potential to harm British–Irish political, social and economic relations. The *Irish Examiner* (14 May 2016) indexed Kenny's argument that, in supporting Remain, the government wanted to 'preserve the strength of the British–Irish relationship'. On a similar theme, the *Irish Independent* (13 June 2016) reported the government's view that Ireland and the UK had worked closely together as member states and had been 'allied on many EU issues'. The *Irish Daily Mail* echoed this line (15 June 2016), describing the UK as having been 'a major ally' of Ireland within the EU.

A related concern was the status of Irish immigrants in Britain. The *Irish Sun* noted (13 June 2016) that 'doubts surround the right of Irish citizens to live and work in Britain, which long predates the EU'. *The Irish Times* (16 June 2016) highlighted former President Mary McAleese's worry that, post-Brexit, the Irish in Britain would not be 'exempt from the box called "immigrants"'. In the main, the newspapers were supportive of the government's interventions. An *Irish Times* column (17 June 2016) endorsed the strategy, arguing that 'this [was] no time for diplomatic squeamishness'. The *Irish Independent* (10 June 2016 (1)) argued that the government had 'done as much as is diplomatically appropriate to get out the Irish Remain vote'. Pointedly, the Irish editions of the *Sun* and the *Daily Mail* criticised the government's approach. The *Irish Sun* (31 May 2016) lambasted Kenny for 'consistently meddling in the Brexit debate' and advised him to 'please shut up'. Meanwhile, the *Irish Daily Mail* (7 June 2016) cautioned that 'the Taoiseach [was] increasingly abandoning accepted policy of keeping out of other countries' affairs'.

Frame 4 relates to the EU. Prominent here was discourse on the government reaffirming its commitment to the EU 'irrespective of the outcome of the UK referendum' (*The Irish Times* 13 May 2016). The reaffirmation pivoted on how the EU benefited Ireland, rather than expressing a transnational commitment to the Union. Nevertheless, *The Irish Times* (15 June 2016 (2)) indexed the government's anxiety that Brexit would damage 'the effectiveness of the EU itself'. The newspaper mirrored the government's view in editorial comment, warning that Brexit would amplify 'instability within the EU at what is already a vulnerable time' (*The Irish Times* 17 June 2016).

However, the Union's cohesion was a secondary concern for the newspapers, which placed a stronger emphasis on how a UK departure would impact Ireland. For instance, the newspapers did speculate on the shape of a future UK–EU relationship but principally in terms of what it would mean for the Irish economy. It was in this light that the *Irish Independent* (10 June 2016) feared there were 'no guarantees' of a UK–EU free trade agreement if Leave won. Irish national interests were woven, also, into discourse suggesting that Brexit would diminish both the UK and the EU geo-politically. *The Irish Times* (15 June 2016 (3)) indexed the view of Minister for Social Protection Leo Varadkar that 'if Britain leaves, we lose an ally and Europe is weakened'.

The newspaper further documented the government's position 'that the EU needs Britain to give it more weight' (*The Irish Times* 22 June 2016).

Finally, Frame 5 explores issues of Irish identity and European identity. The newspapers' framing of the national and cultural identity of the Irish in Britain was more nuanced than the representations portrayed in government speeches and interviews. Much coverage centred on Kenny's appeal to the Irish in Britain to vote Remain to make 'things a little bit easier for our own country' (*Irish Examiner* 17 June 2016). Government discourse tended to assume a comfortable alignment between Ireland's national interests and the voting intentions of Irish immigrants. Wider newspaper coverage revealed a complex picture, in which many immigrants prioritised Brexit's implications for the UK or for their own lives ahead of those for the Irish state.

A case in point was an *Irish Times* piece (8 June 2016 (2)) on older Irish immigrants who were voting Leave because of immigration to the UK from newer member states. A similar theme emerged in an *Irish Independent* interview (10 June 2016 (3)) with an Irish immigrant who acknowledged that Brexit could disrupt the border but who still intended to vote Leave because of 'the difficulties in extraditing migrants who have committed serious crimes [in the UK]'. The *Irish Examiner* (18 June 2016) cautioned that 'anecdotally, many older exiled Irish are finding themselves on the Leave side'. Meanwhile, the *Irish Daily Mail* (18 April 2016) suggested that younger, recent Irish immigrants might ignore the government's pleas if they moved to Britain 'because they couldn't find work here under the Fine Gael–Labour coalition'.

The print media and the potential for a European public sphere

A number of caveats need to be applied to the findings of this study. Irish political interventions comprised just a sliver of the Irish news media's coverage of the campaign. It cannot be assumed that the relatively small sample analysed here was representative of the wider news framing of the referendum. Furthermore, the research focused on a traditional print media case study, which could be viewed as ill-fitting a public sphere concept that aspires to deliberative participation by citizens and increasingly functions within a hybrid and fractured digital media environment.

Nevertheless, the study confirmed many of the enduring difficulties that the EU faces in its news media presentation to national audiences, even when authoritative institutional actors and news media organisations are keen to frame the Union in a positive light. The referendum cut across traditional divisions of news (domestic, Anglo-Irish, EU, foreign) and seemed ripe for the newspapers to move closer to a transnational perspective. But in seeking to define and interpret Brexit's political, economic and social implications in a manner that would be meaningful to Irish audiences, the newspapers' default perspective was inward to national concerns. Frames 1 and 2 dominated the discursive construction of the issue, with strong economistic discourse cutting across both frames. The border was positioned as having dual peace process and economic implications, while Frame 2's discourse prioritised the Republic's economy ahead of the all-island economy or Northern Ireland's. Even the seemingly outward looking Frames 3 and 4 referenced UK and EU considerations back to the domestic arena: what would be the national challenges arising from upheaval in the UK and a changed dynamic to British–Irish relations? Would Ireland's influence in Brussels wane without the UK as an "ally"? Would a less cohesive EU be less beneficial to Ireland?

Government speeches, statements and interviews were central to the frame-building process, as were, to a lesser extent, the views of opposition politicians and noted political figures (Ahern and McAleese). An unusual aspect of the framing contest was the high level of consensus in Irish politics favouring a Remain vote. It was clear that the newspapers amplified the views of certain political actors more than others (the Taoiseach and the Minister for Foreign Affairs, principally). The newspapers also gave primacy to Remain perspectives, notwithstanding instances when they indexed the views of a small number of pro-Brexit politicians.

Indexed official views set the discursive parameters of Frames 1–5, with editorial comment often an extension of government discourse. The newspapers' privileging of official pro-Remain views helps to explain the resilience of the national perspective across the sample. The indexed discourse underpinning Frames 1–5 was, by political actors, calibrated for Irish audiences, either domestically or in Britain, with a low-level encoding of transnational EU considerations.

The main point of divergence between indexed official views and editorial comment and reportage occurred in Frame 5. Newspaper interviews with Irish immigrants found that many were more likely to vote Leave than government discourse suggested. The reportage pointed to a complex array of views, motivations and national and cultural identities among Irish immigrants in Britain. But the discourse did not scale out to consider a wider European identity, or attempt to evaluate what being European meant in light of the issues raised by Brexit. News discourse, both indexed and the newspapers' own reportage/comment, tended to define Irish immigrants' entitlement to vote in the referendum in transactional terms: either they were voting Remain to help their native country (an act of national, rather than EU, support), or were voting Leave to prioritise their economic and social self-interest (to reduce 'other' immigration to the UK).

Also, Frame 5 contained the only instances of discourse criticising the interventions, in the *Irish Examiner*, the *Irish Sun* and the *Irish Daily Mail*. Notably, the *Irish Examiner*'s comments centred not on the legitimacy of the interventions but on a perceived hypocrisy: that, in effect, the government was asking a favour of immigrants the country had deemed 'surplus to requirements' (*Irish Examiner* 18 June 2016). In contrast, the Irish editions of the *Sun* and the *Daily Mail* emphasised the integrity of internal UK sovereignty to decide the referendum outcome. This argument excepted, the six newspapers showed a high degree of consistency in how they presented and interpreted the interventions through Frames 1–5. It reflected the indexing norm of them relying on the same narrow range of official information sources.

A consideration of this study was whether Irish political interventions to encourage another member state to stay in the EU might prompt inclusive news frames of shared union values, challenges and opportunities, broadly in line with Habermas's notions of a European public sphere and of constitutional patriotism. But almost regardless of whether the discursive strands supporting Frames 1–5 originated in indexed official views or in the newspapers' editorial comment or reportage, the study found little contextual explanation of the EU's roles, functions or legitimacy. Similar to their framing of Irish immigrants, the newspapers neglected transnational concerns and positioned the EU in transactional terms: that in return for membership, Ireland attained (mainly) economic benefits but also a supportive environment for the peace process ("invisible" border).

Consistent with a number of multi-country studies on EU news coverage, the sample returned strong evidence that the referendum was nationalised as an Irish issue (particularly around the economy, the border and the peace process), with limited Europeanisation as, also, an EU challenge. Within this discursive context, the EU was framed as "the other" – in this case, as a positive "other". But the result was to curtail a holistic perspective on the collective Union problems arising from Brexit. Overall, the study suggested that Irish journalistic discursive practices, interpretative frameworks and frame-building processes (rooted in indexed Irish political communications) remained rigidly within a national paradigm. Through a public sphere lens, the findings underlined doubts about the capacity of the Irish news media to provide citizens with a nuanced understanding of the EU.

Notes

1   Irish citizens living in the UK have the right to vote in elections and referendums there.

2   Shortly before the official campaign period, the *Independent* titles transitioned to online only publication.
3   The author conducted a supplementary search of *The Irish Times* and *Irish Independent* websites to complete the sample.

References

Baker, S. (2018) 'Whither the "hand of history"? Northern Ireland newspaper coverage of the 2016 referendum campaign', in A. Ridge-Newman, F. León-Solís & H. O'Donnell (eds) *Reporting the road to Brexit: international media and the EU referendum 2016*, pp. 93–109. Basingstoke: Palgrave Macmillan.
Barbieri, G., D. Campus & M. Mazzoni (2019) 'How the EU member states' press represented the euro crisis'. *Journalism* 20(2): 235–255.
Bennett, W.L. (1990) 'Toward a theory of press-state relations in the United States'. *Journal of Communication* 40(2): 103–125.
Bennett, W.L. & B. Pfetsch (2018) 'Rethinking political communication in a time of disrupted public spheres'. *Journal of Communication* 68: 243–253.
Corcoran, F. & D. Fahy (2009) 'Exploring the European elite sphere: the role of the *Financial Times*'. *Journalism Studies* 10(1): 100–113.
Daily Mail (2016) 'Take a bow, Britain', 25 June: 1.
Daily Mirror (2016) 'Don't take a leap into the dark: vote remain today', 23 June: 1.
Deacon, D., J. Downey, E. Harmer, J. Stanyer & D. Wring (2016) 'The narrow agenda: how the news media covered the referendum', in D. Jackson, E. Thorsen & D. Wring (eds) *EU referendum analysis 2016: media, voters and the campaign*, pp. 34–35. Bournemouth: Bournemouth University, CPMR.
De Vreese, C. (2005) 'News framing: theory and typology'. *Information Design Journal* 13(1): 51–61.
Entman, R. (1993) 'Framing: toward clarification of a fractured paradigm'. *Journal of Communication* 43(4): 51–58.
Express (2016) 'Your country needs you: vote leave today', 23 June.
Fenton, N. (2018) 'Fake democracy: the limits of public sphere theory'. *Javnost: The Public* 25(1–2): 28–34.
Gandy, O. (1982) *Beyond agenda setting: information subsidies and public policy*. New York: Ablex.
Habermas, J. (2012) 'The crisis of the European Union in the light of a constitutionalisation of international law'. *The European Journal of International Law* 23(2): 335–348.
Hallin, D. & P. Mancini (2004) *Comparing media systems: three models of media and politics*. Cambridge: Cambridge University Press.
Hepp, A., M. Elsler, S. Lingenberg, A. Mollen, J. Moller, A. Offerhaus, K. Sword & D. Pospielovsky (2016) *The communicative construction of Europe: cultures of political discourse, public sphere, and the euro crisis*. Basingstoke: Palgrave Macmillan.
Irish Daily Mail (2016) 'As we clamour against Brexit, here's why they won't listen', 18 April: 15.
Irish Daily Mail (2016) 'Enda for UK tour to speak against Brexit; Taoiseach intervenes in foreign politics yet again', 7 June: 15.

Irish Daily Mail (2016) 'Brexit vote "as critical for us as Good Friday"; Enda warns of risk to peace process if UK leaves EU', 14 June: 17.

Irish Daily Mail (2016) 'Taoiseach moves fast to bandage wounds from Brexit', 25 June (1).

Irish Daily Mail (2016) 'EU must now look out for Irish citizens … otherwise it will just be proving UK's decision right', 25 June (2).

Irish Daily Mail (2016) 'Will we be next to quit?', 25 June (3).

Irish Examiner (2016) 'Ireland "severely" affected by Brexit, warns Enda Kenny', 14 May. Available at: www.irishexaminer.com/news/arid-20399450.html [accessed accessed 7 June 2019].

Irish Examiner (2016) 'Enda Kenny issues Brexit warning', 14 June. Available at: www.irishexaminer.com/news/arid-20404717.html [accessed 7 June 2019].

Irish Examiner (2016) 'Taoiseach: Brexit would do serious damage', 16 June. Available at: www.irishexaminer.com/news/arid-20405165.html [accessed 7 June 2019].

Irish Examiner (2016) 'Enda Kenny urges Brexit voters to follow the lights home', 17 June. Available at: www.irishexaminer.com/news/arid-20405440.html [accessed 7 June 2019].

Irish Examiner (2016) 'Enda Kenny was appealing to the diaspora to vote not what was best for them, but best for Ireland', 18 June. Available at: www.irishexaminer.com/opinion/columnists/arid-20405620.html [accessed 7 June 2019].

Irish Independent (2016) 'Brexit debate and US presidential race are fuelled by toxic politics', 10 June (1). Available at: www.independent.ie/opinion/columnists/liz-odonnell/brexit-debate-and-us-presidential-race-are-fuelled-by-toxic-politics-34788132.html [accessed 10 June 2019].

Irish Independent (2016) 'Why "Brexit" really matters to the 500,000 Irish living in Britain', 10 June (2). Available at: www.independent.ie/business/brexit/special-report-why-brexit-really-matters-to-the-500000-irish-living-in-britain-34789026.html [accessed 10 June 2019].

Irish Independent (2016) 'It's friendly neighbour "Pascalle" back home in Tyneside', 10 June (3). Available at: www.independent.ie/opinion/comment/its-friendly-neighbour-pascalle-back-home-in-tyneside-34788179.html [accessed 10 June 2019].

Irish Independent (2016) 'Ireland "will have a Plan B" if UK opts for Brexit', 13 June. Available at: www.independent.ie/business/brexit/ireland-will-have-a-plan-b-if-uk-opts-for-brexit-34795059.html [accessed 10 June 2019].

Irish Independent (2016) 'Taoiseach "unashamedly" calls on Irish community in Britain to vote 'Remain', 17 June. Available at: www.independent.ie/business/brexit/taoiseach-unashamedly-calls-on-irish-community-in-britain-to-vote-remain-34810728.html [accessed 10 June 2019].

Irish Independent (2016) 'Project Racism rebounds in Brexit vote: Britain to Remain but EU superstate halted', 23 June. Available at: www.independent.ie/opinion/columnists/ivan-yates/ivan-yates-project-racism-rebounds-in-brexit-vote-britain-to-remain-but-eu-superstate-halted-34826034.html [accessed 10 June 2019].

Irish Independent (2016) 'Five ways Ireland will be poorer following the British decision to exit the EU', 24 June. Available at: www.independent.ie/business/brexit/sinead-ryan-five-ways-ireland-will-be-poorer-following-the-british-decision-to-exit-the-eu-34826798.html [accessed 10 June 2019].

Irish Sun (2016) 'Britain isn't going to become North Korea overnight, but I'd rather they stayed in; fears for Irish firms after Brexit', 13 May. Available at: www.thesun.ie/archives/irish-news/187280/fears-for-irish-firms-after-brexit-britain-isnt-going-to-become-north-korea-overnight-but-id-rather-they-stayed-in/ [accessed 15 June 2021].

Irish Sun (2016) [untitled], 31 May: 11.

The Irish Times (2016) 'Enda Kenny pledges to lobby only Irish people in UK over Brexit', 13 May. Available at: www.irishtimes.com/business/economy/enda-kenny-pledges-to-lobby-only-irish-people-in-uk-over-brexit-1.2646697 [accessed 7 June 2019].

The Irish Times (2016) 'Border assurances "do not stand up", says Bertie Ahern', 1 June. Available at: www.irishtimes.com/news/politics/border-assurances-do-not-stand-up-says-bertie-ahern-1.2667745 [accessed 7 June 2019].

The Irish Times (2016) 'Governments plan high-level meeting after Brexit vote', 8 June (1). Available at: www.irishtimes.com/news/politics/governments-plan-high-level-meeting-after-brexit-vote-1.2676061 [accessed 7 June 2019].

The Irish Times (2016) 'Mary Mitchell O'Connor urges Irish to think of origins in Brexit vote', 8 June (2). Available at: www.irishtimes.com/news/world/uk/mary-mitchell-o-connor-urges-irish-to-think-of-origins-in-brexit-vote-1.2675922 [accessed 7 June 2019].

The Irish Times (2016) 'Brexit fears grows among Irish politicians as referendum approaches', 15 June (1). Available at: www.irishtimes.com/news/politics/brexit-fear-grows-among-irish-politicians-as-referendum-approaches-1.2685443 [accessed 7 June 2019].

The Irish Times (2016) 'David Cameron pulls out of anti-Brexit event with Taoiseach', 15 June (2). Available at: www.irishtimes.com/news/politics/david-cameron-pulls-out-of-anti-brexit-event-with-taoiseach-1.2684807 [accessed 7 June 2019].

The Irish Times (2016) 'Brexit: Fine Gael TDs urge British voters in Ireland to vote remain', 15 June (3). Available at: www.irishtimes.com/news/politics/brexit-fine-gael-tds-urge-british-voters-in-ireland-to-vote-remain-1.2686181 [accessed 7 June 2019].

The Irish Times (2016) 'Brexit: Irish campaign to assure investors of State's EU commitment', 16 June. Available at: www.irishtimes.com/news/world/uk/brexit-irish-campaign-to-assure-investors-of-state-s-eu-commitment-1.2686370 [accessed 7 June 2019].

The Irish Times (2016) 'Remain side hoping for status quo effect', 17 June. Available at: www.irishtimes.com/opinion/noel-whelan-remain-side-hoping-for-status-quo-effect-1.2687669 [accessed 7 June 2019].

The Irish Times (2016) 'Enda Kenny: why Ireland wants the UK to vote Remain', 21 June. Available at: www.irishtimes.com/news/world/uk/enda-kenny-why-ireland-wants-the-uk-to-vote-remain-1.2693196 [accessed 7 June 2019].

The Irish Times (2016) 'Most Irish political parties take active role in Brexit debate', 22 June. Available at: www.irishtimes.com/news/politics/most-irish-political-parties-take-active-role-in-brexit-debate-1.2693651 [accessed 7 June 2019].

The Irish Times (2016) '*Irish Times* View: Brexit a bewildering act of self-harm', 24 June. Available at: www.irishtimes.com/opinion/editorial/irish-times-view-brexit-a-bewildering-act-of-self-harm-1.2698212 [accessed 7 June 2019].

Kunelius, R. (2008) 'Journalism and the EU: a relationship in contexts'. *Journalism* 9(4): 371–376.

McCann, G. & P. Hainsworth (2016) 'Brexit and Northern Ireland: the 2016 referendum on the United Kingdom's membership of the European Union'. *Irish Political Studies* 32(2): 327–342.

Morrow, D. and J. Byrne (2016) 'Playing Jenga? Northern Ireland after Brexit'. *Political Insight* 7(2): 31–32.

Payne, Rita (2018) 'Brexit and the British media'. *The Round Table: The Commonwealth Journal of International Affairs* 107(1): 109–110.

Pfetsch, B. (2018) 'Dissonant and disconnected public spheres as challenge for political communication research'. *Javnost: The Public* 25(1–2): 59–65.

Pfetsch, B., A. Silke & B. Eschner (2008) 'The contribution of the press to Europeanisation of public debates: a comparative study of issue salience and conflict lines of European integration'. *Journalism* 9(4): 465–492.

Picard, R. (2015) *The Euro crisis in the media: journalistic coverage of economic crisis and European institutions*. London: I.B. Tauris.

Preston, P. (2009a) 'An elusive trans-national public sphere: journalism and news cultures in the EU setting'. *Journalism Studies* 10(1): 114–129.

Preston, P. (2009b) *Making the news: journalism and news cultures in Europe*. Abingdon: Routledge.

Ridge-Newman, A., F. León-Solís & H. O'Donnell (2018) *Reporting the road to Brexit: international media and the EU Referendum 2016*. Basingstoke: Palgrave Macmillan.

Rowinski, P. (2016) 'Euroscepticism in the Berlusconi and Murdoch press'. *Journalism* 17(8): 979–1000.

RTÉ (2016) 'Britain votes to leave EU: what does it mean for Ireland?' 24 June. Available at: www.rte.ie/news/2016/0623/797662-brexit-blog/ [accessed 6 April 2020].

Schlesinger, P. and D. Kevin (2000) 'Can the European Union become a sphere of publics?', in E. Oddvar Eriksen and J.E. Fossum (eds) *Democracy in the European Union: integration through deliberation?*, pp. 206–229. Abingdon: Routledge.

Schreier, M. (2012) *Qualitative content analysis in practice*. London: Sage.

Statham, P. (2008) 'Making Europe news: how journalists view their role and media performance'. *Journalism* 9(4): 398–422.

Sweetman, J. (2008) 'Tickle the Republic: the success of Irish versions of UK tabloids – a case-study of the *Irish Daily Mail*'. *Media, Culture and Society* 30(4): 573–580.

Tjernström, V. (2008) 'Nordic newspapers on the EU: European political journalism after "non" and "nee"'. *Journalism* 9(4): 516–536.

Touri, M. (2009) 'News blogs: strengthening democracy through conflict prevention'. *Aslib Proceedings* 61(2): 170–184.

Zelizer, B. (2018) 'Resetting journalism in the aftermath of Brexit and Trump'. *European Journal of Communication* 33(2): 140–156.

10

British–Irish relations: how Brexit unsettled what had been normalised

Brigid Laffan and Jane O'Mahony

Introduction

Brexit unfolded 100 years after the formative events that led to the establishment of an independent Irish state. Prior to independence the history of relations between the two islands was characterised by repeated wars, rebellions and conflict about who should rule Ireland. In 1801, the island of Ireland was incorporated into the Union of Great Britain and Ireland, but Ireland was never a settled or satisfied region of the UK. The "Irish question" bedevilled British politics in the nineteenth century as demands for Home Rule gathered pace driven by modern Irish nationalism. Irish opposition to British rule unfailingly followed a dual track of both constitutional and armed struggle that proved potent enough to take much of Ireland out of the UK by 1922. The turbulent revolutionary years of 1916–1921 led to the establishment of a twenty-six-county state and the partition of the island when the six north-eastern counties remained within the UK, thereby creating a constitutional and political land border on the island. The 300 km-long Irish border was and remains highly contested. The creation of Northern Ireland trapped a large number of Irish nationalists on the wrong side of the border in a political system designed to provide a permanent unionist majority. Decades of discrimination led to the outbreak of communal conflict in 1969, which ended with the 1998 Agreement which provided for new institutions within Northern Ireland, between both states on the island of Ireland, and between the UK and Ireland.

The Agreement did not resolve the conflict between the two communities in Northern Ireland. Rather it morphed into a non-violent phase, an uneasy peace. Brexit was a shock to this settlement and raises complex issues for the two parts of Ireland and between Great Britain and Ireland that have deep historical roots. The core of the 1998 Agreement was to transform the Irish border from a contested space into a border zone across which communities could move with ease to work, avail of health care and socialise. It was about reducing the political and social salience of the border by diluting its effects on everyday life. The border area is heavily populated by nationalists for whom the border was never legitimate. The creation of the single market in the early 1990s was central to normalising border life and joint member-ship of the EU transformed British–Irish relations. The task of disentangling the UK from the EU would have been formidable in any circumstances, but the border on the island of Ireland, the UK's only international land border, added layers of complexity and challenge that were simply not acknowl-edged in the UK during the referendum campaign (Hayward & Murphy 2018; Murphy 2018). Those challenges were understood in Dublin and across the island of Ireland.

This chapter analyses the impact of Brexit on British–Irish relations. The first section examines relations between the UK and Ireland following mem-bership of the EU. Thereafter we assess Ireland's Brexit strategy at two levels, domestic and EU, because Brexit required building and maintaining a domes-tic consensus and ensuring that Ireland's core interests were understood in Brussels and across EU capitals. Next we focus directly on the border because this was a central issue in the negotiations and the following section explores Ireland's membership of the EU beyond Brexit. For Ireland, the UK's exit has a dual quality: it destabilises one of Ireland's geopolitical anchors but it also represents a decisive societal choice for Europe. Brexit is both rupture and launch pad to an Ireland that forges its future with its partners and neigh-bours in Europe. The contingency of Northern Ireland's constitutional future means that British–Irish relations remain salient to both governments given their shared responsibility for maintaining stability and peace.

British–Irish relations in the EU

When Ireland and the UK applied for membership of the EU in 1961, Ire-land was a poor, agricultural country on Europe's north-western periphery, a regional component of the UK economy. Membership of the EU without the UK was unimaginable, but accession to the then EEC offered a route to prosperity and a weakening of economic and political dependence on the UK. Moreover, there was hope that joint membership would gradually diminish the salience of the border. The outbreak of communal conflict in Northern Ireland in the late 1960s, just as Ireland and the UK were negoti-ating accession, was a reminder of the contested nature of the border and the Northern Irish state. From the outset, both governments sought to ring-fence the conflict and did not allow it to spill over into their relations within the EEC.

The two countries joined on 1 January 1973 and within two years it was evident that membership had a dramatic impact on British–Irish relations

(Laffan & O'Mahony 2008). When the UK renegotiated the terms of membership in 1975 and held a referendum, it was already clear that if the UK voted to leave, Ireland would not have followed. It would not have countenanced a return to an asymmetrical relationship outside the EEC. This was a profound shift in Anglo-Irish relations. The then Foreign Minister, Garrett Fitzgerald, concluded that membership released Ireland from the psychological hang-ups of a dependency relationship with the UK and altered perceptions of Ireland among the other member states (Fitzgerald 1975: 2). The pooling of sovereignty enhanced Ireland's sovereignty and sense of autonomy, so that interdependence in Europe was a form of liberation. This was in stark contrast to the UK, which joined the EU at the end of the empire with little affective attachment to the project.

During more than thirty years of shared EU membership, Ireland and the UK grew closer (Tannam 2019). They shared a common language and the degree of social and economic connectivity between the two islands reinforced ties. On core EU policies, both states were part of the liberal North European block supportive of the single market and open trade in contrast to the more protectionist member states of the Mediterranean. As two common law countries in a system dominated by continental codified law, the UK and Ireland had a broadly similar approach to regulation. That said, Ireland supported the development of social legislation that was anathema to UK Conservative governments and was a paid-up member of the Common Agricultural Policy (CAP) supporters club. Ireland joined the European Monetary System in 1979 and twenty years later the euro, marking a major divergence between the two states. The UK's approach towards Schengen and cooperation in Justice and Home Affairs (JHA) meant that Ireland could not contemplate joining Schengen and has opt-in/out arrangements. Successive Irish governments, backed by a more favourable public, were more supportive of European integration than the UK.

Membership of the EU had a significant impact on how the conflict in Northern Ireland was managed. It provided the context in which the two capitals could strive to bring violence under control and EU meetings offered ample opportunities for bilateral talks away from the glare of Anglo-Irish summits. Major changes in EU regimes and policies also contributed to altering the lived experience of the Irish border. When the Interreg programme for cross-border cooperation got underway, EU officials, particularly EU regional development specialists, began to interact with the communities on both sides of the border. These officials offered an outsider perspective and could use their standing to get communities to co-operate on a sectoral rather than a geographic basis. Visits by border communities to other parts of Europe under Interreg offered examples of successful cross-border cooperation and took the political heat out of the concept of cooperation. The most pronounced change came from the single market programme, launched in 1988, that fundamentally altered the regulatory environment in Europe. The core aim of the single market programme was to reduce barriers to economic exchange in Europe including barriers at borders.

Irish Foreign Minister Charlie Flanagan underlined just how important the EU had been for peace in Ireland:

> It is perhaps in Northern Ireland where the EU's positive influence has been most keenly felt. From the outset, joint British-Irish EU membership has facilitated progress with the peace process. The EU has fulfilled an intangible role as a wider Union in which we are all members. The economic impact of EU membership should not be forgotten either ... In short, the EU has been a powerful – if understated – force for good for everyone and every community right across Northern Ireland. (Flanagan 2015)

By the time the 1998 Agreement was signed, the Irish border was no longer a barrier to economic cooperation. All that was needed to transform the border into a communal frontier space was to remove the British army installations, which was part of the Agreement.

In 2011, Queen Elizabeth II became the first British monarch to visit independent Ireland since its foundation. The visit was powerfully symbolic and marked a normalisation of relations after hundreds of years of conflict. However, within two years of the Queen's visit, David Cameron triggered the renegotiation and referendum on continued UK membership. The Dublin government immediately understood the dangers of a UK referendum and the likely impact on Ireland if the decision were to leave the EU. Ireland's worst nightmare materialised on 24 June 2016.

Ireland's Brexit strategy

The Irish government understood that the potential consequences of Brexit for the island of Ireland were existential and demanded a high level of political engagement and policy management. The aim was to protect the 1998 Agreement and minimise the disruption of the UK's exit for Ireland and make Ireland "Brexit ready". Irish political and administrative circles developed a strategy to ensure that Ireland's core interests would be protected. This involved building a domestic consensus, engaging in a diplomatic offensive with EU member states and across the wider world, working with EU institutions and monitoring intensively what was happening in London. Ireland is a small state with limited administrative and institutional resources, but the clarity of the objectives around Brexit meant that the available state capacity was used effectively and with agility.

Once the outcome of the referendum was known, the Taoiseach Enda Kenny immediately launched a Brexit Contingency Plan. The Brexit dossier became one of the most salient agenda items for the government, the Oireachtas and the wider public. The government set out its key concerns, namely the impact of Brexit on Northern Ireland, on trade and the economy, the CTA and for the EU itself (Kenny 2016). The Taoiseach was at pains to say that 'Ireland will, of course, remain a member of the European Union. That is profoundly in our national interest' (Kenny 2016). This was to signal to Ireland's EU partners that it would remain a committed member despite the UK's impending exit.

The domestic strategy consisted of continuously briefing the opposition parties and engaging with parliamentary committees, building a strong domestic political consensus. In autumn 2016, the government established an *All-Island Civic Dialogue* to bring together interested parties for a consultative exercise. This was amplified by up to fourteen sectoral dialogues in such fields as social security, human rights, energy and tourism. This facilitated a two-way flow of communication from the government to key societal actors and enabled the government both to inform the public and to gain an understanding of their concerns and interests. As the negotiations proceeded, state agencies developed a policy toolkit and held Brexit roadshows across the country to assist businesses to prepare for Brexit. In September 2017, stakeholder forums were established which were held every six weeks to inform the government's position and to communicate to key players what was happening with negotiations. Consultation and deliberation in all of these arenas was underpinned by a strong communications strategy to ensure that there was deep societal engagement with the issues and that the public was kept informed of developments. Notably, the Brussels correspondent of RTÉ, Tony Connelly, was one of the most authoritative journalists on Brexit in Europe (see Connelly 2018).

Brexit entailed one of the state's most complex diplomatic exercises since its foundation. This involved maintaining relations with London and Ireland's twenty-six partners in the EU. The objective vis-à-vis London was to impress on the British government the sensitivity of Brexit for the governing of Northern Ireland, the 1998 Agreement and the Irish border. Notwithstanding the fact that the EU would not negotiate with the UK prior to notification, Dublin and London had bilateral discussions in autumn 2016. Interestingly, a House of Lords report of December 2016 argued in favour of a bilateral negotiation between Ireland and the UK to settle the border issue, the outcome of which would then become part of the Withdrawal Agreement (House of Lords 2016). Dublin was never tempted by the bilateral route as Ireland's objectives included both no return to a hard border on the island and the maintenance of Ireland's full obligations and rights as a member state.

The objective vis-à-vis EU institutions and Ireland's twenty-six partners was to ensure that they understood the existential nature of Brexit for the island of Ireland and would elevate the Irish dossier to a central place on the agenda. The historic nature of these negotiations for British–Irish relations cannot be understated. For the first time in a very long and turbulent history, Ireland was a member of a Union of states that the UK was about to exit. If Ireland could make the Irish border an EU issue, it would be on the stronger side of the negotiating table for the first time in its history. The Irish diplomatic service began lobbying its partners on the likely impact of Brexit for the border in the months leading up to the vote. The political and diplomatic effort was intensified between June 2016 and the UK's formal notification of leaving in March 2017 (O'Rourke 2019). Irish ministers and officials spread out across Europe educating their colleagues on the nature of the 1998 Agreement, the EU's contribution to peace on the island of Ireland and the distinctiveness of the Irish border. A senior official from another member state accepted that 'if there is one player which made Ireland go to the top of the agenda, it was Ireland' (McTague 2019).

The fruits of Ireland's efforts were evident in September 2017 when the Commission's Article 50 Task Force published a document on principles for managing the Ireland/Northern Ireland dialogue in the Brexit negotiations. The most significant paragraph stated:

> It is the responsibility of the United Kingdom to ensure that its approach to the challenges of the Irish border in the context of its withdrawal from the European Union takes into account and protects the very specific and interwoven political, economic, security, societal and agricultural context and frameworks on the island of Ireland. These challenges will require a unique solution which cannot serve to preconfigure solutions in the context of the wider discussions on the future relationship between the European Union and the United Kingdom. (European Commission 2017)

The document placed responsibility firmly on the UK and signalled that the EU would be open to a "unique solution" for Northern Ireland that would not be available to the remainder of Great Britain. The EU commitment to the island of Ireland was evident in the EU negotiating guidelines where Northern Ireland was one of three issues to be settled in the Withdrawal Agreement.

Brexit and the Irish border

The question of the Irish border was always going to be one of the most difficult issues to resolve in the Brexit negotiations for underlying historical reasons, on the one hand, and the contingency of the UK government's preferences, on the other. Put simply, UK preferences transformed the Irish border from an extremely complex challenge into an almost intractable one. The border was where the ambition to "take back control" came face to face with the realities of commitments made in the 1998 Agreement and the wishes of the people of Northern Ireland who voted to remain in the EU. Theresa May's Lancaster House speech in January 2017 outlined what her core negotiating objectives were:

- Taking back control of UK law by leaving the jurisdiction of the European Court of Justice.
- Controlling immigration by leaving the single market and the free movement of people. The Prime Minister framed this in the following manner: 'I want to be clear. What I am proposing cannot mean membership of the Single Market'.
- Ending contributions to the EU budget.
- Gaining freedom to agree trade agreements globally, which meant leaving the customs union. The Prime Minister framed this as follows: 'that means I do not want Britain to be part of the Common Commercial Policy and I do not want us to be bound by the Common External Tariff'.
- In relation to Ireland, the Prime Minister acknowledged that 'nobody wants to return to the borders of the past, so we will make it a priority to deliver a practical solution as soon as we can'. (UK Government 2017a)

Theresa May's objectives consisted of a set of incompatible preferences. It was possible for the UK to maintain a frictionless and invisible border on the island of Ireland by remaining part of the customs union and by joining the European Economic Area (EEA). If, however, the UK prioritised leaving the customs union and the common market, there would have to be special arrangements for the Irish border. The UK created a trilemma whereby it could have two of its three core preferences but not all three. Yet when the UK government published a paper on the negotiations in February 2017 the UK government said:

> [w]e recognise that for the people of Northern Ireland and Ireland, the ability to move freely across the border is an essential part of daily life. When the UK leaves the EU we aim to have as seamless and frictionless a border as possible between Northern Ireland and Ireland, so that we can continue to see the trade and everyday movements we have seen up to now. (UK Government 2017b)

The possibility of achieving this was undermined in May 2017 when the Prime Minister called an election with the intention of strengthening her majority. When her electoral gamble failed, she needed the support of the DUP to remain in power. The DUP was the only political party in Northern Ireland that favoured Brexit and as the dominant unionist party, was seized of the dangers to Northern Ireland's constitutional position in the event of special arrangements for Northern Ireland. The UK government was faced with a veto player on the Withdrawal Agreement.

The Irish government for its part wanted the UK to fulfil its commitment of no return to the borders of the past. In autumn 2016, as UK preferences on exit became clearer, the Irish government began to intensify its efforts to ensure that the Irish border would be a key item on the EU's agenda. It impressed on the EU's chief negotiator, Michel Barnier, the salience of the issue when he visited Dublin in autumn 2016 and two very large Irish delegations went to Brussels to meet him and Task Force 50 at this time. The outcome of Irish agenda setting was that Task Force 50 and the Council understood Irish concerns and were determined to support Ireland. After the UK triggered the Article 50 process, Ireland requested that if the 1998 Agreement led to a united Ireland, Northern Ireland would automatically accede to the EU. The UK objected but according to a Council official, the response was 'if this is what the Irish want, we're going to do it. They are around the table. You are not around the table' (Connelly 2018: 20). This was a harbinger of things to come as Ireland found itself on the stronger side of the table for the first time in centuries of Anglo-Irish relations. When the EU's negotiating guidelines were published in April 2017, Ireland was one of three issues that had to be negotiated in the first phase of negotiations. The guidelines stated:

> The Union has consistently supported the goal of peace and reconciliation enshrined in the Good Friday Agreement in all its parts, and continuing to support and protect the achievements, benefits and commitments of the Peace Process will remain of paramount importance. In view of the unique circumstances on the island of Ireland, flexible and imaginative solutions will be required, including with the aim of avoiding a hard border, while respecting the integrity of the Union legal order. (European Council 2017)

The EU was signalling that it was willing to find flexible and imaginative solutions to avoid a hard border, but this could not impact on the integrity of the Union's legal order. The inclusion of Ireland at this stage had implications for the manner in which the Irish border was addressed, because in order to move the negotiations to the second phase, the European Council required sufficient progress to have been achieved on the three key issues in the first phase. This meant that the UK had to confront the incompatibility of its position. Following the UK election in May 2017, the two sides got down to formal negotiations in July 2017. Two working groups were set up to address citizens and budget, but a dialogue on Ireland was established under the responsibility of the two deputy negotiators. In autumn 2017, progress was made on the first two issues but little on Ireland. The UK was hoping that if it made concessions on citizens and budgetary contributions, that solidarity with Ireland might ebb. This did not happen; at a meeting with President Tusk on 24 November 2017, Theresa May is alleged to have said that 'one country cannot hold up progress' and the UK was a 'much bigger and much more important country than Ireland' (Connelly 2018).

In autumn 2017, the idea of a "backstop" that would keep the border open became a serious proposition. During this time, the UK government found it difficult to engage seriously on the border, partly because of the DUP and partly because of the intrinsic difficulty of the problem. Time began to bear down on the UK negotiators as the Prime Minister wanted agreement on a transition and a move to phase two of the negotiations. The European Council requested a joint report from the two negotiating teams so that they could assess the issue of opening phase two of the negotiations at their December summit. However, Michel Barnier said that 'What is unclear is what rules will apply in Northern Ireland after Brexit. And what the UK is willing to commit to, in order to avoid a hard border' (Barnier 2017). The UK could not avoid addressing the border issue. On the brink of agreement with the EU, Theresa May had to cut off negotiations when she was in Brussels finalising the Joint Report because the DUP, on whom her government depended, would not agree to the draft report. The unfolding drama of that week was no surprise to anyone with even a cursory knowledge of the island of Ireland and the delicate balances that had kept Northern Ireland in an uneasy peace. The two parties managed to agree a joint report which was sufficiently ambiguous for both sides to live with, but the border issue was still far from settled.

The final Joint Report addressed the Irish border in two paragraphs, paragraph 49 and 50. Paragraph 50 was added following DUP objections to the first draft. In paragraph 49, the UK committed to protecting North–South cooperation on the island of Ireland and to avoiding a hard border. It agreed three ways of doing this:

1   via the overall UK–EU relationship but if this were not possible it pledged to
2   propose specific solutions that took into account the special circumstances of the island of Ireland but in the absence of agreed solutions
3   the United Kingdom would maintain full alignment with those rules of the Internal Market and the Customs Union which, now or in the future, supported North–South cooperation, the all-island economy and the protection of the 1998 Agreement. (Joint Report 2017)

The guarantees in paragraph 49 were comprehensive and the third element was effectively a backstop to ensure that in all circumstances, a hard border would be avoided. The additional paragraph 50 offered the DUP a guarantee that there would be no border between the Northern Ireland and the UK.

The Joint Report proved sufficient to move the negotiations to the next phase, but it was not clear on just how the agreed aim might be achieved. The credibility of the UK commitment was quickly undermined when the UK negotiator, David Davis, suggested that the agreement was largely symbolic and the UK would not be held to it. This caused considerable disquiet in Brussels and Dublin as they were very serious about the commitment and intended to hold the UK government to its pledges.

A feature of the Brexit negotiations was the failure of the UK to offer a legal text. At no stage during the negotiations did the UK government draft a protocol on how it would fulfil its commitments to Ireland, because once it had to translate paragraph 49 into legal commitments, it was clear that there were no easy choices. Task Force 50 produced a colour coded draft Withdrawal Agreement in March 2018 which showed that there was considerable agreement on citizens and the budget but much less on Ireland. The Agreement contained a protocol on Ireland that met with an immediate adverse reaction from London. In July 2018, the UK government produced two papers, one on the Irish border and a second known as the Chequers proposals that outlined the UK's approach to the negotiations and the future relationship. Although negotiations were opened in July 2017, it took the UK government a year to outline their perspective on the future partnership with the EU. The proposals were received with scepticism in Brussels and the other capitals, but given Theresa May's domestic difficulties, there was no immediate rejection of them. This came at the Salzburg European Summit in September when the discussion between May and the other heads of state and government did not go well. At a press conference following the Salzburg meeting, Council President Donald Tusk informed the press that although the Chequers proposals had some positive elements, 'they will not work' and went on to say that the heads 'reconfirmed that there will be no Withdrawal Agreement without a solid, operational and legally binding Irish backstop' (Tusk 2018). The Irish border would not disappear as a priority issue.

Having accepted that there would have to be a backstop, the UK changed strategy and asked that all of the UK be part of a customs union while the backstop was in place. This was regarded as a major demand and raised concerns that the UK would use this to undermine the single market. The EU insisted on provisions ensuring a level playing field but did make this major concession to the UK. In November 2018, the two sides signed a Withdrawal Agreement that was endorsed by the governments of the EU27 and the UK. The Brexit process then move into ratification phase. May tried three times to get the Agreement through the House of Commons and failed before finally announcing her decision to resign. During the discussion on the Agreement in the House of Commons, there was considerable debate on alternatives to the backstop and a vote in favour of what was known as the

Malthouse compromise, which essentially focused on replacing the backstop with 'alternative arrangements' (Hayward 2019). This was unacceptable to the EU although there were a number of efforts to clarify what the backstop implied, especially that it was a temporary device that would remain in place unless and until it was replaced by agreed measures that kept the border open.

The backstop was the key issue that prevented ratification of the Withdrawal Agreement by the House of Commons. There were objections from the DUP, fearing its impact on the constitutional status of Northern Ireland. Members of the European Research Group, a hard core of Conservative pro-Brexit MPs, agreed with the DUP but were also concerned about the all-UK customs union because they felt that this was a trap that would keep the UK in the orbit of the EU and prevent trade negotiations with non-European states. There were also concerns about the absence of political consent in Northern Ireland because the Assembly had not met since January 2018. The 2019 European Parliament elections returned two pro-remain MEPs in Northern Ireland, which suggested that a majority in Northern Ireland still preferred to remain in the EU. For its part, the Irish government and its partners in the EU remained committed to the Withdrawal Agreement and refused to re-open it. Following a series of extensions granted by the European Council, domestic political developments in the UK brought the first phase of the Brexit negotiations to a close. When Theresa May resigned, she was replaced by Boris Johnson, which marked a fundamental shift in UK politics as a leading Brexiteer was in power and the composition of his cabinet was strongly Leave-orientated.

Immediately on becoming Prime Minister, Johnson identified the Irish backstop as the biggest impediment to agreement and vowed to leave the Union by October 31 with or without a deal. This transformed the negotiations into a high stakes game with potentially very serious consequences for Ireland. As the clock ticked through autumn 2019, the chances of a no deal exit increased significantly although Boris Johnson ultimately was unwilling to follow through with his threat. By early October 2019, when it became apparent that member state support for Ireland remained firm, the UK began to soften its stance on the backstop. In a letter to Commission President Juncker, the Prime Minister set out the elements of a new plan that included:

- An all-island regulatory zone for goods, particularly for agri-food, which would be governed by EU regulations;
- A consent mechanism for Northern Ireland;
- Northern Ireland would remain in the UK customs territory. (Johnson 2019)

This demonstrated that the UK wanted a deal but the terms were not acceptable to the EU27. The vital breakthrough came at a bilateral meeting between the Taoiseach and Prime Minister on 10 October. The two political leaders spoke without advisers and achieved agreement on a possible path to agreement (Joint Statement 2019). The Irish government and the EU had always said that it was willing to examine alternatives to the backstop provided they achieved the desired outcome. Over the next week, the details of a new protocol on Ireland were agreed that went beyond Boris Johnson's initial offer. At the October European Council, the Protocol was agreed and following ratification of the Withdrawal Agreement, the UK left the Union on 31 January 2020. The Brexit negotiations entered the second phase on the future relationship and the Withdrawal Agreement including the Protocol on Ireland became a matter of implementation. A Joint Committee involving the EU and the UK is responsible for overseeing the implementation. Effectively there is a border in the Irish Sea, but the implementation of the Protocol remains highly sensitive and subject to differing interpretations.

EU membership beyond Brexit

Brexit forced Ireland out of its comfort zone within the EU. The government had no choice but to place Ireland at the centre of the EU agenda on Brexit. It amassed its available political and institutional capacity to secure the support of EU institutions and its twenty-six partners in the Union. It was conscious when doing so that less than a decade earlier Ireland had exchanged interdependence within the Union for dependence on international funding to finance the state. The most significant consequence of Brexit for Ireland's membership of the Union was that it brought to light the fact that the EU was Ireland's geopolitical anchor in the twenty-first-century world. Relations with the UK and the United States would remain critical, but neither is more important than Ireland's membership of the Union. Ireland has now made a decisive choice for Europe and membership is intrinsic to Ireland's state identity and place in the world.

The UK's future relationship with the Union remains vital for Ireland, but its EU concerns go well beyond this. The sensitive dossiers for Ireland include the climate crisis, corporate tax, defence and security, and the future architecture of the EU. Commission President Ursula von der Leyen elevated the climate crisis to the centre of the EU agenda with a new green deal. Ireland is a climate change laggard and, according to the Environmental Protection Agency, 'Ireland is not on the right long-term trajectory in meeting national 2050 targets in the electricity generation, built environment and transport sectors' (EPA 2018). The participation of the Green Party in the 2020 coalition involving Fianna Fáil and Fine Gael offered the possibility of altering the domestic politics on climate issues and provide impetus to move Ireland beyond its laggard status. Corporation tax has been a key component of the Irish model of political economy since it opted for export-led economic growth. In 2016, Ireland's corporate tax rate of 12.5% was the second lowest in the EU. This came under increased scrutiny from the EU and in summer 2016, the Commission deployed its powers under competition law to rule that Apple had received unfair tax incentives in Ireland (see Killian, Chapter 4, this volume). However, the Commission's decision and subsequent parliamentary and media debates exposed an unease about aggressive tax planning by MNCs and the damage to Ireland's reputation if it is classified as a tax haven.

Ireland's role in European security and defence also continued to test successive governments. According to Tonra, 'a distance; geographic, strategic and psychological that generates negative Irish attitudes towards European security and defence where cooperation is still seen as a cost, even a penalty of EU membership. It is a bill we reluctantly pay in return for markets and membership' (Tonra 2019: 10). This may not be tenable in future as geopolitical pressures bear down on Europe. Ireland's positioning during the Covid-19 crisis in the Union signalled an important shift. Ireland was one of nine countries supporting debt mutualisation at an early stage and as a net contributor, Ireland did not position itself with those opposing a significant financial response. It was not tempted to join the frugal four – the Netherlands, Austria, Denmark and Sweden – on the Covid Recovery Fund. Thus Ireland finds itself at the beginning of the third decade of the twenty-first century as a committed EU member state, albeit like all member states with some testing dossiers.

Conclusion

Brexit is of greater consequence and carries greater dangers for Ireland than for any other member state because of history, geography and a shared border. Brexit was a predominantly English phenomenon that was caught up in the complex territorial and constitutional politics of the island of Ireland. Historically, the UK political system has struggled to address both what was known as the "Irish question" and relations between Great Britain and the continent. Brexit brought these two issues together making it even more difficult for the UK to disentangle itself from the EU. Having ratified a Withdrawal Agreement, the UK finally left in January 2020 but the challenge of negotiating the future relationship and the implementation of the

Irish Protocol remains. Faced with the existential challenge of Brexit, Irish politicians and diplomats engaged proactively to shape Brexit in practice, especially in relation to the Irish border, and did not concede to a reintroduction of border checks on the island of Ireland. Brexit forced Ireland out of its comfort zone in the EU and the wider international system.

As Ireland approached 100 years since the foundation of the state, developments since June 2016 have vindicated Ireland's choice for Europe in 1972. The contrast between the exercise of Irish sovereignty in the EU and Scotland's devolved authority within the UK could not be more sharply underlined. Although 62% of Scottish voters wanted to remain in the EU, they left with the rest of the UK. Moreover, Ireland as a small state has seen its essential interests protected and promoted by the EU and has learned that a London government can never again power Ireland against its will. As it embarks on its second century of statehood, Ireland does so a member state of Europe's essential Union, the only available institution in Europe for managing deep interdependence in an increasingly unstable and disorderly world.

References

Barnier, M. (2017) 'Speech at the Centre of European Reform on the "Future of Europe"'. 20 November. Available at: https://ec.europa.eu/commission/press-corner/detail/en/SPEECH_17_4765 [accessed 29 June 2020].

Connelly T. (2018) *Brexit and Ireland: the dangers, the opportunities, and the inside story of the Irish response*. London: Penguin.

EPA (2018) 'Ireland's greenhouse gas emissions projections 2017–2035'. Dublin: Environmental Protection Agency. Available at: www.epa.ie/pubs/reports/air/airemissions/ghgprojections2017–2035/EPA_2018_GHG_Emissions_Projections_Summary_Report.pdf [accessed 2 July 2020].

EU Commission (2017) *Guiding principles for the Dialogue on Ireland/Northern Ireland*. Brussels: European Commission Task Force 50.

European Council (2017) *European Council (Art. 50) guidelines for Brexit negotiations*. 29 April. Available at: www.consilium.europa.eu/en/press/press-releases/2017/04/29/euco-brexit-guidelines/ [accessed 29 June 2020].

Fitzgerald, G. (1975) 'Irish foreign policy within the context of the EEC'. Address delivered by Minister for Foreign Affairs, 10 November. Available at: http://aei.pitt.edu/8545/1/8545_1.pdf [accessed 30 June 2020].

Flanagan, C. (2015) 'Irish Foreign Minister address to Chatham House'. Available at: www.dfa.ie/news-and-media/press-releases/press-release-archive/2015/september/flanagan-addresses-chatham-house-on-brexit/ [accessed 1 July 2020].

Hayward, K. (2019) 'Weighing up alternatives arrangements to the backstop'. Available at: https://ukandeu.ac.uk/research-papers/weighing-up-alternative-arrangements-to-the-backstop/ [accessed 19 February 2020].

Hayward, K. & M.C. Murphy (2018) 'The EU's influence on the peace process and agreement in Northern Ireland in light of Brexit'. *Ethnopolitics* 17(3): 276–291.

House of Lords (2016) 'Brexit: UK–Irish relations'. House of Lords European Union Committee, 6th Report of Session 2016–17, 12 December 2016, HL Paper 76. Available at: https://publications.parliament.uk/pa/ld201617/ldselect/ldeucom/76/7602.htm [accessed 24 June 2019].

Johnson, B. (2019) 'Letter from PM Johnson to President Juncker', 2 October 2019. Available at: https://assets.publishing.service.gov.uk/government/uploads/system/uploads/attachment_data/file/836029/PM_letter_to_Juncker.pdf [accessed 4 October 2019].

Joint Report (2017) 'JR from the negotiators of the European Union and the United Kingdom Government to the European Council, 8 December 2017'. Available at: https://ec.europa.eu/commission/sites/beta-political/files/joint_report.pdf [accessed 28 June 2020].

Joint Statement (2019) 'Joint Statement issued following a meeting of Taoiseach Leo Varadkar and PM Boris Johnson'. 10 October. Available at: https://merrionstreet.ie/en/News-Room/News/Spotlights/Joint_Statement_by_An_Taoiseach_Leo_Varadkar_and_Prime_Minister_Boris_Johnson.html [accessed 12 October 2019].

Kenny, E. (2016) 'Statement by An Taoiseach Enda Kenny on the UK vote to leave the European Union'. Available at: https://merrionstreet.ie/en/News-Room/Speeches/Statement_by_An_Taoiseach_Enda_Kenny_TD_on_the_UK_Vote_to_Leave_the_European_Union.html [accessed 29 June 2020].

Laffan, B. & J. O'Mahony (2008) *Ireland and the European Union*. Basingstoke: Palgrave Macmillan.

McTague, T. (2019) 'How the UK lost the Brexit battle'. *Politico*, 4 February. Available at: www.politico.eu/article/how-uk-lost-brexit-eu-negotiation/ [accessed 9 April 2019].

Murphy, Mary C. (2018) *Europe and Northern Ireland's future. Negotiating Brexit's unique case*. Newcastle: Agenda Publishing.

O'Rourke, K. (2019) *A short history of Brexit: from Brentry to Backstop*. London: Pelican.

Tannam, E. (2019) Brexit and the future of UK–Irish relations. Dublin: DCU Working Paper No. 3/2019. Available at: https://papers.ssrn.com/sol3/papers.cfm?abstract_id=3357165 [accessed 25 March 2019].

Tonra, B. (2019) *Brexit and Irish security and defence*. Dublin: Spire Working Paper Series, No. 12. Available at: www.ucd.ie/spire/t4media/Ben%20Tonra_WP122019_final.pdf [accessed 2 July 2020].

Tusk, D. (2018) 'Remarks following the Salzburg Informal European Council, 20 September 2017'. Available at: www.consilium.europa.eu/en/press/press-releases/2018/09/20/remarks-by-president-donald-tusk-after-the-salzburg-informal-summit/ [accessed 18 June 2021].

UK Government (2017a) 'The government's negotiating objectives for exiting the EU: PM speech'. London: The Stationery Office. Available at: www.gov.uk/government/speeches/the-governments-negotiating-objectives-for-exiting-the-eu-pm-speech [accessed 20 September 2020].

UK Government (2017b) 'The United Kingdom's exit from, and new partnership with, the European Union'. London: The Stationery Office. Available at: www.gov.uk/government/publications/the-united-kingdoms-exit-from-and-new-partnership-with-the-european-union-white-paper [accessed 22 September 2020].

11

Brexit and the economy of Ireland

Stephen Kinsella

Introduction

The Republic of Ireland and the UK have functioned as separate sovereign entities for almost a century. They have functioned as a single labour and product market for at least seven times as long. They have functioned as a common energy market for only slightly more than a decade. Brexit was at once a labour, energy, capital and balance of payments shock to this deeply integrated shared territory.

The purpose of this chapter is to examine the state of integration between the two nations before Brexit. It argues the Brexit separation was a shock to three, and not two, economies. The core assumption of the European project since the 1950s has been ever deeper integration across labour, goods and services markets. This core assumption will be examined precisely because it was the key assumption challenged by Brexit. This chapter traces the evolution of each distinct economy – and the joint entity it functionally exists as – in several sectors. It then discusses key risks and opportunities by sector for each economy.

In trying to understand the impact of Brexit on the UK and Irish economies, three important characteristics need to be highlighted and understood. Ireland's economy is small, open and connected to its former colonist by centuries of ties which exist mostly at the sectoral level. These three features define much of Ireland's economic existence and their disruption is, in some sense, the lasting legacy of Brexit.

That Ireland is small is, in some sense, obvious: slightly under 5 million people lived and worked within the Republic of Ireland before Brexit. Some 67.53 million lived within the UK, of which about 1.8 million lived in Northern Ireland. The landmass of the Republic is roughly 69,000 km², versus the UK's 242,000 km². The average population density in the Republic was seventy persons per km² in 2016, up from sixty-seven persons in 2011 and sixty-two persons per km² recorded in 2006. The UK's population density varies widely, as one might expect, but on average it was 255 people per km² in 2018.

The UK economy is open, with a ratio of trade to GDP of 61% in 2019, and is one of the world's most financialised economies. The Irish economy, however, is one of the most open in the world, with a ratio of trade to GDP of 210% and an equally financialised economy, thanks mainly to the links between the two countries' financial systems (Sokol 2007). Only Hong Kong and Singapore have higher trade ratios. This ratio is one measure of the openness of the Irish economy. Ireland has followed many of the precepts of small, high income, trading nations, in that they are international rule-takers, club-joiners and employ a range of multinational enterprise-friendly industrial policies.

Finally, the Irish and UK economies are deeply connected at a sectoral level, thanks to their shared colonial histories. These sectors represent the relationships which existed before the islands were partitioned in terms of sovereignty, and so are based around agriculture, light manufacturing and transport. The changes in the sectoral composition of the Irish economy since its independence in 1922 were also in evidence in terms of the dwindling importance of the UK as an export destination. In 1945, 94% of Irish exports went to the UK. In 2018, that figure was 11%. The other key connection to consider is the connection between Northern Ireland and the Republic.

One island, three economies, different productivity

A key feature uncovered by the Brexit debate was the difference in economic potential of the economies that share the island of Ireland. Though they share an island, the Republic of Ireland and Northern Ireland are, economically speaking, quite different places. We can talk of three economies in Ireland. The first is the domestic economy of the Republic. The second is the multinational-dominated sectors of the Republic, which are mainly in the pharmaceutical, ICT, finance, agri-food and manufacturing sectors, and which have historically driven much of its growth. The third is the economy of Northern Ireland. Each "Ireland" is quite distinct from the others, and Brexit, therefore, has had differential effects on each.

For example, relative to both the UK and the Republic, Northern Ireland's labour market has typically had a much higher rate of labour market inactivity and a lower employment rate. Sectorally, the Republic has a far higher proportion of service jobs (Barry 2007). The North is still quite manufacturing based. In terms of gross-value added, a simple measure of productivity, the Republic was about 1.5 times as productive as the North in

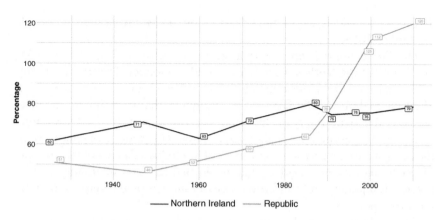

Figure 11.1 GDP per person in Northern Ireland and Ireland, percentage of UK
average GDP per person, 1926–2010
Source: Eurostat.

2019. Much of this productivity differential can be attributed to the presence of multinationals in the Republic's economy. Even using a modified
measure of gross national income per person, which strips out much of the
influence of multinational activity, the differential in value added is more
than 10% higher than in the UK and more than 45% higher than Northern
Ireland.

Figure 11.1 shows the economic outputs of the two new regions over
much of the past century, expressed as a percentage of the UK's average
economic output per person. This is intended as a measure of relative living
standards over the long run. Much of the deforming influence of multinational activity on the Republic's GDP statistics takes place after 2010, so I
report the statistics from 1926 to 2010 to retain some measure of direct comparability.

In Figure 11.1, which begins in 1926, Northern Ireland stood at about
62% of the UK's living standard. The Republic[1] was about 51% of UK GDP
per capita. By 1973, as both the UK and the Republic joined the European
project, Northern Ireland was at 73% of the UK's living standard, while the
Republic was at 59%. Thereafter the fortunes reversed. The main difference
was the drive to openness pursued by the Republic as its key industrial strategy. The courting of FDI from the late 1950s drove the large sectoral changes
that saw the Republic's fortunes change very rapidly after it joined the
European project. Living standards in the Republic increased sharply in the
late 1980s and 1990s, during the Celtic Tiger period. The Republic's standard of living surpassed the UK in the early 2000s, as a property bubble,
which would eventually become the fourth most expensive in the world

once it burst, took hold. Today, as discussed earlier, the economies are different when measured in sectoral, regional and productivity terms. Brexit has deep implications when viewed through each of these lenses.

Brexit as trade shock

Evidence on cross-border investment shows the UK's economy as already suffering from the uncertainty caused by the 2016 Brexit decision, but before any final settlement. Born et al. (2019) estimated the impact of Brexit to the UK since 2016. They found UK economic output, measured by GDP, was between 1.7% and 2.5% lower at the end of 2018 than it otherwise would have been had the referendum result been to remain within the EU. The largest element of the drop in economic output was the loss of real investment in UK firms by the rest of the world.

No estimate of the effects of Brexit showed a positive outcome for the Irish economy, and very few have estimated a positive effect for the UK economy. In addition to estimates by HM Treasury and Ireland's Department of Finance, academic studies by Barrett et al. (2015), Bergin et al. (2017), Chen et al. (2018), Dhingra et al. (2017), Ebell et al. (2016) and Gudgin et al. (2018) produced a range of estimates for the impact of Brexit. All of them found negative outcomes.

Most estimates of the impact of Brexit on the Irish economy ranged in severity from –0.5% to –7% of GDP over the medium term. The median estimate for the impact of Brexit on the Irish economy for the eight studies analysed in this chapter was –3% of Irish gross national income over a ten-year period. Translated into per-person terms, Brexit was expected to cost each Irish person just over €2,000 per annum by 2030. These costs will not be evenly distributed, either over time or over household type.

A summary of the many economic effects and their various channels was contained in Hantzsche et al. (2019). Other groups, including lobby groups, private research firms and large banks, have produced various Brexit impact estimates. Only those closely aligned with pro-Brexit groups have produced estimates showing a positive effect of Brexit, and even then, under relatively unlikely and implausible conditions.

Using different assumptions, models and estimation approaches, a consensus view has emerged that in any Brexit event, the UK would suffer a permanent loss of real income relative to remaining in the EU. A summary of fifteen studies of these effects, in cumulative percentages of UK GDP, is shown in Figure 11.2. Five scenarios are modelled. The central scenario was a free trade area, where UK goods and services have access to the single market, where there was little or no financial contribution from the UK

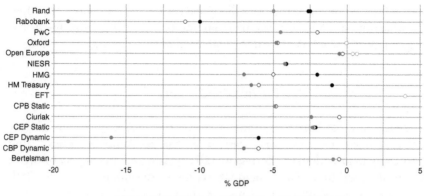

Figure 11.2 Estimates of long-term Brexit impact, percentage of GDP over ten years
Source: Institute for Government.

government for this access, where UK exporters must comply with EU rules and regulations when exporting to the single market, where there was no formal influence over the rules governing the single market, and where there was no obligation on the UK to accept free movement of people.

The other major scenario modelled was the "hard" Brexit, where World Trade Organisation rules come into force. In this scenario, tariffs of between 1.5% and 19% are applied by sector across the full range of UK exports. Many export categories attract little or no tariffs. Many do. Chilled bovine carcasses, for example, would attract a 12.8% tariff, while cotton fibres would attract a 4% tariff. Additionally, a range of non-tariff barriers to trade would apply to all goods and services.

The three other scenarios the figure details are: unilateral trade openness, where the UK drops all tariffs to the rest of the world; membership of the EEA, which confers more rights on the UK to influence regulations, but which comes at a considerable financial cost to the UK exchequer; and a Swiss Bilateral arrangement, which replicates the relationship Switzerland enjoys with the EU.

Only one study of the fifteen displayed in Figure 11.2, by the pro-Brexit group Economists for Free Trade, estimates a medium-term benefit from Brexit of 4% GDP growth, and only under conditions where the UK economy trades freely with the rest of the world, that is, when the automatic operation of tariff laws are not brought into force once the UK leaves. Across all the studies and types of Brexit assumed, the median estimate of the impact was –2.6%. Across the two major scenarios assumed in all the estimation processes, the creation of a new free trade area and a "hard" Brexit where the World Trade Organisation's third-country rules pertain, the median estimates across all studies are –4.7% for free trade areas and –4.85% for the World Trade Organisation option.

As mentioned earlier, the imposition of tariffs was equivalent to a balance of payments shock. This was because, at once, by automatic operation of law, imports to the UK become more expensive. All tariffs are taxes on domestic consumption. Imagine two countries, each producing a single commodity that they trade with one another. A well-known result in international economics first developed by Ozga (1957) argues that the effect of the imposition of tariffs on the balance of trade between the two countries is stronger the more substitutable "home" produced goods are for import goods in the country imposing the tariff. The effect of tariffs on the balance of trade is also stronger the greater the sum of the marginal propensities to import in both countries. The question of the impact of tariffs can be estimated by computing trade elasticities. Lawless and Morgenroth (2019) examined detailed trade flows between the UK and all other EU member states. They matched over 5,200 UK products to the relevant World Trade Organisation tariff applicable to external EU trade. They found significantly different impacts across countries. Reductions in trade to the UK fall by between 5% (Finland) and 43% (Bulgaria), taking into account the new tariffs and the elasticity of the trade response to this price increase.

Both Ireland and the UK are large importers of each other's goods and services. The UK trade surplus with Ireland was the UK's second largest trade surplus in 2018. Ireland was one of four EU countries the UK had a trade surplus with in 2018.[2] Overall, Ireland was the UK's fifth largest export market and ninth largest source of imports in 2018. The bulk of the cost of doing business across borders comes from non-tariff barriers. Examples of non-tariff barriers include border checks, custom controls and compliance with different product standards and regulations. Unlike tariffs, these barriers cannot be removed unilaterally because they require trade partners to agree on a set of rules and regulations which they can both accept. The immediate implication of a non-tariff barrier was the imposition of a hard border between Northern Ireland and the Republic. The security and political implications of such an imposition are studied in Durant and Stojanovic (2018). No outcome in these studies was modelled as positive for either Northern Ireland or the Republic.

Brexit is a sectoral shock, in that the costs of even a "soft" Brexit will be borne by a subset of key sectors with high employment intensities, like farming, agri-food, manufacturing and transport. For example, Ireland is particularly reliant on trade with the UK in agriculture, for exports and in manufacturing goods, for imports. Byrne and Rice (2018) estimated the

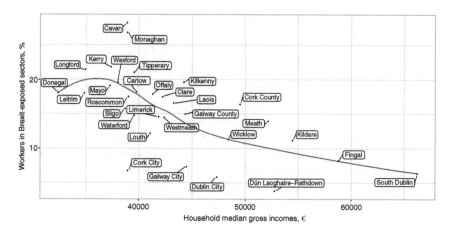

Figure 11.3 Household incomes and employment in Brexit-exposed sectors by county (Ireland)
Source: IBEC.

effects on the potential loss of trade between the two nations, just from the imposition of non-tariff barriers to trade. They estimate a 9.6% decline in trade flows between the UK and Ireland, simply from an increase in border waiting times. This equates in their model to a 1.4% decline in total Irish exports and a 3.1% decline in total Irish imports. At a sectoral level, they found fresh foods, raw materials like metals, some intermediate inputs into firms' supply chains, and bulky goods were particularly exposed to delays.

The regional differences can be understood as a shock to different households with different income levels. Figure 11.3 shows the percentage of workers in Brexit-exposed sectors relative to the median gross household income by county. The relationship was fit using a Loess method.[3] Counties near the border between Ireland and Northern Ireland like Cavan and Monaghan, which are also lower down on the income rank, are very exposed to Brexit and lack the larger incomes of other counties. Counties like Louth and South Dublin are less exposed, with South Dublin enjoying both the largest gross median household income and one of the lowest employment exposures to Brexit.

Reflecting the sectoral, and primarily rural, nature of the Brexit shock, the cities have a lower risk of large-scale employment shocks, while the largely rural areas, such as Kerry, Tipperary and Kilkenny, will be disproportionately affected. Compare, for example, Cork County to Cork City, to see this difference clearly.

At a regional level, it is clear a "hard" Brexit can also be understood as a regional shock for Northern Ireland. In 2018, 36% of Northern Ireland's goods exports were to the Republic of Ireland (compared to 6% for the UK as a whole), while 28% of Northern Ireland's goods imports were from the Republic of Ireland (compared to 3% for the UK as a whole). In 2018, Northern Ireland accounted for 15.2% of all UK goods exports to Ireland and 16.1% of all UK goods imported from Ireland. InterTrade Ireland, a cross-border initiative, found that if the UK becomes a third country reliant on WTO rules, with the requisite checks at the border, cross-border trade between Northern Ireland and the Republic could fall by between 9% and 17%. This shock would be equivalent to the 2007–2008 crisis for many sectors in Northern Ireland, especially. The nature of each type of shock – regional, regulatory, or balance of payments – is conditional on the character of the economies experiencing those shocks. It is to this set of characteristics that we now turn.

Migration

This chapter began by discussing Brexit in terms of a balance of payments shock, a regional and sectoral shock. Brexit is also a labour market and migration shock. Irish nationals comprise the largest foreign born group in the UK across a sample of EU member states when measured as a percentage of home country population, with almost 400,000 people born in Ireland residing in the UK.

The two economies function as a single labour market. A quasi-equilibrium relationship exists between wages and unemployment rates between Ireland and the UK. If wages grow in the UK relative to Ireland, or the rate of unemployment in the UK falls relative to Ireland, this results in increased net migration flows. Studies have shown that a deteriorating performance of the UK economy can put upwards pressure on unemployment rates in Ireland and downwards pressure on wages (Barrett et al. 2015). The labour market issues have been largely resolved, as all parties agreed Irish and UK workers could be treated reciprocally under any Brexit scenario. The same terms have not been applied to other EU workers.

Ireland is a country with a long history of both inwards and outwards migration. Barrett et al. (2015) highlighted the jointly determined migration and labour market equilibria between both countries. The Irish experience is often caricatured as mass outwards migration since the 1840s. While net migration has been outwards in several periods, in fact the modern record on migration into Ireland has been more nuanced. To illustrate the complexity of the situation, Figure 11.4 shows the evolution of inwards migration and outwards migration to Ireland in thousands since the late 1980s. The bars show inwards and outwards migration (expressed as a negative figure for illustrative purposes) each year.

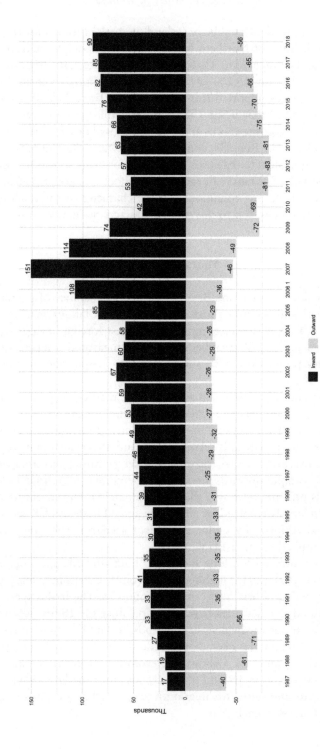

Figure 11.4 Inwards and outwards migration from Ireland, 1987–2018, thousands of persons
Source: Central Statistics Office.

We can use Figure 11.4 to say a few things. First, inwards and outwards migration are persistent features of the Irish economic and social experience. Ireland's size means that regardless of Ireland's position in the business cycle in a given year, people will choose to leave and people will choose to come. The size and openness of Ireland as a small island is the often unspoken context. Outwards migration is a benefit and a cost of being so small. The Brexit dimension to the migration issue is how it alters the benefits and costs. Migration is a benefit because Ireland needs people to travel, to increase their skills, and to come back and enrich it with their diverse experiences, not to mention their accumulated capital.

Outwards migration is a cost because many who leave do not return, especially after the 2007–2008 crisis. As Gilmartin (2018) writes, places and social relationships themselves change because people leave, implying the social effects, especially on extended families, are almost entirely negative from the perspective of those left behind on the island.

There are benefits and costs to inwards migration as well. Inwards migration brings labour when it is needed to help the economy grow. In this discussion, I am separating out economic migrants from student migrations and of course from migrants who apply for international protection and refugee status. Economic migrants make up the bulk of the numbers we are looking at here. I am quite hesitant to define these people just in terms of the supply of labour they afford us, because most migration is actually family migration in practice, either to, or with family, but 'economic migrant' is a recognised category, so I will stick with it.

It is obvious from Figure 11.4 that the Irish economy's growth during the period from about 1994 to 2007 was helped by inwards migration. The remarkable recovery we experienced from 2014 to today has also been helped by net inwards migration. The costs to inwards migration are typically in terms of integration, and these are mostly born by the inward migrants themselves. For example, there is no state-level national English training policy. A migrant arriving here without English must either pay to learn or learn in an unstructured way. The Government's Office for the Promotion of Migrant Integration does not have a programme to help integrate migrants. They bear that cost themselves.

Figure 11.5 breaks down the estimates of where people are coming from. Again, the story is nuanced. Many inwards migrants are Irish – about 30,000 per year or so. Some inwards migrants are from the UK, typically 5,000 to 6,000. Some are from the EU15, the 'old school' EU members, typically 8,000 to 10,000. Some are from the EU13, the newer EU members such as Poland, Lithuania and Slovenia. The non-EU or "rest of the world" component has grown markedly since 2008, when it was roughly 18,000. Today it is around 30,000. As a proportion of overall

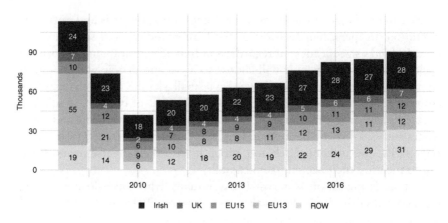

Figure 11.5 Estimated inwards migration to Ireland, 2008–2018, thousands of persons
Source: Central Statistics Office.

inwards migrants, non-EU migrants make up around 34% of the total. In order of size, the top ten registered nationalities from non-EU countries are Brazil, India, China, the United States, Pakistan, Nigeria, Philippines, Malaysia, Canada and South Africa. The recurring themes of size, openness and connectedness are shown clearly in Figure 11.5, as is a recognition that UK citizens are part of the labour market experience of the Irish economy, and vice versa.

Energy

The island of Ireland has had a single energy market since November 2017. This single energy market has improved the security of Ireland's energy supply as well as facilitating higher rates of renewable energy penetration. A large proportion of Ireland's energy needs are met through imports, some 66% in 2017. Electricity generated in Ireland has increased from 12% of the total primary energy supply in 2015 to 34% in 2016. If supply were interrupted due to Brexit, or to a mechanical fault at either the Moyle gas interconnector or the East–West interconnection, Ireland could probably cope. But coping and thriving are very different things. They are almost opposites. In a Brexit scenario where the all-island energy generation system is disrupted, the North would suffer greatly.

This is because at a given moment, and in any electricity system, supply and demand must always be equal. In an isolated system, this implies electricity generation must always be sufficient to meet any demand.

Connecting Northern Ireland and the Republic through the single energy market made it far easier to meet the demands of each region. As in the long-run living standards discussion earlier, initially there was a surplus of power generation in the North. This helped meet shortages in the South, but with the building of ever more data centres and a growing population, the North found its position reversed by 2020. As a result, it is now imperative for security of supply in the North that a second North–South interconnector be built to allow surplus power in the Republic to be transferred to the North. This large-scale capital project is exactly the kind of project that would have been imperilled by a hard Brexit, which breaks, via the automatic operation of law, the regulatory alignment between the two territories necessary to continue operating as a single market.

The key risk to the energy security of the island of Ireland posed by Brexit is the reduction in capital spending by both the Republic and the UK on interconnection. Curtin (2018) estimated that leaving the internal energy market would cost the UK economy as much as £500 million a year by the early 2020s as a result of planned infrastructure investments as well as increased costs of financing. The result of a hard Brexit would have been higher prices paid by consumers in both Ireland and the UK, potential distribution disruption, and a failure to treat a single geographic area in a manner that would be the most efficient from both engineering and investment perspectives.

Conclusion

Brexit was a sectoral shock, a migration shock and a balance of payments shock. The 2016 Brexit referendum result altered expectations enough to depress real investment in the UK economy before the eventual legal settlement took place. It is appropriate to consider the island of Ireland as having three economies with different productivity levels, different income profiles and different sectoral strengths. The Republic contains two distinct economies: one dominated by foreign-owned multinationals, the other by domestic-orientated firms and households. The third economy, that of Northern Ireland, has lagged both of the Republic's in terms of productivity and growth in living standards for more than 30 years.

In the Republic, the trade shock has been both sectoral and regional, with rural and border areas more intensely hit than urban, service-based areas. The migration shock has been mitigated by a bilateral agreement to continue the provisions of a CTA which has existed for centuries in practice, and for seven decades in law.

For all their complexity, economies are remarkably resilient when considered through a decadal lens. Brexit is a structural shock, but sectors on the islands of Great Britain and Ireland are adjusting. The more profound shock has been a diplomatic reordering within the EU. Deprived of its natural ally, Ireland has had to push outwards towards Europe and develop new diplomatic allies. The success of this diplomatic reordering has yet to be gauged.

Notes

I thank Gerard Brady of IBEC for generously providing the data underlying Figure 11.2. I thank the editors for their constructive comments which have improved the chapter. The usual disclaimer applies.

1   Ireland formally became a Republic on 18 April 1949. It was a dominion between 1922 and 1948. I retain the "Republic" nomenclature in the text for expositional simplicity and comparability.
2   The other three countries were Sweden, Malta and Luxembourg.
3   The 'Loess' (Locally Weighted Least Squares Regression) regression is a polynomial non-parametric method where least squares regression was performed in localised subsets. This makes it a suitable candidate for smoothing any numerical vector. Standard errors are not shown.

References

Barrett, A., A. Bergin, J. FitzGerald, D. Lambert, D. McCoy, E. Morgenroth & Z. Studnicka (2015) *Scoping the possible economic implications of Brexit on Ireland*. Dublin: Economic and Social Research Institute.

Barry, F. (2007) 'Foreign direct investment and institutional co-evolution in Ireland'. *Scandinavian Economic History Review* 55(3): 262–288.

Bergin, A., A. Garcia-Rodriguez, E. Morgenroth & D. Smith (2017) 'Modelling the medium-to long-term potential macroeconomic impact of Brexit on Ireland'. *The Economic and Social Review* 48(3): 305–316.

Born, B., G.J. Müller, M. Schularick & P. Sedláček (2019) 'The costs of economic nationalism: evidence from the Brexit experiment'. *The Economic Journal* 129(623): 2722–2744.

Byrne, S. & J. Rice (2018) *Non-tariff barriers and goods trade: a Brexit impact analysis (No. 6/RT/18)*. (Dublin: Central Bank of Ireland.

Chen, W., B. Los, P. McCann, R. Ortega-Argilés, M. Thissen & F. van Oort (2018) 'The continental divide? Economic exposure to Brexit in regions and countries on both sides of The Channel'. *Papers in Regional Science* 97(1): 25–54.

Curtin, J. (2018) 'Brexit and electricity cooperation between Northern Ireland and Ireland'. *IIEA Brexit Report Series*. Available at: www.iiea.com/publication/brexit-and-electricity-cooperation-between-northern-ireland-and-ireland/ [accessed 1 June 2021].

Dhingra, S., H. Huang, G. Ottaviano, J.P. Pessoa, T. Sampson & J. Van Reenen (2017) 'The costs and benefits of leaving the EU: trade effects'. *CEP Discussion Paper* No. 1473, April.

Durrant, T. & A. Stojanovic (2018) 'The Irish border after Brexit'. *IfG Insight*. London: Institute for Government.

Ebell, M., I. Hurst & J. Warren (2016) 'Modelling the long-run economic impact of leaving the European Union'. *Economic Modelling* 59: 196–209.

Gilmartin, M. (2015) *Ireland and migration in the twenty-first century*. Manchester: Manchester University Press.

Gudgin, G., K. Coutts, N. Gibson & J. Buchanan (2018) 'The macro-economic impact of Brexit: using the CBR macro-economic model of the UK economy (UKMOD)'. *Journal of Self-Governance and Management Economics* 6(2): 7–49.

Hantzsche, A., A. Kara & G. Young (2019) 'The economic effects of the UK government's proposed Brexit deal'. *World Economy* 42(1): 5–20.

Lawless, M. & E.L. Morgenroth (2019) 'The product and sector level impact of a hard Brexit across the EU'. *Contemporary Social Science* 14(2): 1–19.

Ozga, S.A. (1957) 'Tariffs and the balance of payments'. *The Quarterly Journal of Economics* 71(4): 630.

Sokol, M. (2007) 'Space of flows, uneven regional development, and the geography of financial services in Ireland'. *Growth and Change* 38(2): 224–259.

12

Northern Ireland and Brexit: a unique challenge in unique circumstances

David Phinnemore and Lisa Whitten

Introduction

Northern Ireland was largely ignored during the 2016 Brexit referendum. It became, however, the main stumbling block to the conclusion of the withdrawal negotiations and almost jeopardised an orderly UK withdrawal from the EU. The central issue was how to avoid a physical hardening of the border on the island of Ireland once the UK left the EU's customs union and its internal markets. There was also the question of how to ensure Brexit did not compromise implementation of the 1998 Agreement and especially North–South cooperation on the island. The solution was to develop differentiated post-Brexit arrangements for Northern Ireland, a tortuous process that culminated in the Protocol on Ireland/Northern Ireland annexed to the Withdrawal Agreement.

This chapter explores key themes that shaped Brexit debates in and on Northern Ireland. It considers the positions taken by political parties in Northern Ireland in and following the 2016 referendum before considering UK and EU responses to the challenges that Brexit posed for the land border and the 1998 Agreement and the role these played in the withdrawal negotiations. The chapter proceeds with an analysis of the Protocol and discusses its implications for Northern Ireland. A final section assesses the impact on the politics and future of Northern Ireland of the Brexit process.

The 2016 referendum and its aftermath

Northern Ireland's political parties have always differed on European integration with views in advance of the 2016 referendum ranging from the vehemently pro-Leave Traditional Unionist Voice (TUV) through the 'considered' pro-Leave stance of the DUP (Foster 2016a), the respectively qualified and muted pro-Remain of the Ulster Unionist Party (UUP) and Sinn Féin, to the unashamedly pro-Remain stances of the Social Democratic and Labour Party (SDLP), Alliance and the Green Party. For the TUV, the referendum provided an opportunity to free the UK from the 'tentacles of Brussels bureaucracy and diktats' (TUV 2016: 3). The then DUP leader, Arlene Foster, was less gung-ho, announcing in February 2016 that her party would 'on balance recommend a vote to leave the EU', but recognising that 'DUP members and voters will hold a range of differing personal views' on the issue (Foster, 2016a).[1] Within the UUP, there were concerns about what a Leave vote might mean economically and politically for Northern Ireland; the party leadership eventually concluded that 'on balance Northern Ireland is better remaining in the EU' (UUP 2016a). Beyond unionism, Sinn Féin committed to 'campaigning against Brexit' while remaining 'euro-critical' and insisting it would 'continue to resist the dilution of national sovereignty' and campaign for 'greater democratisation' of the EU (Sinn Féin 2016: 4, 17–18). Far less equivocal pro-Remain positions were taken by Alliance, the SDLP and the Green Party. Alliance declared itself 'whole-heartedly pro-European' (Alliance 2016), while the equally enthusiastic SDLP declared it would 'lead the fight [in] convincing Northern Ireland to stay IN Europe' (SDLP 2016: 9).

The EU referendum campaign in Northern Ireland was, however, generally lacklustre. Political energies had been focused on the fiercely contested Assembly election on 5 May 2016 and its aftermath: Alliance, the SDLP and the UUP abandoning the power-sharing executive and entering 'opposition'; and the DUP and Sinn Féin seeking to agree a Programme for Government. Hence, although Remain-supporting parties sought in the referendum campaign to highlight the unique political, economic and constitutional exposure of Northern Ireland to the UK leaving the EU, their endeavours came late in the day and received limited attention. The same was true of the interventions of others. Former UK Prime Ministers, John Major and Tony Blair, warned that a Leave vote would 'jeopardise the unity' of the UK and risk 'destabilising [Northern Ireland's] complicated and multi-layered constitutional settlement' (BBC 2016a). Former US President, Bill Clinton, expressed similar concerns, stating that Northern Ireland 'will really get whacked' if the UK left the EU (*Daily Telegraph* 2016). George Osborne, the then Chancellor of the Exchequer, also warned that there 'would have to be a hardening of the border' in the event of a Leave vote (BBC 2016b).

These and other pro-Remain positions were dismissed by Leave supporters, notably the Secretary of State for Northern Ireland, Theresa Villiers, and her predecessor, Owen Patterson, as well as the DUP. Not that these issues received much attention at all beyond Northern Ireland. Indeed, subsequent accounts from insiders and close observers of the various Leave and Remain campaigns describe Northern Ireland as an 'afterthought' – assuming it was considered at all – by the two camps (Oliver 2016; O'Toole 2016). The region of the UK most vulnerable to the impact of a UK withdrawal from the EU received the least attention.

That a majority of voters in Northern Ireland voted Remain was not unexpected, but the size of the vote at 56% was lower than anticipated. The overall victory for Leave surprised many and tensions between the DUP and Sinn Féin were immediately apparent. For Deputy First Minister and Sinn Féin leader, Martin McGuinness, there was now a 'democratic imperative for a border poll' on Northern Ireland's constitutional future to avoid 'the north [being] dragged out on the tails of a vote in England'. Foster described the call as 'opportunistic' and the referendum outcome as a 'good result' with the UK backing 'hope ... aspiration' and 'future potential' (*Belfast Telegraph* 2016).

Despite differences, a fragile Executive consensus did emerge. In late June 2016, Foster declared that she and McGuinness were 'agreed and determined that our specific circumstances in Northern Ireland must be accounted for in any new arrangements that are developed ... we [will] work together to do what is right for Northern Ireland' (Foster 2016b). There then followed on 16 August 2016 a joint letter to the new UK Prime Minister, Theresa May, that outlined shared positions and priorities (The Executive Office 2016). Foster and McGuinness acknowledged the 'difficult issues relating to the border throughout our history and the peace process' and the multifaceted nature of Northern Ireland's vulnerability to Brexit due to its history, geography and economic structure. They set out several Northern Ireland-specific priorities, notably no impediment to free movement of goods, people or services across the land border.

May responded by pledging to account for the 'specific interests of the people of Northern Ireland' during the withdrawal process (UK Government 2016). However, her language was noticeably less robust in characterising the nature of Northern Ireland's vulnerability. She made no commitment to policy, only process and 'full engagement' with the Northern Ireland Executive, the Joint Ministerial Committee, the Irish government and the EU to achieve the 'wish' of all involved that 'free movement of people and goods across the island of Ireland' would continue (UK Government 2016). She also repeated an earlier assertion that 'no one wants to see a return to the borders of the past' and declared 'the future of the border with Ireland is of the *highest priority* for Northern Ireland, and indeed is an *important priority* for the UK as a whole' (UK Government 2016). Little did May realise how difficult – and ultimately fatally damaging for her Prime Ministership – addressing this priority would be.

The August 2016 letter provided the only articulation of an official Northern Ireland position on Brexit. Although it set out 'initial thoughts', there was no follow-up owing to differences over how to address Northern Ireland's unique position. These were apparent in the debate on whether there should be some form of Brexit 'special status' for Northern Ireland. Sinn Féin and the SDLP advocated for 'Special Status within the EU' (SDLP 2017; Sinn Féin 2017); Alliance (2016) and the UUP (2016b), to differing degrees, were open to some form of differentiated treatment. The DUP, increasingly fearful of the consequences for 'the union', initially baulked and then, with increasing vehemence, opposed any notion that Northern Ireland might be treated differently from the rest of the UK.[2] Ultimately, these differences mattered little. In January 2017, following unheeded calls for Foster's resignation for her part in the Renewable Heat Incentive scandal,[3] McGuinness resigned and the Executive collapsed. Fresh elections to the Assembly were held on 2 March 2017, but no new Executive emerged. For the duration of the withdrawal negotiations and until January 2020 Northern Ireland was without a sitting Assembly and a functioning Executive. There was no official Northern Ireland voice in the withdrawal negotiations.

Addressing Northern Ireland's unique circumstances

Calls for some form of differentiated treatment for Northern Ireland were not enthusiastically received by the UK government. For May, a key priority was ensuring that the referendum result – which saw a 62% majority for Remain in Scotland – did not undermine the Union. With the question of independence still not settled, despite the 55% vote against in the 2014 referendum, calls from the Scottish government for their own differentiated withdrawal from the EU had to be resisted. Despite the spectre of Scotland looming large, the UK government could not ignore the unique situation of Northern Ireland. May stressed in her letter triggering Article 50 that the UK and the EU had 'an important responsibility to make sure that nothing is done to jeopardise the peace process in Northern Ireland, and to continue to uphold the Belfast Agreement' (UK Government 2017a). She also noted that the UK wanted 'to avoid a return to a hard border' on the island of Ireland. With the UK committed to leaving the EU customs union and internal market, it was unclear how this could be achieved.

The EU, however, offered a way forward. In its guidelines for the withdrawal negotiations, the European Council in April 2017 noted that 'in view of the unique circumstances on the island of Ireland, flexible and imaginative solutions will be required, including with the aim of avoiding a hard border, while respecting the integrity of the Union legal order' (European Council 2017: 11). The door was open to suggestions from the UK for differentiated arrangements for Northern Ireland. The scope for differentiation, however, was narrowed down considerably by the result of the hastily called UK general election on 8 June. May's Conservative government lost its parliamentary majority and opted for a confidence and supply agreement with the DUP's ten MPs who became increasingly vociferous in their opposition to any differentiated treatment of Northern Ireland. As Nigel Dodds, the DUP leader in Westminster, subsequently argued, keeping Northern Ireland 'in lockstep with the rest of the United Kingdom, for us that's the fundamental point' (Conservative Home 2018).

Addressing the unique circumstances on the island of Ireland was deemed a priority issue – at least for the EU – for the withdrawal negotiations when they opened on 19 June 2017. A dedicated "Dialogue on Ireland/Northern Ireland" was launched and progress to a second phase of the withdrawal negotiations made conditional on sufficient progress being made on the Irish dimension. This frustrated the UK government, which preferred to leave arrangements for avoiding a hard border to the negotiations on the future UK–EU relationship. Equally, however, it strengthened the Irish government's position since it had a veto over the move to the second phase. Also causing frustration for the UK was the European Council's insistence that negotiations be conducted exclusively through the EU's appointed negotiator, Michel Barnier. There was no scope for bilateral negotiations with Ireland, and no opportunity, formal or informal, for May to negotiate directly with other heads of government or state.

A further concern for the UK government was the need, despite its reluctance to consider differentiated arrangements, to engage with the EU's offer of 'flexible and imaginative solutions' (see Phinnemore 2017). Indeed, only in August 2017 did the UK government issue a *Position Paper on Northern Ireland and Ireland* (UK Government 2017b). It focused on the need to uphold the 1998 Agreement, maintain the CTA 'and associated rights', avoid a hard border for the movement of goods, and the aim to preserve North–South and East–West cooperation. It was disappointingly light, however, on how to proceed, notably regarding the preservation of North–South cooperation where the only issue really considered in any detail was the future of the all-island single electricity market. Moreover, on the border and customs arrangements, it advocated an untested 'customs partnership arrangement' (UK Government 2017c) regarded by the EU as impractical and a thinly veiled attempt to leverage special arrangements for the UK as a whole and not just Northern Ireland.

Frustrated with the limited UK engagement and noting "insufficient progress" on the Irish dimension, the European Council in October 2017 postponed a decision on moving to the second phase of the withdrawal negotiations. Progress was gradually made, but objections from the DUP over a UK commitment to continued regulatory alignment between Northern Ireland and the EU came close to jeopardising agreement on a key Joint Report on the negotiations.[4] Adjustments and the addition of a paragraph committing the UK government to ensure 'no new regulatory barriers' between Northern Ireland and the rest of the UK unless the NI Executive and Assembly agree (European Commission 2017: 50) eventually allowed the Joint Report to be adopted. Key was paragraph 49. It noted the UK's commitment 'to protecting North–South cooperation and its guarantee of avoiding a hard border' and the agreement that 'any future arrangements must be compatible with these overarching requirements' (European Commission 2017: 49). The UK government's intention was to achieve these objectives through the future EU–UK relationship. However, if this were not possible – a likely prospect given the UK government's red lines – the UK would propose 'specific solutions to address the unique circumstances of the island of Ireland' (European Commission 2017: 49). For the EU, the problem was that there was scant evidence that the UK had any such 'specific solutions' to propose, or at least not ones acceptable to the EU. So, it was agreed that 'in the absence of agreed solutions, the United Kingdom will maintain full alignment with those rules of the Internal Market and the Customs Union which, now or in the future, support North–South cooperation, the all-island economy and the protection of the 1998 Agreement' (European Commission 2017: 49). The principle of a "backstop" had been agreed.

In the absence of any 'specific solutions' from the UK government, EU negotiators produced a Protocol on Ireland/Northern Ireland as part of a first draft of the Withdrawal Agreement (European Commission 2018a). It proposed "backstop" arrangements that would see Northern Ireland remain part of the EU customs territory and in a "common regulatory area" with the EU so that the free movement of goods across the border could be assured. The UK government response was swift and firm. May declared that the proposed arrangements would 'undermine the UK common market and threaten the constitutional integrity of the UK by creating a customs and regulatory border down the Irish Sea, and no UK prime minster could ever agree to it' (BBC 2018). The principle of a backstop was not, however, being rejected. Indeed, as the colour-coding on a revised draft Protocol a month later indicated, there was agreement, at least in principle, on the lengthy preamble and provisions on the rights of individuals under the 1998 Agreement, the CTA, areas of North–South cooperation, state aid, the single electricity market, a specialised committee to oversee the implementation of the Protocol, safeguards, and arrangements for the replacement of the Protocol 'in whole or in part' by subsequent UK–EU agreements (European Commission 2018b). No agreement was signalled on the common regulatory area, the customs territory question, the related issues of agriculture, fisheries and the environment, and supervision and enforcement. Further negotiations would be necessary.

It took eight months to reach agreement (Official Journal 2019). Key to the deal was EU acceptance that the backstop would include a UK-wide customs union with the EU thereby reducing – but not eliminating – the need for increased checks and controls on the movement of goods between the rest of the UK and Northern Ireland. The problem was, however, that the May government could not secure parliamentary approval for what had been agreed. At issue was less the principle of differentiated arrangements for Northern Ireland, but more the fact that remaining in a customs union with the EU would impose serious constraints on the UK pursuing an independent trade policy, at least in terms of goods. For the most pro-Brexit members of May's government and party, the backstop as such would have to go. For the DUP too, the fact that the Protocol included the potential for differentiated treatment of Northern Ireland meant that it could not be supported. With successive ratification attempts failing and the UK having to seek extensions to the Article 50 process, thus delaying withdrawal, May's position as Prime Minister became untenable. She was replaced in July 2019 by Boris Johnson who swiftly demanded that the EU renegotiate the Withdrawal Agreement and "ditch" the backstop (*Guardian* 2019).

Technically, Johnson succeeded. The "backstop" and its UK-wide customs union with the EU were abandoned. The remainder of the Protocol with its Northern Ireland-specific arrangements was, however, retained. Moreover, rather than only applying if the post-transition UK–EU relationship failed to address the "unique circumstances" on the island of Ireland and in so doing inter alia avoid a physical hardening of the border, the Protocol's arrangements for Northern Ireland would automatically enter into force on 1 January 2021. As such, the revised Protocol, formally adopted with the signing of the Withdrawal Agreement on 23 January 2020, actually entailed greater differentiated treatment of Northern Ireland than the backstop version and importantly involved a much greater increase in formalities, checks and controls on the movement of goods between the rest of the UK and Northern Ireland. Indeed, depending on the nature and scope of the UK–EU relationship, tariffs could also be applicable. Despite this, the Withdrawal Agreement was approved by the UK Parliament, although not one MP representing a Northern Ireland political party voted in favour.[5]

The Protocol on Ireland/Northern Ireland

In terms of its effects, the Protocol on Ireland/Northern Ireland annexed to the UK–EU Withdrawal Agreement that entered into force with the UK's departure from the EU on 31 January 2020 (Official Journal 2020) differs only marginally from the initial drafts discussed in February 2018

(European Commission 2018a, 2018b).[6] The text is not the same, however, having been substantially rewritten during 2018–2019 in an attempt to de-dramatise the content and assuage – unsuccessfully – unionist concerns. References to a "common regulatory area" were removed, for example, and language respecting Northern Ireland's constitutional status under the 1998 Agreement and 'the essential State functions and territorial integrity' of the UK (Article 1) were added. There were two major substantive differences, however: the backstop mechanism was removed and a 'democratic consent' provision was introduced. The full Protocol's entry into force was therefore no longer conditional on the substance of the post-transition UK–EU relationship, but automatic from 1 January 2021.[7] However, from 2024, and potentially every four years thereafter, members of the NI Assembly (MLAs) will have an opportunity to decide whether core elements of the Protocol concerning customs and regulatory alignment should be abandoned.

The essential purpose of the Protocol is to 'set out arrangements necessary to address the unique circumstances on the island of Ireland, to maintain the necessary conditions for continued North–South cooperation, to avoid a hard border and to protect the 1998 Agreement in all its dimensions' (Article 1(3)). The primary focus is how to avoid a physical hardening of the border. This is achieved by allowing for the maintenance of the free movement of goods on the island of Ireland by keeping Northern Ireland in effect in the EU customs territory and, through continued regulatory alignment, in the EU internal market for goods. There is also alignment with EU VAT, excise, sanitary and phytosanitary, and state aid rules. Although Northern Ireland remains formally part of the UK customs union and its internal market – and the UK government is committed to the 'unfettered' access of goods from Northern Ireland into the rest of the UK – the effect of the Protocol is to require increased customs and regulatory formalities, checks and controls, and potentially tariffs on the movement of goods from the rest of the UK into Northern Ireland. How extensive these will be will depend on the nature and substance of the post-transition UK–EU relationship: the closer the relationship is in terms of tariff-free trade, customs cooperation and regulatory alignment, the less differentiation between Northern Ireland and the rest of the UK.

Beyond the movement of goods, the Protocol sees the UK, in line with obligations under the 1998 Agreement, committing to 'no diminution of rights, safeguards or equality of opportunity' (Article 2) as a resulting of leaving the EU. It also recognises the CTA and confirms that the UK and Ireland 'may continue to make arrangements between themselves relating to the movement of persons between their territories' (Article 3). Provision is made for the continued operation of the single electricity market on the island of Ireland as well as the regulatory alignment necessary to maintain North–South cooperation in areas including the environment, energy,

telecommunication, justice and security.[8] The Protocol also sets out dedicated governance arrangements including responsibilities around monitoring
and enforcement as well as decision-making and information exchange. Two
Protocol-specific bodies were established: a Specialised Committee to oversee
its implementation and application and a Joint Consultative Working Group
for the 'exchange of information and mutual consultation'. Both involve representation from the UK and the EU. The Specialised Committee can also
receive views from the North–South Ministerial Council, the 1998 Agreement's North–South implementation bodies, the Northern Ireland Human
Rights Commission, the Equality Commission for Northern Ireland, and the
Joint Committee of representatives of the Human Rights Commissions of
Northern Ireland and Ireland. Overall responsibility for the Protocol's implementation and for decision-making lies with the UK–EU Joint Committee.

Dedicated institutional arrangements therefore provide opportunities for
the interests of Northern Ireland to be represented in the implementation of
the Protocol. This is necessary given the Protocol's impact on Northern Ireland. Moreover, regulatory alignment under the Protocol is dynamic:
changes to the EU customs code and future EU acts amending or replacing
other EU acts covered by the Protocol will automatically apply in Northern
Ireland. Additions require the agreement of the Joint Committee. Also, there
is the matter of the Court of Justice in Luxembourg having jurisdiction over
the application of EU law in Northern Ireland. All this, as well as the perceived permanency of the original "backstop" version of the Protocol,
proved highly controversial, hence the insertion of the democratic consent
provisions and the opportunity for MLAs to vote for the disapplication en
bloc of the Protocol's provisions on customs, regulatory alignment, state aid,
VAT, excise and the single electricity market. The effect, unless alternative
arrangements are agreed, would be a hardening of the land border.

Assessing the Protocol

The Protocol places Northern Ireland in a unique relationship with the EU
and one few envisaged following the 2016 referendum. It exists because of
the shared UK–EU commitment to the peace process in Northern Ireland, to
protecting the 1998 Agreement and to avoiding a physical hardening of the
border on the island. For its supporters, the Protocol delivers. The unique
circumstances on the island of Ireland are addressed, the necessary conditions
for continued North–South cooperation are maintained, a hard border is
avoided and the 1998 Agreement is protected in all its dimensions. However,
these objectives are achieved through essentially a minimalist arrangement
focused on the movement of goods. There is no provision, for example, for

the free movement of services or of people, although Irish citizens can move freely under the CTA. Any claims that the objective of supporting the 'all-island economy' – originally included in the preamble to the "backstop" version of the Protocol but then quietly dropped to accommodate DUP objections – is met are somewhat tenuous. Other criticisms focus on the extent to which the Protocol imposes additional checks and controls on the movement of goods between the rest of the UK and Northern Ireland (and to a lesser extent in the other direction). This not only imposes additional burdens on business, it adds to unionist concerns that the Protocol undermines the integrity of the UK 'internal market'. Indeed, Foster has described the effects of the Protocol as tantamount to the 'annexation' of Northern Ireland (RTÉ 2018). For many unionists, Johnson's revised Protocol was an act of 'betrayal' (BBC 2019).

Beyond unionism, however, the "backstop" version of the Protocol was broadly welcomed by Northern Ireland's pro-Remain political parties, although their clear preference was for the UK to remain in the EU, a position supported by a majority of the electorate and reflected in the result of the 2019 European Parliament election which saw Alliance take the third Northern Ireland seat from the UUP. There has been far less enthusiasm among political parties as well as business organisations and some civil society groups, however, for the revised Protocol, primarily because of the increased friction it introduces for trade between Northern Ireland and the rest of the UK. Concerns about what this will mean for business were only heightened by the Johnson government's reluctance during 2000 to confront the realities of the Protocol, provide certainty as to what it would involve, or engage honestly in preparation for its effective implementation from 1 January 2021.

Brexit and the politics of Northern Ireland

Brexit's most immediate challenge for Northern Ireland has been political. Almost as soon as the result of the 2016 referendum was announced, the border returned to the political centre stage and for a period the creative ambiguity of the 1998 Agreement that has allowed diverging constitutional visions and understandings of the border to coexist was almost shattered. Political discourse in and on Northern Ireland became increasingly imbued with the language of "the Union", "the border" and the "constitutional integrity" of the UK as a state, in ways that only deepened divisions between unionists and nationalists. And, while disagreements over Brexit cannot be directly blamed for the three-year hiatus between 2017 and 2020 in devolved government, at the very least they exacerbated existing tensions and served as a disincentive to a return to power-sharing government.

The negotiation of the Protocol and the UK's orderly exit from the EU on 31 January 2020 de-escalated debates about the border, but only to see them replaced by mounting concerns, particularly for unionists, over the border down the Irish Sea. The reality of the Protocol, exacerbated by the "hard" Brexit preferences of the Johnson government, has increased east–west formalities, checks and controls, and a palpable sense of abandonment of unionists by London. Not that debates about 'the border' have gone away. The prospect of MLAs voting every four – possibly eight – years on the future of the Protocol ensures as much. The danger is that each vote becomes a proxy border poll: a vote denying consent is a vote to safeguard Northern Ireland's position in the UK; a vote in favour is a vote for weakening the union.

Political debate in Northern Ireland has therefore been re-constitutionalised by Brexit. The evidence can be found both in party political pronouncements and in public opinion. In 2016, a quarter of voters (26%) believed the UK leaving the EU would make a united Ireland more likely, with 16% indicating they were personally now more in favour of such an outcome. By 2019, the respective figures had risen to 39% and 25% (ARK 2016, 2020). While polling data still does not indicate the level of support for a united Ireland that would allow the Secretary of State for Northern Ireland to call a border poll, Brexit has led to an increased sense that such a poll is an inevitability and that a united Ireland is more likely than it has ever been.

Brexit has undoubtedly disrupted politics in Northern Ireland. The results of elections in 2019 demonstrate as much. Local elections in May saw a surge of support for the pro-Remain Alliance and a corresponding decline in support for unionist and nationalist parties across the board. Alliance also saw significant gains in the European Parliamentary election in June 2019, taking a seat from the UUP. Indeed, with transfers, the Alliance candidate received most votes. In the general election of December 2019, support for the DUP and Sinn Féin dropped by 5.4 and 6.7 percentage points respectively, with the DUP losing two seats. The Alliance and SDLP saw their votes increase by 8.8 and 3.1 percentage points respectively. With the SDLP gaining two seats and Sinn Féin securing seven, Northern Ireland for the first time returned more nationalist than unionist MPs. With Alliance winning a seat, the majority of MPs were opponents of Brexit. For the DUP, there was clearly no reward for having been in a confidence and supply agreement with May and then Johnson. Despite the UK government's dependency on DUP votes in Westminster during the withdrawal negotiations, the result was a set of post-Brexit arrangements for Northern Ireland that many unionists considered a betrayal of the Union.

This is clearly a major concern for unionism. The wilful abandonment by Johnson of the DUP also reflected a general disregard for others' interests in the pursuit of the UK government's interest. Throughout the withdrawal

process, the engagement of the UK government with the devolved administrations, for example, was generally superficial and sporadic. On how to
address the unique circumstances on the island of Ireland, consultation with
interests in Northern Ireland was minimal, a situation not helped by the
absence of a NI Executive. What engagement there was tended to be with
and through the DUP, or when the May government worked with business
interests and others – ultimately unsuccessfully – to secure parliamentary
support for the "backstop" Protocol. Moreover, reliance on the DUP in
Westminster meant that the UK government, particularly with Johnson as
Prime Minister, abandoned any pretence to act impartially in respect of
Northern Ireland. An obvious effect was that the standing of the UK government in Northern Ireland was further undermined. Whether it can redress
the situation is a major challenge for the UK government. How seriously it
takes implementation of the Protocol and how far it genuinely takes Northern Ireland's interests into account will be telling. It cannot afford to ignore
either the Protocol or Northern Ireland. To do so would be to run the risk
of exacerbating the tensions that Brexit has either created or revived.

Conclusion

Withdrawing from the EU would be a demanding process for any state. It
has proved to be extremely fraught and complex for the UK. An important
reason has been Northern Ireland. Its position and constitutional status
posed particular challenges barely acknowledged at the time of the 2016
referendum. While the economic, social and political need to avoid a physical hardening of the border was gradually acknowledged, the UK government's appreciation of the challenges involved and the difficulties of squaring
them with its red lines of leaving the EU customs union and the internal
market took time to develop. The same was true of the solution: differentiated withdrawal arrangements for Northern Ireland; an outcome almost
impossible for an avowedly unionist government to accept, particularly
when dependent on DUP votes in Westminster for its survival.

The effect of Brexit for Northern Ireland is a reinforced uniqueness: constitutionally within the UK and occupying its own particular, more integrated
position with the EU in the wider UK–EU relationship. How stable this new
reality will be remains to be seen. Brexit by its nature is disruptive and has evi-
dently proven to be so for Northern Ireland. Further disruption can be expected
as the realities of Brexit play out and the UK moves away from the EU and the
Protocol is implemented. Economic disruption is certain, particularly with the
inevitable increased friction on east–west trade. All this will have implications
for politics in and the politics of Northern Ireland. Brexit has unsettled

Northern Ireland; tensions have been revived; the constitutional question is once again to the fore. Few were willing in 2016 to consider the implications of a Leave vote for Northern Ireland. More now might wish they had.

Notes

1 Notwithstanding its pro-Leave position, several DUP policies set out in its 2016 Assembly election manifesto were based on an assumption of continued access to EU funding (DUP 2016).
2 In October 2016 the SDLP moved a motion for 'special status' in the Northern Ireland Assembly; this was narrowly defeated, indeed by only one vote. The DUP was not always entirely opposed to some special arrangements for Northern Ireland. Foster accepted that a special status could be a matter for negotiation (*Reuters* 2016), and the DUP manifesto for the 2017 general election asserted the need for 'Northern Ireland-specific solutions' and ones that 'fully reflect' its 'particular circumstances' (DUP 2017: 18–19).
3 The Renewable Heat Incentive scheme was a subsidy to encourage switching to renewable heating methods and away from oil and gas. It was introduced in Northern Ireland in 2012, based on a similar system already in use in England, Scotland and Wales. However, the Northern Irish scheme omitted to include any cost controls, and the subsidy was higher than the actual fuel cost. The scandal came to light in 2016 (BBC 2020).
4 For a detailed account of the near collapse of the negotiations in November–December 2017, see Connelly (2018).
5 Neither did then Secretary of State for Northern Ireland, Julian Smith. Smith was unceremoniously sacked by Johnson three weeks later. However, his successor, Brandon Lewis, and his four predecessors – Karen Bradley, James Brokenshire, Theresa Villiers and Owen Paterson – all voted in favour.
6 For further analysis of the Protocol, see Phinnemore (2020) and Weatherill (2020).
7 Any agreement concluded by the UK and the EU can, however, indicate the parts of the Protocol that it supersedes (Article 13(8)).
8 Fourteen areas are specified: environment, health, agriculture, transport, education and tourism, as well as in the areas of energy, telecommunications, broadcasting, inland fisheries, justice and security, higher education and sport. The non-exhaustive list draws on a joint UK–EU mapping exercise of the impact of Brexit on North–South cooperation (see European Commission 2019).

References

Alliance (2016) *Forward. Faster. Manifesto 2016: An agenda to increase the speed of change in Northern Ireland.* Available at: https://cain.ulster.ac.uk/issues/politics/docs/apni/apni_2016–04–19_nia-man.pdf [accessed 22 May 2019].

ARK (2016) *Northern Ireland Life and Times Survey 2016*. Available at: www.ark. ac.uk/nilt/2016/Political_Attitudes/ [accessed 22 May 2019].

ARK (2020) *Northern Ireland Life and Times Survey 2019*. Available at: www.ark. ac.uk/nilt/2019/Political_Attitudes/ [accessed 15 July 2020].

BBC (2016a) 'Major and Blair say an EU exit could split the UK'. BBC News, 9 June. Available at: www.bbc.co.uk/news/uk-politics-eu-referendum-36486016 [accessed 5 April 2019].

BBC (2016b) 'Reality check: would Brexit mean border controls for NI?' BBC News, 7 June. Available at: www.bbc.co.uk/news/uk-politics-eu-referendum-36462023 [accessed 5 April 2019].

BBC (2018) 'Theresa May rejects EU's draft option for Northern Ireland'. BBC News, 28 February. Available at: www.bbc.co.uk/news/uk-politics-43224785 [accessed 14 July 2020].

BBC (2019) 'NI newspapers: Unionist fury over Brexit "betrayal"'. BBC News, 18 October. Available at: www.bbc.co.uk/news/uk-northern-ireland-50094038 [accessed 14 July 2020].

BBC (2020) 'Renewable Heat Incentive scheme: what is it?' BBC News, 13 March. Available at: www.bbc.com/news/uk-northern-ireland-50521782 [accessed 20 September 2020].

Belfast Telegraph (2016) 'First Minister Arlene Foster: our nation is safe and Northern Ireland will be front and centre of Brexit negotiations'. *Belfast Telegraph*, 24 June. Available at: www.belfasttelegraph.co.uk/news/brexit/first-minister-arlene-foster-our-nation-is-safe-and-northern-ireland-will-be-front-and-centre-of-brexit-negotiations-34829817.html [accessed 24 May 2019].

Connelly, T. (2018) *Brexit and Ireland: the dangers, the opportunities, and the inside story of the Irish response*. London: Penguin (updated edition).

Conservative Home (2018) 'Interview: the Brexit negotiation – Dodds warns against the "annexation" of Northern Ireland'. 25 April. Available at: www.conservative-home.com/highlights/2018/04/interview-the-brexit-negotiation-dodds-warns-against-the-annexation-of-northern-ireland.html [accessed 23 May 2019].

Daily Telegraph (2016) 'Bill Clinton urges Britain to stay in the EU as he warns Northern Ireland will get "whacked" if voters back Brexit'. *Daily Telegraph*, 31 March. Available at: www.telegraph.co.uk/news/2016/03/31/bill-clinton-urges-britain-to-stay-in-the-eu-as-he-warns-norther/ [accessed 12 July 2019].

DUP (2016) *Our plan for Northern Ireland: The DUP manifesto for the 2016 Northern Ireland Assembly Election*. DUP, 4 April. Available at: www.mydup. com/images/uploads/publications/DUP_Manifesto_2016_v8_LR.pdf [accessed 22 May 2019].

DUP (2017) *Standing strong for Northern Ireland*, May. Available at: www.stratagem-ni. com/media/1203/dup-westminster-manifesto-2017.pdf [accessed 14 July 2020].

European Commission (2017) *Joint report from the negotiators of the European Union and the United Kingdom Government on progress during phase 1 of nego- tiations under Article 50 TEU on the United Kingdom's orderly withdrawal from the European Union, TF50 (2017) 19 – Commission to EU 27*. 8 December. Available at: https://ec.europa.eu/commission/sites/beta-political/files/joint_report. pdf [accessed 14 July 2020].

European Commission (2018a) *European Commission draft Withdrawal Agreement on the withdrawal of the United Kingdom of Great Britain and Northern Ireland from the European Union and the European Atomic Energy Community*, TF50

180   *Ireland the European Union*

(2018) 33 – Commission to EU 27. Brussels, 28 February. Available at: https://ec.europa.eu/commission/sites/beta-political/files/draft_withdrawal_agreement.pdf [accessed 19 July 2019].

European Commission (2018b) *European Commission draft Withdrawal Agreement on the withdrawal of the United Kingdom of Great Britain and Northern Ireland from the European Union and the European Atomic Energy Community highlighting the progress made (coloured version) in the negotiation round with the UK of 16–19 March 2018,* TF50 (2018) 35 – Commission to EU 27. Brussels, 19 March. Available at: https://ec.europa.eu/commission/sites/beta-political/files/draft_agreement_coloured.pdf [accessed 19 July 2019].

European Council (2017) *Special meeting of the European Council (Art. 50) (29 April 2017) – Guidelines,* EUCO XT 20004/17. Brussels, 29 April. Available at: www.consilium.europa.eu/media/21763/29-euco-art50-guidelinesen.pdf [accessed 13 July 2019].

Foster, A. (2016a) 'DUP to recommend vote to leave the EU'. News Letter, 20 February. Available at: www.newsletter.co.uk/news/dup-to-recommend-vote-to-leave-the-eu-1-7224491 [accessed 20 May 2019].

Foster, A. (2016b) *First Minister's statement to Assembly following EU referendum result.* 27 June. Available at: www.mydup.com/news/article/first-ministers-statement-to-assembly-following-eu-referendum-result [accessed 18 May 2019].

Guardian (2020) 'Johnson sends "ditch the backstop" message to EU via Brexit adviser'. *Guardian,* 31 July. Available at: www.theguardian.com/politics/2019/jul/31/johnson-sends-ditch-the-backstop-message-to-eu-via-brexit-adviser [accessed 14 July 2020].

Official Journal (2019) *Agreement on the withdrawal of the United Kingdom of Great Britain and Northern Ireland from the European Union and the European Atomic Energy Community,* C 66, 19 February.

Official Journal (2020) *Agreement on the withdrawal of the United Kingdom of Great Britain and Northern Ireland from the European Union and the European Atomic Energy Community,* L 29, 31 January.

Oliver, D. (2016) *Unleashing demons: the inside story of Brexit.* London: Hodder & Stoughton.

O'Toole, M. (2017) 'Ireland an afterthought during Brexit campaign when I was Cameron adviser'. *The Irish Times,* 4 October. Available at: www.irishtimes.com/opinion/ireland-an-afterthought-during-brexit-campaign-when-i-was-cameron-adviser-1.3242732 [accessed 5 April 2019].

Phinnemore, D. (2017) 'The language of "flexible and imaginative" solutions is unique to the Irish dimension of Brexit'. LSE Blog, 6 November. Available at: https://blogs.lse.ac.uk/brexit/2017/11/06/the-language-of-flexible-and-imaginative-solutions-is-unique-to-the-irish-dimension-of-brexit/ [accessed 20 September 2020].

Phinnemore, D. (2020) 'The Protocol on Ireland/Northern Ireland: a flexible and imaginative solution for the unique circumstances on the island of Ireland?', in M. Westlake (ed.) *Outside the EU: options for Britain,* pp. 163–175. Newcastle: Agenda Publishing.

Reuters (2016) 'Northern Ireland leader says special status for province possible after Brexit'. Reuters, 29 October. Available at: www.reuters.com/article/us-britain-eu-nireland/northern-ireland-leader-says-special-status-for-province-possible-after-brexit-idUSKCN12T0JI [accessed 13 July 2019].

RTÉ (2018) 'Foster says no deal better than EU "annexation" of Northern Ireland'. 13 October. Available at: www.rte.ie/news/2018/1013/1002900-brexit/ [accessed 21 July 2019].

SDLP (2016) *Build a better future: SDLP manifesto 2016*. Available at: www.sdlp. ie/site/assets/files/43032/sdlp_manifesto_web-1.pdf [accessed 23 May 2019].

SDLP (2017) *Securing our place in Europe: proposals for a special status for Northern Ireland within the EU*, Belfast, January. Available at: www.newry.ie/attachments/article/4720/eustatus.pdf [accessed 12 July 2019].

Sinn Féin (2016) *Better with Sinn Féin: Sinn Féin manifesto – Assembly Election 2016*. Available at: www.sinnfein.ie/files/2017/2016_Assembly_Manifesto.pdf [accessed 23 May 2019].

Sinn Féin (2017) *Securing designated special status for the North within the EU*, Sinn Féin, Dublin/Belfast, April. Available at: www.sinnfein.ie/files/2017/Brexit-MiniDocs_April2017_Final.pdf [accessed 12 July 2019].

The Executive Office (2016) *Letter to the Prime Minister, The Rt Hon Theresa May MP*, 10 August. Available at: www.executiveoffice-ni.gov.uk/publications/letter-prime-minister-rt-hon-theresa-may-mp [accessed 12 July 2019].

TUV (2016) *Assembly election manifesto 2016: Straight talking – Principled politics*. Available at: https://cain.ulster.ac.uk/issues/politics/docs/tuv/tuv_2016–04–13_nia-man.pdf [accessed 22 May 2019].

UK Government (2016) *Prime Minister's letters to Arlene Foster and Martin McGuiness [sic]*. London, 14 October. Available at: www.executiveoffice-ni.gov.uk/publications/letter-first-minister-arlene-foster-and-deputy-first-minister-martin-mcguinness-prime-minister-rt [accessed 12 July 2019].

UK Government (2017a) *Prime Minister's letter to Donald Tusk triggering Article 50*. London, 29 March. Available at: www.gov.uk/government/publications/prime-ministers-letter-to-donald-tusk-triggering-article-50 [accessed 13 July 2019].

UK Government (2017b) *Northern Ireland and Ireland: Position Paper*. HM Government, London, 16 August. Available at: www.gov.uk/government/publications/northern-ireland-and-ireland-a-position-paper [accessed 13 July 2019].

UK Government (2017c) *Future customs arrangements: a future partnership paper*. HM Government, London, 15 August. Available at: www.gov.uk/government/publications/future-customs-arrangements-a-future-partnership-paper [accessed 13 July 2019].

UUP (2016a) 'Statement from the Ulster Unionist Party'. UUP, 5 March. Available at: http://uup.org/news/4155/21/Statement-from-the-Ulster-Unionist-Party#.XOKeXi-ZPfY [accessed 20 May 2019].

UUP (2016b) *A vision for Northern Ireland outside the EU*, Belfast, September. Available at: https://uup.org/assets/images/a%20vision%20for%20ni%20outside%20the%20eu.pdf [accessed 19 July 2019].

Weatherill, S. (2020) 'The Protocol on Ireland/Northern Ireland: protecting the EU's internal market at the expense of the UK's'. *European Law Journal* 45(2): 222–236.

13

Making it up as we go along: Brexit and constitutional politics in Great Britain and Ireland

Jonathan Evershed

Constitutional integrity

This chapter explores the 'lived detail of the politico-legal landscape' (Scheppele 2004: 395) in Great Britain and Ireland as it was disrupted and reshaped by Brexit. Examining Brexit's impact on the UK's devolution settlement, its territorial constitution and its political-legal and rights frameworks, it suggests that Brexit highlighted the contingency of Britain's constitutional arrangements and the inconsistency of political claims about them. This created profound uncertainties about the UK's commitments vis-à-vis the island of Ireland and undermined its reliability as a co-guarantor of the 1998 Agreement. Ireland was in turn forced to confront and attempt to manage this uncertainty. The chapter examines how Ireland and the EU sought to address the political-legal challenges posed by Brexit and with what successes, limitations and enduring consequences. Brexit may yet have profound constitutional implications for Ireland, not least of which is represented by the potential break-up of the UK and the renewed prospect of Irish unity.

The Brexit process was marked by sustained conflict over how the 'unique circumstances' on the island of Ireland could be addressed, a hard border avoided and the 1998 Agreement protected 'in all its dimensions' as the UK left the EU (European Commission 2018: 105). From the outset, this appeared likely to involve some form of special settlement for Northern Ireland, by which its future relationship with the EU would be different – to a lesser or greater extent – than that of Great Britain's (Hayward 2018). Over the course of the Brexit negotiations, this manifested in multiple (re)draftings of a Protocol on Ireland/Northern Ireland, which was to be included in any Withdrawal Agreement signed by the UK and the EU (see Phinnemore & Whitten, Chapter 12, this volume). The terms of each iteration of this Protocol were fiercely contested by British politicians on both sides of the House of Commons (even after the fact of the Withdrawal Agreement having been signed into law), but particularly by Conservatives (Kenny & Sheldon 2020) and the DUP (Murphy & Evershed 2019). Between late 2017 and 2019, final agreement on a Brexit deal foundered for several months on deeply fractious debate about the Protocol, and this eventually contributed to Theresa May's ousting as Prime Minister. These debates hinged on claims that, by creating new forms of de jure and de facto divergence between Great Britain and Northern Ireland (however minimal), the Ireland/Northern Ireland Protocol was thereby undermining of the "constitutional integrity" of the UK (Murray 2018; Skoutaris 2020).

It is a foundational contention of this chapter that such arguments about the UK's "constitutional integrity" do not have any stable basis in some set of fundamental constitutional principles. As Weale asks, 'what does it [even] mean to say that the UK is acting in accordance with its own constitutional requirements, when those requirements have to be made up as we go along?' (2018: 28). Similarly, Griffith suggests that 'the constitution is no more and no less than what happens' (1979: 19). Claims about what is and is not "constitutional" in the context of Brexit have been profoundly political: 'performative utterances' (Adler-Nissen et al. 2017: 575) that do not simply reflect the constitutional nature of the problems they purport to describe, but actively attempt to (re)construct those problems as ones of constitutional principle rather than of politics per se. These principles are thereby revealed to be fluid, unstable and, in the end, negatable.

Certain features and requirements of the UK's constitution have intervened in Brexit's conflicted politics – often in unexpected or unforeseen ways – but more enduringly these politics have also served to destabilise and reshape the constitution. The conventions of British parliamentary democracy, the nature of the devolution settlement and, in particular, the UK government's commitments under the terms of the 1998 Agreement have all been disrupted or undermined during their encounter with Brexit and its volatile politics. Brexit has thereby highlighted and magnified the deficiencies of the UK's 'improvised' (Weale 2018: 28) and uncodified constitution. In particular, Brexit has revealed that there are no enduring, unequivocal or 'normatively thick' (McHarg 2018: 953) constitutional understandings on which the British political-legal order ultimately rests. Crucially, reflecting a long, conflicted and dynamic history of British–Irish constitutional entanglement (Carty 1996: 158; see also Bogdanor 2019: 198; de Mars et al. 2018: 137–138), as a consequence of both governments' roles as co-guarantors of the 1998 Agreement and given that the Irish border has provided the political backdrop against which Brexit's constitutional drama has been staged, this has had (potentially deeply) destabilising implications for the Irish political-legal order.

Brexit and the British Constitution

It is worth recalling that Brexit was never meant to happen. Prime Minister David Cameron's 2013 pledge to hold an in–out referendum on the future of the UK's EU membership was made in the hope of lancing the Eurosceptic boil which had bedevilled his Conservative Party for two decades, with a minimum of disruption to his wider domestic programme and with no plans for any outcome other than Remain (Evans & Menon 2017: 26–30; Shipman 2016). Little to no consideration was given to the referendum's constitutional ramifications because it was not thought that there would be any. There was not, for example, an effort to determine whether and how the "will of the people" as expressed in an advisory referendum might need to be reconciled to the principle of parliamentary sovereignty. Neither was the question as to what might happen if the four constituent parts of the UK returned different referendum results explored with any rigour. Very little heed was paid in Westminster to the potential ramifications of a Leave result for the UK's obligations under the terms of the 1998 Agreement, and with what consequences for the peace and political processes in Northern Ireland (Murphy 2018a; O'Toole 2017). This reflects what was defined as a generalised paucity of understanding that the conclusion of the peace talks in 1998 represented a 'constitutional moment' (Todd 2017: 57) for the UK, and that the 1998 Agreement is a central pillar of the UK's constitutional order (interview 1).

The folly of holding an "in–out" referendum of which the potential political-legal consequences of a Leave vote were so (deliberately) obscure revealed a great deal of misassumption not only about the proclivities of the British – and, more particularly, the English (see Henderson et al. 2017) – electorate, but also about the inherent stability of the British state and its institutions. Assumptions about a certain unassailable permanence and a presumption of continuity are perhaps the defining features of British constitutional understandings. These assumptions are underpinned by a Whiggish teleology and Burkean notions of tradition and custom which are stubbornly predominant. And crucially, they stem from a very particular and selective perception of the UK's constitutional history, eliding or largely ignoring the many ruptures and radical departures which have defined it.

In the 1990s and 2000s, the UK's territorial constitution underwent a series of transformations. But perhaps paradoxically, these changes were understood within the context of wider assumptions about the uninterruptedness of British constitutional tradition (see Wincott 2018). As noted by one senior Irish official, with a long history of involvement in British–Irish relations:

You know, the Good Friday Agreement, part of it was about devolved government in Northern Ireland. But that went on alongside devolution in Wales and
Scotland. What did the world look like in 2000? It was Labour in government
in London with a huge majority, Labour in government in Scotland with a
huge majority, Labour in government in Wales with a huge majority, and the
SDLP as the second major party, holding the Deputy First Minister's job in
Belfast. So, it was this sort of homogeneous Labour-land. And I think that
there was a sense that this would never end. (interview 2; see also Bogdanor
2019: 246)

By 2016, political change and divergence across the four constituent parts of
the UK had disturbed the 'unusually benign' (Wincott 2018: 23) political
environment which had prevailed during the early years of devolution.
However, and as noted in a report by a House of Lords Select Committee,
subsequent UK governments had nonetheless continued to take the Union's
longevity and stability for granted (House of Lords 2016). That they were
able to do so arguably owed much to the UK's membership of the EU. European legal frameworks took precedence and thereby guaranteed a level of
institutional, political and economic integration across the UK's devolved
jurisdictions and, indeed, between the UK and Ireland. This played no small
part in maintaining the illusion of the UK's overall constitutional "integrity". Indeed, as Bogdanor (2019) has demonstrated, where consistency and
the durability of legal principle had become a feature of the UK's constitutional order during the late twentieth and early twenty-first centuries, this
was in large part a function of the UK law's entanglement with wider European legal frameworks. According to a 2017 report by the House of Lords
European Committee:

> The European Union has been, in effect, part of the glue holding the United
> Kingdom together since 1997. The supremacy of EU law, and the interpreta-
> tion of that law by the Court of Justice of the EU, have in many areas ensured
> consistency of legal and regulatory standards across the UK, including in
> devolved policy areas, such as environment, agriculture and fisheries. In prac-
> tice, the UK internal market has been upheld by the rules of the EU internal
> market. (House of Lords 2017: 12)

In Northern Ireland, joint British–Irish enrolment in common political, legal
and economic frameworks had also been pivotal in advancing the peace
process (Hayward & Murphy 2018; Murphy 2014). What Murphy (2019a:
3–5) has called the 'Europeanisation' of British–Irish relations underpinned
and was fundamental in shaping Northern Ireland's particular devolution
settlement. Prior to 2016, questions about the legitimate scope and limits of
devolution and the restrictions placed on British sovereignty by international frameworks were the subject of what were thought to be largely

benign and accommodating constitutional silences (Foley 2012 [1989]). In the wake of Brexit, these questions have been revealed to be of jarring and immediate significance. And emerging answers to them have not often been encouraging, least of all when viewed from the island of Ireland. Above all, Brexit has revealed that a UK constitutional order stripped of its European legal underpinning is highly unstable: resting ultimately on a weak foundation of contingent and even mutable political-legal principles. This has served to undermine the UK government's dependability as a negotiating partner and the reliability of its role as co-guarantor of the Northern Ireland peace and political processes.

Contingent commitments

The Miller case[1] (re)established the primacy of parliamentary sovereignty as a justiciable constitutional principle. But it also established that it was the only such principle. The Supreme Court ruled that there was no constitutionally protected role for the devolved governments of Wales, Scotland and Northern Ireland in the Brexit process, and that Westminster retained the full legal competence to legislate even in devolved policy areas if it so chose, with or without the consent of the devolved administrations. In Northern Ireland, this judgement represented a stark and jarring reassertion of Westminster's sovereignty, which had come to be seen and exercised in subtler, more ambiguous ways since 1998. That there was no legally enforceable role for the Northern Ireland Assembly in the Brexit process appeared to fly in the face of the ethical and normative imperative, if not the letter, of Northern Ireland's unique constitutional requirements; the need to seek balance between divergent unionist and nationalist demands, interests and aspirations; and particularly the "principle of consent" (Harvey 2016; Murphy 2018b: 31), which holds that change in the constitutional status of Northern Ireland requires precisely the kind of majority support among Northern Irish voters which Brexit so conspicuously lacks. In sum, in its judgment on Miller, the Supreme Court 'adopted a view of the British constitution at odds with what is required to accommodate Northern Ireland's evolving constitutional development, potentially undermining the Good Friday Agreement' (McCrudden & Halberstam 2017: 1–2).

As de Mars et al. (2018) have speculated, the collapse of power-sharing in Northern Ireland in January 2017, in the wake of the Renewable Heat Initiative (RHI) scandal[2] may have suited the UK government's approach to the Brexit process. Had the Assembly been functioning, then the imperative of obtaining consent for Brexit legislation would have been 'undeniable and the nationalist parties would, in all likelihood, have had the votes to frustrate it' (de Mars et al. 2018: 124). The suspension of devolution in Northern Ireland gave the UK government the freedom to treat it as something of a political football, deploying it as leverage in Brexit negotiations – often to the frustration of its European interlocutors – with no need for agreement and no political push-back from Stormont (Boffey 2018; Evershed 2018a). Concurrently, an incremental process of returning powers from Belfast to London, and of passing Brexit legislation in areas of previously devolved competence, went largely unopposed (Emerson 2019).

The confidence and supply agreement signed between the DUP and the Conservatives in 2017 further called into question the probity of the UK's approach to devolution and the peace and political processes in Northern Ireland. Despite the deal's explicit claim to the contrary (Cabinet Office 2017: 2–3), the Conservative government's pact with the DUP undermined the 1998 Agreement-mandated claims to 'rigorous impartiality' and neutrality in respect of the rights, culture, identity and political aspirations of both political "communities" in Northern Ireland (Harvey 2017). The confidence and supply deal facilitated a partisan mirroring of the DUP's rhetoric on the primacy of the 'precious' Union by Theresa May (*Belfast Telegraph* 2018) and saw the UK's "constitutional integrity" come to be understood and represented on the DUP's exclusivist, inconsistent and even contradictory terms (Barry 2018; Evershed 2018b, 2019). As Tannam (2018) has examined, it contributed to critically undermining the intergovernmental cooperation between the UK and Irish governments on which the overall stability of the peace settlement in Northern Ireland rests, including through acting to limit the depth and scope of issues the UK government has deemed apt to be discussed at the reconvened British–Irish Intergovernmental Conference (BIIGC).[3] At the same time, it fostered an invidious and divisive, if ultimately unstable, relationship between the DUP and Brexit hardliners in the Conservative Party, which played a key role in frustrating attempts at securing the UK's orderly withdrawal from the EU.

Brexit has revealed in stark terms the instability of the British constitutional order and the UK government's questionable fidelity to key political-legal commitments as they are outlined in the 1998 Agreement. Crucial features of the constitutional landscape on which the protection of the 1998 Agreement is dependent are revealed to rely, ultimately, on little more than Westminster's good faith. Key statutes underpinning the UK's constitutional settlement, including as enshrined in the various pieces of devolution legislation and the Human Rights Act 1998, have, in the final analysis, no special protections or privileged constitutional status. There are no fail-safe legal protections by which to guard, for example, against:

[t]he UK Parliament taking clear and direct steps to repeal the [Northern Ireland Act 1998][4] or alter its terms … Even the principle of consent, by which the people of Northern Ireland have to approve any change in its status as part of the UK … could be ignored by the Westminster Parliament if a majority of MPs insisted on doing so. (de Mars et al. 2018: 130)

The apparent ease with which Brexit has overridden long-standing political-legal commitments – including to rigorous governmental impartiality, equality of citizenship and non-diminution of rights in Northern Ireland – has called into question the extent to which good faith can be assumed (BrexitLawNI 2018a, 2018b). This has not been helped by claims from influential Brexiteers that the 1998 Agreement has outlived its usefulness (Geoghegan 2018). And this has presented a deep-seated challenge for the EU, and for Ireland, in particular. In sum:

[t]he realities of the UK constitution, confirm precisely why a guarantee like [the Protocol on Ireland/Northern Ireland] is necessary. It would be unwise of either the EU or the UK – given the volatility of political life – to make too many assumptions about what might happen next. Given historical relations, and the scope for mutual misunderstanding, no Irish government could simply rely on political assurances that everything will be fine or that solutions (so far absent) will suddenly appear. (Harvey 2019)

Ireland's English question

As Laffan (2018; see also Laffan & O'Mahony, Chapter 10, this volume) has outlined, if UK politics in the twentieth century were shaped, to a lesser or greater extent, by the "Irish question", then Brexit has (re)opened something of an "English question" for contemporary Irish law and politics. It is worth asking at the outset whether this has been a universally negative development, or whether it may have helped to catalyse new and progressive forms of political understanding and behaviour, fostering 'domestic elite cohesion and domestic institutions that reinforce a capacity for domestic adjustment to external conditions' (Laffan 2018: 2). It is interesting to contrast the relative stability of Irish politics with the "Brexit chaos" across the Irish Sea. Progressive constitutional developments have built on the institutionalisation of forms of deliberative citizen engagement with important political-legal questions (Farrell et al. 2018). The constitutional ambiguity of referendums in the UK is at odds with their clearly defined place in Ireland's constitutional order, including in addressing questions about Ireland's relationship with the EU. And effective monitoring of referendums by Ireland's Referendum Commission contrasts markedly with the UK Electoral Commission's failure to prevent rule-breaking and the influence of dark money in the Brexit referendum in 2016 (O'Toole 2018).

There can be little doubt that Brexit has posed profound risks and been immensely challenging for the Republic of Ireland. Upending decades of avowedly joined-up thinking on Northern Ireland, Brexit has put the British and Irish governments squarely on opposite sides of the negotiating table. While this has been portrayed in terms of a rapid souring of British–Irish relations from their highpoint in 2011–2014, it is worth asking whether it instead reflects something of the superficiality or one-sidedness of this British–Irish rapprochement. Arguably, while they have both reflected and helped to drive deep-rooted political-cultural changes on the island of Ireland, Queen Elizabeth II's visit and wreath-laying in 2011; her handshake with then Northern Ireland Deputy First Minister, Martin McGuinness, in 2012; and President Michael D. Higgin's state visit to the UK in 2014 have provoked very little by way of deep or enduring transformation in British mindsets or behaviours (Pennell 2017).

Whatever the "maturation" of British–Irish relations in recent years, Brexit has precipitated something of a crisis of trust between Ireland and the UK. The tenor of the Brexit negotiations has raised concerns for Ireland about the prejudices, intentions and reliability of its closest neighbour, in general, and its political class, in particular (McTague 2018). What is a somewhat equivocal commitment to the 1998 Agreement on the part of the UK government has contrasted with the prioritisation and more expansive interpretation of the Agreement which has pertained in Dublin during the Brexit process. As argued by one senior Irish official close to Brexit negotiations, since 2016 the Irish government has sought to elevate protection of the 1998 Agreement, and the open border both which it enables and on which it relies, as an issue of existential importance, ahead of other (more material) concerns and interests:

> We are actually putting our economy *behind* protection of the Good Friday Agreement on our list of priorities. Brexiteers can't believe that, but it's true … We believe that the open border is so crucial to achieve, even if this results in any impediments for East–West trade … What they don't always get in London is that this is not just about trade. (interview 2)

EU solidarity with Ireland in this regard has been more or less consistent throughout the Brexit process. In 2017, the European Commission's Task Force 50 was charged with negotiating with the UK the terms of its withdrawal from the EU. The Task Force, with the backing of both the European Council and the European Parliament, moved quickly to ensure that the protection of the Good Friday Agreement in all its parts became a priority for the negotiations: one of the three issues to be satisfactorily resolved before any final agreement on the future relationship between the EU and the UK could be reached. This was owed in no small part to what amounted to an all-out diplomatic offensive on the part of the Irish government – in concert with all of Ireland's main political parties and wider civic society – following the Brexit referendum (Laffan 2018; Murphy 2018b: 35).

The EU's commitment to full protection of the 1998 Agreement was in part reflected in a declaration by the European Council on 29 April 2017 that a newly united Ireland – for which the 1998 Agreement makes provision on the basis of majorities in concurrent referendums North and South of the border – would be guaranteed EU membership without an accession process (Connelly 2018: 321–343; Humphreys 2018: 69–70). This leaves open the possibility that Irish unity may yet prove to be a viable route back to full EU rights and entitlements on the part of Northern Irish citizens after Brexit. However, it merely leaves open this possibility: it does not represent its active pursuit on the part of either the Irish government or the EU. The principle out-working of Ireland and the EU's commitment to the 1998 Agreement has been the various iterations of the Protocol on Ireland/ Northern Ireland. And it is noteworthy that the mechanisms enshrined therein have been concerned, above all and as far as practicable, with maintaining and reinforcing the political, legal and constitutional status quo (Hayward & Phinnemore 2019; McGarry & O'Leary 2019; Phinnemore & Whitten, Chapter 12, this volume).

All iterations of the Ireland/Northern Ireland Protocol have explicitly paid due regard to the "constitutional integrity" of the UK, proposing a bespoke form of post-Brexit participation in the EU's single market and customs union for Northern Ireland only insofar as this is required to maintain an open border and facilitate the North–South cooperation enshrined in the 1998 Agreement. The Protocol is ultimately a compromise intended to guarantee a minimum level of political-legal stability for the island of Ireland in an unknown post-Brexit future. None of its iterations has been, despite unionist and Brexiteer claims to the contrary, a pitch for Irish unity by the backdoor. As suggested in a series of opinion polls (Faith 2019a 2019b; Garry et al. 2018), its proposed measures have enjoyed broad public support in Northern Ireland. And, ultimately, it is precisely that which the Protocol has been designed to prevent – namely, a hard border on the island of Ireland – which may precipitate the most decisive swing in favour of unity among Northern Irish voters.

As Murphy (2019b) has identified, a united Ireland was emphatically not one of the Brexit priorities of the Fine Gael government led by Leo Varadkar. After the UK's 2016 EU referendum, the Irish government took quick, decisive and strategic action in seeking to mitigate the worst (potential) effects of Brexit, including with its Brexit Omnibus Act 2019 – one of the largest pieces of legislation ever signed into law in the history of the Irish State (Murphy 2019a: 11–13). It also demonstrated its willingness to make provision for some of the constitutional uncertainty which Brexit has engendered across the Irish Sea, and a tacit understanding of some of the centrifugal forces it may have unleashed, including through the reopening of its consulate in Wales. However, it remained reticent to engage proactively in a debate about potentially profound constitutional change closer to home. In August 2017, an Oireachtas report included recommendations on preparing for Irish unity, such as the convening of a "New Ireland Forum 2" and a full constitutional and legal audit (Oireachtas 2017), but these were not implemented.

On the face of it, this was repudiated by the incoming Fianna Fáil, Fine Gael and the Green Party government formed in the wake of the 2020 general election, whose Programme for Government included a proposal to form a "Shared Island Unit" in the Taoiseach's office. However, the wording of this proposal deliberately shied away from any discussion of "unity" and was couched in a broader approach to repairing and normalising British–Irish relations after Brexit (Tannam 2020). The Irish government's approach to the debate about Irish unity remains markedly hesitant. In light of the uncertainty that Brexit has engendered, this may become increasingly unsustainable (Gillespie 2019: 1). While, as de Mars et al. (2018: 149) have suggested, Brexit places far greater strains on the British constitution than it does on Ireland's, it has thrown into sharp relief some important politico-legal tensions in the latter.

Although the Irish Constitution is more 'proactive' (de Mars et al. 2018: 136) in its protection of the 1998 Agreement than the UK's (with Article 29.7 of the Constitution granting the Agreement constitutional status), there are nonetheless a series of important lacunae in Ireland's constitutional order in this regard. For example, after Brexit, Irish citizens living in Northern Ireland will be deprived of the same right to representation in the European Parliament which is afforded to citizens in the South. This contravenes the principles of equality and non-diminution of rights on both sides of the border, as well as pledges on the part of the government to protect, guarantee and uphold the rights of Irish citizens in the North (see Murphy 2019b). Ireland's citizens' rights frameworks are additionally incompatible with the requirements of the 1998 Agreement – which asserts parity of esteem and equality of citizenship between unionists and nationalists – in that they confer the full gamut of political rights exclusively on those who hold Irish (as opposed to British) citizenship. Humphreys has argued that:

> It is hard to avoid the conclusion that the failure of [the Irish] Constitution to confer virtually any express rights on non-Irish citizens is simply incompatible with the Agreement's provisions giving entitlement to any member of the people of Northern Ireland to regard themselves as British. (Humphreys 2018: 203)

He therefore proposes a range of legislative and constitutional changes which may be needed in order to secure Ireland's full compliance with its commitments to the 1998 Agreement, regardless of the final outcome of the Brexit process and whether or not the debate on Irish unity continues to gather momentum (Humphreys 2018: 189–230). These range from measures to confer key rights on non-Irish (and particularly British) citizens, through provision for the continuation of devolved power-sharing in Northern Ireland in the event of Irish unity, to changes to the constitutional preamble, the symbols and even the name of the state.

In light of the ongoing uncertainty that Brexit has precipitated, Irish unity represents a plausible constitutional future for which the Irish government should seek to make relevant preparations. It is worth noting that there is another such future which merits some attention. Brexit seems to have precipitated a deepening of the process of Europeanisation of law and politics in Ireland (Murphy 2019a: 12–13). Levels of support for European integration in Ireland remain among the highest in Europe and this has only been bolstered by Brexit (see Simpson, Chapter 8, this volume). At present, an "Irexit" from the EU remains the interest of only a few marginal groups and parties whose wider policy agendas are generally as antisemitic, sexist, homophobic and racist as they are lacking in popular support. However, 'in the broader European context, and in the longer term, Brexit will challenge some of the fundamentals of Ireland's relationship with the EU' in a way which may have 'political ramifications that affect the Irish party system and the relative strength of political parties' (Murphy 2018b: 37). According to Murphy:

> The Brexit crisis effectively restricted the extent to which Ireland could explore and investigate the merits, or the potential for 'goodness of fit', between Irish and evolving EU policy preferences … Resistance to EU pressures for adaptation and reorientation may strengthen when discussions turn to issues which are not explicitly related to Brexit including Eurozone reform, taxation, Irish neutrality, climate change or an increased EU budget. Throughout the Brexit period, the EU enjoyed strong public support among Irish voters … However, the Brexit referendum result dramatically illustrated how fickle public support can be, and attuned the EU and its members to the conditionality of the EU's future. (Murphy 2019a: 16)

To consider Ireland simply immune to the same forces which have transformed the question of the UK's EU membership from the concern of an extremist fringe to the defining issue in contemporary British politics would be a mistake (Fanning & Farrell 2018). Amid the constitutional upheaval which Brexit has precipitated, vigilance against these forces should be the order of the day.

Conclusion

Brexit represents a constitutional moment for the UK – one marked by the potential for radical and potentially enduring structural change within the British state. Once thought to be its key strength, in the context of the UK's withdrawal from the EU, the improvised and intangible nature of the British constitution has become its primary weakness. The Brexit process has revealed the fundamental fragility of the UK's constitutional infrastructure and placed it under a series of stresses and strains which may, eventually, prove its undoing. It has seen many of the political-legal commitments which underpinned its territorial constitution and devolution settlement, in general, and the peace and political processes in Northern Ireland, in particular, rapidly and worryingly overturned. And it has undermined the UK's reliability as a co-guarantor of the 1998 Agreement, giving the question of Irish unity a renewed salience, and raised new questions about the nature of the future relationship between the EU and Ireland.

Brexit unexpectedly signalled something of a constitutional moment for Ireland. There are undoubtedly dangers in this, including those represented by the (albeit marginal) political risk posed by those exclusivist and ethno-chauvinist political forces currently advocating an "Irexit". However, it also represents something of an opportunity for a new 'open, deliberative and dialogical' engagement with constitutional issues: one based on North–South dialogue and the creation of deliberative political communities in and across the two jurisdictions on the island (Todd 2017). While the exogenous shock of Brexit is not of its making, the Irish government is nonetheless forced to confront its fallout. And in doing so, it could and arguably should seek to play a leading role in the emerging discussion about Ireland's constitutional future(s).

Notes

1 The Miller case is a case heard by the UK Supreme Court in 2017, which ruled that the British government had to receive parliamentary approval before initiating the Article 50 withdrawal procedure.
2 For details on the scandal surrounding the RHI scheme and its role in the collapse of devolved power-sharing in Northern Ireland, see McBride (2019).
3 The BIIGC is a pillar of the 1998 Belfast (Good Friday) Agreement's third strand. In light of the apparent success of power-sharing in Northern Ireland, it had gone into abeyance since the mid-2000s. Reconvened in 2018, the Conference provides the Irish government with a consultative role in non-devolved policy areas as they pertain to Northern Ireland.

4   The Northern Ireland Act 1998 gave (incomplete) legal effect to the Good Friday
    Agreement in British law, establishing, inter alia, the devolved power-sharing
    Assembly and Executive, its powers and functions, and the Secretary of State for
    Northern Ireland's power to call a border poll.

References

Adler-Nissen, R., C. Galpin & B. Rosamond (2017) 'Performing Brexit: how a post-Brexit world is imagined outside of the United Kingdom'. *The British Journal of Politics and International Relations* 19(3): 573–591.

Barry, J. (2018) 'Unionists should spell out why they reject NI in customs union'. *News Letter*, 14 March. Available at: www.newsletter.co.uk/news/opinion/unionists-should-spell-out-why-they-reject-ni-in-customs-union-1-8414653 [accessed 4 October 2019].

Belfast Telegraph (2018) 'Theresa May's keynote address at Belfast's Waterfront Hall [full speech]'. 20 July. Available at: www.belfasttelegraph.co.uk/news/northern-ireland/theresa-mays-keynote-address-at-belfasts-waterfront-hall-full-speech-37138123.html [accessed 4 October 2019].

Boffey, D. (2018) 'May's plan to give Stormont a backstop veto enrages EU envoys'. *Guardian*, 24 September. Available at: www.theguardian.com/politics/2018/sep/24/mays-plan-to-give-stormont-a-backstop-veto-enrages-eu-envoys [accessed 5 August 2019].

Bogdanor, V. (2019) *Beyond Brexit: towards a British constitution*. London: I. B. Tauris.

BrexitLawNI (2018a) *BrexitLawNI policy report: Brexit and the peace process*. Belfast: BrexitLawNI.

BrexitLawNI (2018b) *BrexitLawNI policy report: Brexit, human rights and equality*. Belfast: BrexitLawNI.

Cabinet Office (2017) *Agreement between the Conservative and Unionist Party and the Democratic Unionist Party on support for the Government in Parliament*. Available at: https://assets.publishing.service.gov.uk/government/uploads/system/uploads/attachatta_data/file/621794/Confidence_and_Supply_Agreement_between_the_ConservConse_Party_and_the_DUP.pdf [accessed 15 January 2019].

Carty, A. (1996) *Was Ireland conquered? International law and the Irish question*. London: Pluto Press.

Connelly, T. (2018) *Brexit and Ireland: the dangers, the opportunities, and the inside story of the Irish response*. London: Penguin.

de Mars, S., C. Murray, A. O'Donoghue & B. Warwick (2018) *Bordering two unions: Northern Ireland and Brexit*. Bristol: Policy Press.

Emerson, N. (2019) 'How much direct rule has crept in since Stormont collapsed?' *The Detail*, 8 March. Available at: https://thedetail.tv/articles/how-much-direct-rule-has-crept-in-since-stormont-collapsed [accessed 4 October 2019].

European Commission (2018) *European Commission Draft Withdrawal Agreement on the withdrawal of the United Kingdom of Great Britain and Northern Ireland from the European Union and the European Atomic Energy Community*. 28 February. Available at: https://ec.europa.eu/commission/sites/beta-political/files/draft_withdrawal_agreement.pdf [accessed 23 September 2019].

Evans, G. & A. Menon (2017) *Brexit and British politics*. Cambridge: Polity Press.

Evershed, J. (2018a) 'The Ghost at the Feast: The Northern Ireland Executive and Assembly and the Brexit backstop'. *Irish Association for Contemporary European Studies*, 28 September. Available at: www.iaces.ie/blog/the-ghost-at-the-feast-the-northern-ireland-executive-and-assembly-and-the-brexit-backstop [accessed 29 September 2019].

Evershed, J. (2018b) 'What is special about customs?' *Centre on Constitutional Change*, 25 July. Available at: www.centreonconstitutionalchange.ac.uk/opinions/what-special-about-customs [accessed 28 July 2018].

Evershed, J. (2019) 'The DUP and no-deal tariffs: double standards?' *Centre on Constitutional Change*, 14 March. Available at: www.centreonconstitutionalchange.ac.uk/opinions/dup-and-no-deal-tariffs-double-standards [accessed 4 October 2019].

Faith, P. (2019a) 'Northern Ireland voters back Brexit backstop'. *The Times*, 18 August. Available at: www.thetimes.co.uk/article/northern-ireland-voters-back-brexit-backstop-lbrjn0f5g [accessed 3 October 2019].

Faith, P. (2019b) 'Poll shows increased Northern Ireland majority backs remain'. *The Times*, 27 October. Available at: www.thetimes.co.uk/article/poll-shows-increased-northern-ireland-majority-backs-remain-njpt2fr2h [accessed 28 October 2019].

Fanning, B. & D. Farrell (2018) 'Ireland cannot be complacent about populism'. *The Irish Times*, 17 August. Available at: www.irishtimes.com/opinion/ireland-cannot-be-complacent-about-populism-1.3598461 [accessed 4 October 2019].

Farrell, D., J. Suiter & C. Harris (2018) '"Systematising" constitutional deliberation: the 2016–18 citizens' assembly in Ireland'. *Irish Political Studies* 34(1): 113–123.

Foley, M. (2012 [1989]) *The silence of constitutions: gaps, 'abeyances' and political temperament in the maintenance of government*. Abingdon: Routledge.

Garry, J., K. McNicholl, B. O'Leary & J. Pow (2018) *Northern Ireland and the UK's exit from the EU: what do people think?* London: The UK in a Changing Europe.

Geoghegan, P. (2018) 'Brexiteers launch broadside at Northern Ireland peace deal'. *Politico*, 22 February. Available at: www.politico.eu/article/brexiteers-broadside-northern-ireland-peace-deal-good-friday-agreement/ [accessed 3 October 2019].

Gillespie, P. (2019) 'Constitutional futures after Brexit'. *Institute of British–Irish Studies*, 26 February. Available at: www.ucd.ie/ibis/t4media/IBIS%202019%20Constitutional%20Futures%20Final.pdf [accessed 30 September 2019].

Griffith, J.A.G. (1979) 'The political constitution'. *The Modern Law Review* 42(1): 1–21.

Harvey, C. (2016) 'Northern Ireland's transition and the constitution of the UK'. *UK Constitutional Law Association*, 12 December. Available at: https://ukconstitutionallaw.org/2016/12/12/colin-harvey-northern-irelands-transition-and-the-constitution-of-the-uk/ [accessed 3 October 2019].

Harvey, C. (2017) 'Northern Ireland and rigorous impartiality: untangling a constitutional mess'. *Queen's Policy Engagement*, 13 June. Available at: http://qpol.qub.ac.uk/ni-rigorous-impartiality/ [accessed 3 October 2019].

Harvey, C. (2019) 'Why is the backstop needed?' *The UK in a Changing Europe*, 15 February. Available at: https://ukandeu.ac.uk/why-is-the-backstop-needed/ [accessed 3 October 2019].

Hayward, K. (2018) 'The pivotal position of the Irish border in the UK's withdrawal from the European Union'. *Space and Polity* 22(2): 238–254.

Hayward, K. & M.C. Murphy (2018) 'The EU's influence on the peace process and agreement in Northern Ireland in light of Brexit'. *Ethnopolitics* 17(3): 276–291.

Hayward, K. & D. Phinnemore (2019) 'Breached or protected? The "principle" of consent in Northern Ireland and the UK government's Brexit proposals'. *LSE Brexit*, 9 January. Available at: https://blogs.lse.ac.uk/brexit/2019/01/09/breached-or-protected-the-principle-of-consent-in-northern-ireland-and-the-uk-governments-brexit-proposals/ [accessed 15 March 2019].

Henderson, A., C. Jeffery, D. Wincott & R. Wyn Jones (2017) 'How Brexit was made in England'. *The British Journal of Politics and International Relations* 19(4): 631–646.

House of Lords (2016) *Select Committee on the Constitution 10th report of session 2015–16: The Union and devolution*, HL Paper 149. London: The Stationery Office.

House of Lords (2017) *European Union Committee 4th Report of Session 2017–19: Brexit: devolution*, HL Paper 9. London: The Stationery Office.

Humphreys, R. (2018) *Beyond the border: the Good Friday Agreement and Irish unity after Brexit*. Newbridge: Merrion Press.

Kenny, M. & J. Sheldon (2020) 'When planets collide: the British Conservative Party and the discordant goals of delivering Brexit and preserving the domestic Union, 2016–2019'. *Political Studies*, online first, DOI: 10.1177/0032321720930986.

Laffan, B. (2018) 'Brexit: re-opening Ireland's "English question"'. *The Political Quarterly* 89(4): 568–575.

McBride, S. (2019) *Burned: the inside story of the 'Cash-for-Ash' scandal and Northern Ireland's secretive new elite*. Newbridge: Merrion Press.

McCrudden, C. & D. Halberstam (2017) 'Northern Ireland's Supreme Court Brexit problem (and the UK's too)'. *UK Constitutional Law Association*, 21 November. Available at: https://ukconstitutionallaw.org/2017/11/21/christopher-mccrudden-and-daniel-halberstam-northern-irelands-supreme-court-brexit-problem-and-the-uks-too/ [accessed 2 October 2019].

McGarry, J. and B. O'Leary (2019) 'Matters of consent: the Withdrawal Agreement does not violate the Good Friday Agreement'. *LSE British Politics and Policy*, 28 October. Available at: https://blogs.lse.ac.uk/politicsandpolicy/brexit-good-friday-agreement/ [accessed 28 October 2019].

McHarg, A. (2018) 'Navigating without maps: constitutional silence and the management of the Brexit process'. *International Journal of Constitutional Law* 16(3): 952–968.

McTague, T. (2018) 'The British and Irish are fighting again'. *Politico*, 2 November. Available at: www.politico.eu/article/how-brexit-burned-uk-irish-friendship-theresa-may-leo-varadkar/ [accessed 4 October 2019].

Murphy, M.C. (2014) *Northern Ireland and the European Union*. Manchester: Manchester University Press.

Murphy, M.C. (2018a) *Europe and Northern Ireland's future: negotiating Brexit's unique case*. Newcastle: Agenda Publishing.

Murphy, M.C. (2018b) 'Brexit and the Irish case', in P. Diamond, P. Nedergaard & B. Rosamond (eds) *The Routledge handbook of the politics of Brexit*, pp. 27–39. Abingdon: Routledge.

Murphy, M.C. (2019a) 'The Brexit crisis, Ireland, and British–Irish relations: Europeanisation and/or de-Europeanisation?' *Irish Political Studies*, 27 September. Available at: www.tandfonline.com/doi/full/10.1080/07907184.2019.1669564 [accessed 4 October 2019].

Murphy, M.C. (2019b) 'What are the Irish government's Brexit priorities? A united Ireland is not one of them'. *LSE Brexit*, 17 January. Available at: https://blogs.lse.

ac.uk/brexit/2019/01/17/what-is-the-irish-governments-brexit-wish-list/ [accessed 4 October 2019].

Murphy, M.C. & J. Evershed (2019) 'Between the Devil and the DUP: the Democratic Unionist Party and the politics of Brexit', *British Politics*, online first, DOI: 10.1057/s41293-019-00126-3.

Murray, C. (2018) 'Brexit and the "constitutional integrity" of the United Kingdom'. *UK Constitutional Law Association*, 25 September. Available at: https://ukconstitutionallaw.org/2018/09/25/colin-murray-brexit-and-the-constitutional-integrity-of-the-united-kingdom/ [accessed 2 October 2019].

Oireachtas (2017) *Brexit and the future of Ireland: uniting Ireland and its people in peace and prosperity*. Dublin: Houses of the Oireachtas (Oireachtas Joint Committee on Implementation of the Good Friday Agreement).

O'Toole, M. (2017) 'Ireland an afterthought during Brexit campaign when I was Cameron adviser'. *The Irish Times*, 4 October. Available at: www.irishtimes.com/opinion/ireland-an-afterthought-during-brexit-campaign-when-i-was-cameron-adviser-1.3242732 [accessed 4 October 2019].

O'Toole, F. (2018) 'If only Brexit had been run like Ireland's referendum'. *Guardian*, 29 May. Available at: www.theguardian.com/commentisfree/2018/may/29/brexit-ireland-referendum-experiment-trusting-people [accessed 4 October 2019].

Pennell, C. (2017) '"Choreographed by the angels"? Ireland and the centenary of the First World War'. *War & Society* 36(4): 256–275.

Scheppele, K.L. (2004) 'Constitutional ethnography: an introduction'. *Law & Society Review* 38(3): 389–406.

Shipman, T. (2016) *All out war: the full story of Brexit*. London: William Collins.

Skoutaris, N. (2020) *What's in an Irish border? Brexit, the backstop(s) and the constitutional integrity of the UK*, DCU Brexit Institute Working Paper No. 02–2020. Dublin: DCU Brexit Institute.

Tannam, E. (2018) 'The Good Friday Agreement, Brexit and British–Irish intergovernmental co-operation'. *Ethnopolitics* 17(3): 243–262.

Tannam, E. (2020) 'Shared island? There's hope for British–Irish intergovernmental relations'. *LSE Brexit Blog*, 2 July. Available at: https://blogs.lse.ac.uk/brexit/2020/07/02/shared-island-theres-hope-for-british-irish-intergovernmental-relations/ [accessed 21 September 2020].

Todd, J. (2017) 'From identity politics to identity change: exogenous shocks, constitutional moments and the impact of Brexit on the island of Ireland'. *Irish Studies in International Affairs* 28: 57–72.

Weale, A. (2018) 'Brexit and the improvised constitution', in B. Martill & U. Staiger (eds) *Brexit and beyond: rethinking the futures of Europe*, pp. 28–36. London: UCL Press.

Wincott, D. (2018) 'Brexit and the state of the United Kingdom', in P. Diamond, P. Nedergaard & B. Rosamond (eds) *The Routledge handbook of the politics of Brexit*, pp. 15–26. Abingdon: Routledge.

Interviews

1   Member of Labour Party Shadow Ministerial Team for Northern Ireland, 23 February 2018.
2   Official of Irish Department for Foreign Affairs and Trade, 17 July 2018.

14

Taking back control, without going back to conflict: weighing up the impact of Brexit on Northern Ireland's peace process

James Pow

Peace and reconciliation in Europe and Ireland

The EU originated as a peace process on a continental scale, laying the foundations for cooperation and reconciliation in the wake of the Second World War. The preamble of the Treaty of Paris acknowledged that peace 'can be safeguarded only by creative efforts commensurate with the dangers that threaten it' (Treaty of Paris 1951: 3). It is through this lens that we can understand the EU as, at its foundation, an ambitious peace process on a continental scale (Birchfield et al. 2017). Devastated by the impact of the Second World War, six countries chose to enter the pioneering European Coal and Steel Community with the explicit intention of preventing war and healing its raw wounds. This founding mission played an enduring role through the subsequent widening and deepening of the integration project, particularly in the wake of the Cold War (Unwin 2014). But the continued relevance of this mission and the extent of its impact were not equally perceived by all member states.

In 2012, the EU was awarded the Nobel Peace Prize, with the citation praising how 'the Union and its forerunners have for over six decades contributed to the advancement of peace and reconciliation, democracy and human rights in Europe' (Nobel Committee 2012). The British government responded by issuing a 37-word official statement celebrating 'the EU's historic role in promoting peace and reconciliation in Europe, particularly through its enlargement to Central and Eastern Europe' (FCO 2012). Without inferring too much from this brief response, it neatly encapsulates the UK's self-image as more of an *observer* of a continental peace process than as a direct *participant*. For the UK, accession to the EEC was overwhelmingly motivated by strategic economic considerations; its membership served a largely transactional purpose (George 1998; Wall 2008).

Although not widely recognised at the time, the simultaneous accession of the UK and Ireland in January 1973 helped to lay part of the framework that would eventually transform another conflict on European soil: the Troubles in Northern Ireland. The EU's institutions promoted diplomatic relations between the British and Irish governments, facilitating cooperation that would eventually culminate in the 1998 Agreement. The participation of the two states in the EU provided a framework in which key provisions of the settlement could be implemented, notably on developing cross-border relations on the island of Ireland, and further deepening relations between the UK and Ireland. And yet, it is the UK's departure from the EU that has exposed the importance of its membership for an ongoing peace process on its own soil.

This chapter considers the peace process in Northern Ireland in the light of the UK's decision to leave the EU. It begins by setting out the significance of the European dimension to the peace process before addressing the potential challenges posed by Brexit to a crucial set of relationships. The UK's decision to leave the EU poses two main challenges to the peace process developed over the last two decades. Firstly, it risks undermining inter-group relations within Northern Ireland by increasing the salience of its constitutional status and by reinforcing polarisation along communal lines. Secondly, it risks undermining the implementation of the Agreement by testing relationships between Northern Ireland and its immediate environment: either with the rest of the island of Ireland, the rest of the UK, or both.

This chapter will examine these dual effects through the lens of public opinion in Northern Ireland. Drawing on cross-sectional survey data from the Northern Ireland Life and Times Survey (ARK 2018) and Garry et al. (2018), it will explore group-level attitudes towards different possible forms of Brexit, identifying the positive and/or negative consequences for the stability of Northern Ireland's peace process. The chapter concludes with a discussion as to how the EU may most effectively play a constructive role in Northern Ireland in a post-Brexit context.

Ending conflict and promoting peace: the EU dimension

When the European Parliament commissioned the Haagerup Report in 1983, it marked the first time that the EU directly engaged with the conflict in Northern Ireland (Hayward 2006). Published the following year, the report concluded that the conflict represented a clash between two national identities, British and Irish: 'it is like two nations deeply distrustful of each other living in each other's midst' (Haagerup 1984: 13). By framing the conflict in these terms, it identified its resolution primarily through greater

British–Irish cooperation. While it was acknowledged that the European institutions could support such cooperation, conflict resolution was ultimately seen as a matter for the two national governments – and their willingness to work together. It is, therefore, important not to overstate the role of the EU in the development of the 1998 Agreement (Bew et al. 1997).

Rather than playing an active role in conflict resolution, the EU's role can be more reasonably described as facilitative.[1] The joint accession of Ireland and the UK in 1973 was not immediately accompanied by an improvement in relations between the two member states, but the institutions of the EU, particularly the Council, provided a forum for elite-level contact that did not previously exist (Arthur 1999; Hayward 2006; Meehan 2000). As Meehan put it, common membership of the EU 'helped to open up a space for contending parties to talk about solutions to old problems in a new way – and to act upon that' (2000: 96). A reduction in mutual distrust and the development of constructive collaboration resulted in the bilateral Anglo-Irish Agreement of 1985 and the Downing Street Declaration of 1993, both recognised to be important waypoints on the journey to the 1998 Agreement (McGarry & O'Leary 1997).

It is worth briefly setting out some of the key provisions of this Agreement, broadly understood to constitute a peace settlement (Bell 2006). Of particular significance is the principle of consent, stipulating that Northern Ireland's constitutional status in the UK can only change if it is the wish of a majority of voters to join a united Ireland, democratically expressed in a referendum.[2] There is a related protection for citizenship, guaranteeing the right of the people of Northern Ireland to identify as British, Irish, or both, regardless of the constitutional status of Northern Ireland. In this sense, the Agreement follows the nationality-based logic of the Haagerup Report. Technically speaking, however, it consists of *two* interlocking documents: both an international treaty between the two national governments (the British–Irish Agreement) *and* a multi-party agreement between the majority of Northern Ireland's political parties (the Multi-Party Agreement). In other words, an accord at the level of the two governments was a necessary but insufficient element of the 1998 Agreement.

In a broader sense, the Agreement does not narrowly define the conflict simply in terms of competing national identities. Instead, it refers to Northern Ireland's *communities*, allowing for a more holistic understanding of group divisions that can encompass other salient dimensions, including community background and ethno-national ideology.[3] Similarly, the Agreement does not in itself constitute an immediate resolution to competing claims of national self-determination (Stevenson 2017). Instead, its preamble emphasises the cultivation of three sets of *relationships*: 'within Northern Ireland, within the island of Ireland and between the peoples of these islands' (NIO 1998). Each relationship is the subject of a complementary yet distinct strand of the

Agreement. Strand One sets out a series of power-sharing arrangements for the government of Northern Ireland, inclusive of representatives from across its communities (see McGarry & O'Leary 2006). Strand Two specifies arrangements for cooperation across the island of Ireland, notably through the North–South Ministerial Council (see Coakley 2002). Strand Three, finally, institutionalises the relationships between the national and devolved governments of the UK and Ireland, both through the British–Irish Council and the British–Irish Intergovernmental Conference (see Coakley 2014).

While there is little direct reference to the EU across these provisions, Strand Two of the Multi-Party Agreement tasks the North–South Ministerial Council with considering 'the European Union dimension of relevant matters, including the implementation of EU policies and programmes and proposals under consideration in the EU framework' (NIO 1998: 16). This includes arrangements 'to ensure that the views of the Council are taken into account and represented appropriately at relevant EU meetings' (NIO 1998: 16). There is, therefore, an explicit expectation that the EU would provide a vehicle for the development of a cooperative North–South relationship on issues of common interest. Further, in the preamble of the British–Irish Agreement, the two governments pledge 'to develop still further the unique relationship between their peoples and the close co-operation between their countries as friendly neighbours and as partners in the European Union' (NIO 1998: 32). The Agreement was reached in the clear assumption that Ireland and the UK would continue to share membership of the EU, facilitating the aims of the broader settlement.

The most active role played by the EU itself came in the form of financial support. As early as 1989, the EU promoted the peace process through its regional policy and the International Fund for Ireland (IFI). Between 1995 and 2013 the EU provided €1.3 billion through three rounds of a dedicated Peace Programme, funding projects that promote reconciliation as well as social and economic development in Northern Ireland and the border region of Ireland (SEUPB 2019). The Peace IV round of the programme allocated €229 million from the European Regional Development Fund (ERDF) between 2014 and 2020. The EU agreed to continue funding the programme until its scheduled expiry in 2020, regardless of the UK's withdrawal.

The experience of Northern Ireland between two referendums

The 1998 Agreement was endorsed by over 70% of voters in Northern Ireland in a referendum. In the two decades that followed, it is difficult to dispute that the conflict has been transformed. Violence, and the threat of it, has not disappeared; Republican and Loyalist paramilitary organisations

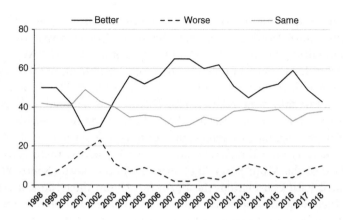

Figure 14.1 Relations between Protestants and Catholics ('What about relations between Protestants and Catholics? Would you say they are better than they were five years ago, worse or about the same now as then?'), 1998–2018
Source: ARK (2018).

still exist, still exert control over communities and still engage in terrorist activity (Wilson 2016). However, the scale of such activity has declined significantly in the wake of the 1998 Agreement. During the Troubles between 1969 and 1998, more than 3,200 people were killed; in the 20 years that followed, 107 security-related deaths were recorded (PSNI 2018).

Time series data show that this less violent political climate has been accompanied by largely positive subjective assessments of inter-group relations. Each year, the Northern Ireland Life and Times (NILT) survey asks a representative sample of the population whether they think relations between Catholics and Protestants have improved, worsened or stayed the same over the last five years, and whether they think relations between the two groups will be better, worse or the same in five years' time. The retrospective evaluation trends (presented in Figure 14.1) and prospective evaluations (in Figure 14.2) are highly correlated. In the immediate aftermath of the 1998 Agreement, initial optimism declined. However, despite some volatility – largely owing to shifts in the relative number of people thinking the quality of inter-group relations were or would be the *same* compared to better – only a small minority of citizens offered a negative assessment throughout the period. These trends tell an important story about citizens' attitudes in Northern Ireland: despite many setbacks to the peace process in the wake of the 1998 Agreement (see Knox 2016; McCrudden et al. 2016; Smyth 2004), optimism has consistently remained more prevalent than pessimism.

Attitudinal evidence does not suggest that people regarded the EU as a major contributing factor to the origins of the peace process. While the 1998 NILT survey asked respondents to evaluate the extent to which they thought

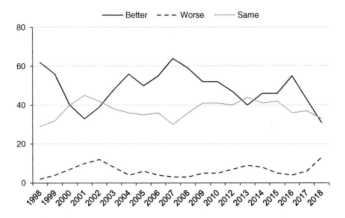

Figure 14.2 Relations between Catholics and Protestants ('In five years' time, do you think relations between Protestants and Catholics will be better than now, worse than now, or about the same as now'?), 1998–2018
Source: ARK (2018).

the British government, the Irish government, the US government, paramilitary groups and general public opinion had been 'helpful in the search for peace' (ARK 1998), it is telling that this battery of questions did not include an item on the perceived role of the EU. However, there was much greater public awareness of the more visible *post*-Agreement role of the EU in supporting Northern Ireland's peace process. In 2002, far more respondents said they thought that Northern Ireland's participation in the EU was a good thing (46%) than a bad thing (4%); financial support for the peace process was by far the most commonly cited reason among those expressing a favourable opinion (ARK 2002).[4] Our ability to establish a causal relationship between EU membership and Northern Ireland's peace process is constrained by the lack of a counterfactual scenario in which the UK or Ireland, or both, lay outside the EU. That said, the UK's exit from the EU offers the closest thing to a natural experiment. Inevitably, it will be some time before the full impact of Brexit on Northern Ireland is clear, but even at this early stage we can make some preliminary observations of its possible effect on the delicate set of relationships that the 1998 Agreement seeks to support.

Testing relationships within Northern Ireland

A majority of voters across the UK chose to leave the EU in the 2016 referendum but with significant geographical variation in voting behaviour. Notably, in Northern Ireland, a majority of voters supported remaining in

Table 14.1 2016 EU referendum vote choice (self-reported)

	Protestant	Catholic	Other	All
Remain	40	88	73	63
Leave	60	12	27	37
Total	*100*	*100*	*100*	*100*

Source: Garry et al. (2018).

the EU by a margin of 56% to 44%. This divergence in aggregate preferences presents two main challenges for the successful implementation of the 1998 Agreement within Northern Ireland. Firstly, it places a strain on the principle of consent, namely that 'it would be wrong to make any change in the status of Northern Ireland save with the consent of a majority of its people' (NIO 1998: 33). However, responding to a legal challenge, the UK Supreme Court deemed that the principle of consent only applied to the future of Northern Ireland's constitutional status as a constituent part of the UK or a united Ireland, not to its future inside or outside the EU (see McCrudden & Halberstam 2017).

Secondly, it reinforces, rather than undermines, communal divisions. As Table 14.1 shows, an overwhelming majority of Catholic voters (88%) supported the UK's continued membership of the EU, as did a majority of those identifying with neither of the two traditional communities. In contrast, most Protestant voters, albeit by a smaller majority, opted to leave the EU. These divisions have increased the relative salience of Northern Ireland's constitutional position, creating a difficult backdrop against which political parties representing divergent preferences must govern together. Indeed, the very dominance of Brexit on the political agenda, coupled with the protracted uncertainty over its unique effect on Northern Ireland, has contributed to the difficulty in restoring Northern Ireland's devolved power-sharing institutions.[5]

Still, beneath these divisions lies a significant degree of common ground. Beyond the binary choice of leaving or remaining in the EU, much greater cross-community consensus exists when people were asked to consider the *type* of exit they would prefer, assuming that there are three basic forms this could take. Among those expressing an opinion, 61% of people in Northern Ireland wanted to see a "soft" exit for the whole of the UK, defined as the UK leaving the EU but essentially remaining in the single market and customs union. This included 62% of Protestants, 61% of Catholics and 60% of those identifying with neither of the two traditional communities. The other two scenarios presented in Table 14.2 received significantly lower levels of support and were more polarising. A quarter of Protestants preferred

Table 14.2 Support for various forms of Brexit

	Protestant	Catholic	Other	All
Hard	24	5	17	15
Mixed	14	34	24	24
Soft	62	61	60	61
Total	*100*	*100*	*100*	*100*

Source: Garry et al. (2018).

to see a "hard" exit for the whole of the UK, defined here as leaving the single market and customs union, compared to just 5% of Catholics. In contrast, over a third of Catholics supported a "mixed" exit, involving the whole of the UK leaving the EU, but with Northern Ireland uniquely remaining in the single market and customs union. This option was supported by just 14% of Protestant respondents.

Therefore, while it was true that leaving the EU was not the first preference of a majority of voters in Northern Ireland, and that the fundamental issue of the UK's withdrawal divided citizens along existing communal lines, the extent to which Brexit undermined inter-communal relations was likely to be conditional on the extent to which it disrupted the status quo ante.

Testing the North–South relationship

Few people in Northern Ireland have much awareness of the North–South Ministerial Council, the institutional mechanism that facilitates policy cooperation and the promotion of shared interests between the Northern Ireland Executive and the Irish government.[6] At the popular level, it is the symbolic open border between Northern Ireland and the Republic of Ireland that best encapsulates a positive relationship between the two jurisdictions, one that has manifestly changed since the signing of the 1998 Agreement. Historically, customs posts demarcated the boundary between the UK and Ireland (Denton & Fahy 1993). As targets for Republican terrorists, these stations were militarised during the Troubles, with many additional military checkpoints and the security-related closure of many crossings. The text of the Agreement does not explicitly require the absence of customs or trade-related regulatory checks along the border – it was written with the implicit assumption that both jurisdictions would remain in the EU's single market and customs union – but it *does* explicitly call for the absence of military installations: 'the development of a peaceful environment on the basis of this agreement can and should mean a normalisation of security arrangements

Table 14.3 If Northern Ireland leaves the single market and customs union, how likely do you think it is that this will result in manned checkpoints and cameras at the North–South border?

	Protestant	Catholic	Other	All
Likely	61	73	57	65
Not likely	21	18	25	21
Don't know	18	9	18	15
Total	100	100	100	100

Source: Garry et al. (2018).

and practices should mean a normalisation of security arrangements and practices' (NIO 1998: 25). It is important that these two types of border infrastructure are not conflated.

Nonetheless, the UK's exit from the EU poses a clear challenge to the maintenance of this symbolically important open border, which has become the frontier between an EU member state and a third country. In the UK, the Leave campaign's call to "take back control" resonated with many citizens in the 2016 referendum, many of whom were attracted to the prospect of ending the free movement of citizens from the rest of the EU into the UK – a key pillar of the single market – and the idea of the UK, not the EU, being responsible for negotiating trade deals with other countries (Goodwin & Milazzo 2017). The potential consequences of such changes for the UK's only land border received marginal attention during the referendum campaign itself. They have weighed more heavily in its aftermath.

In her Lancaster House speech, then Prime Minister Theresa May insisted that the UK would leave both the customs union and single market, *and* that there would be no 'return to the borders of the past' (UK Government 2017). These goals appear irreconcilable. Indeed, as far as the majority of citizens in Northern Ireland were concerned, there was a widespread expectation that leaving the single market and customs union on a UK-wide basis would require some form of checks at the border (see Table 14.3). This was true for a firm majority of Catholics, Protestants, and those who are neither, and likely formed part of the explanation for the high level of cross-community support for the UK staying in both the single market and customs union: to avoid the need for infrastructure at the border. The issue had an obvious economic dimension, but it was the psychological dimension that was most relevant to the broader peace process.

Figure 14.3 shows the extent to which people in Northern Ireland would find it "impossible to accept" a range of new features at the border with the Republic of Ireland. Relatively unobtrusive installations, such as cameras,

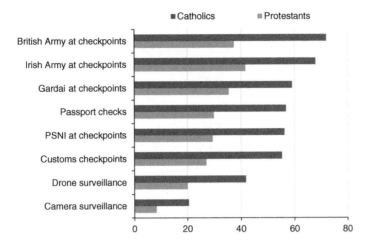

Figure 14.3 Percentage of Catholic and Protestant respondents who would find each possible feature at the North–South border "almost impossible to accept" Source: Garry et al. (2018).

receive a relatively modest amount of opposition. Any form of manned checkpoint would be tolerated far less, especially those involving British or Irish soldiers. Significantly, we can see that the intensity of opposition varies strongly along communal lines; a majority of Catholics consistently oppose any form of manned checkpoints, even those without a military presence, whereas only a minority of Protestants would find any of these changes "almost impossible to accept". It is notable, however, that a sizeable minority of Protestants hold these attitudes. These non-trivial levels of opposition may reflect concerns that customs checks would have a negative economic impact, but this does not explain the significantly higher level of opposition towards militarised checkpoints compared to customs checkpoints among Protestants. This difference may be better explained by concerns that militarised checkpoints would undermine the peace process, either symbolically or materially.

Figure 14.4 shows what types of opposition may emerge in the event of a hardening of the UK's border with Ireland. Among respondents who said they would find it "impossible to accept" new forms of infrastructure at the border, seven in ten expressed support for non-violent opposition, such as peaceful demonstrations and petitions. Only a very small proportion expressed any support for illegal direct action, including vandalising technology or other installations at the border, and 2% said they would support violence against persons in the event of new border checks. It is perhaps a sign of the resilience of the peace process to date that support for

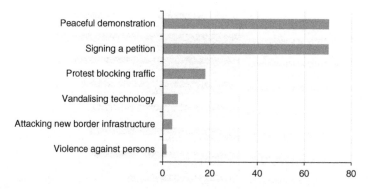

Figure 14.4 Support for various forms of protest against new North–South border checks among those who would find at least one form of check "almost impossible to accept"
Source: Garry et al. (2018).

non-peaceful activity is as low as it is. However, this finding comes with two important caveats. Firstly, and most obviously, it stems from self-reported responses to a survey and so levels of support for violence are likely to be underestimated. Secondly, more broadly, many people in Northern Ireland will be aware that while civil rights protests in the 1960s involved peaceful demonstrations, they were followed by an escalation of events that precipitated protracted conflict.[7] If widespread direct action were to take place in the context of deep political tensions, there would be a risk that peaceful forms of protest would be exploited by malevolent actors.

A new East–West challenge

Recognising the sensitivity of the North–South border and the unique position of Northern Ireland, geographically and historically, the UK government made an early 'commitment to the avoidance of a hard border (with Ireland), including any physical infrastructure or related checks and controls' (European Commission 2017: 7). However, the UK's simultaneous commitment to withdrawing from the EU's single market and customs makes it difficult to maintain border arrangements in their pre-Brexit form. The so-called "backstop" offered a potential solution. Under this insurance mechanism, Northern Ireland would remain in the customs union, relevant parts of the single market, and the EU's VAT system, even if the rest of the UK did not, and that technological solutions would be found to prevent a hardening of the border. In turn, this would result in new checks on goods between Northern Ireland and Great Britain. While these checks would be

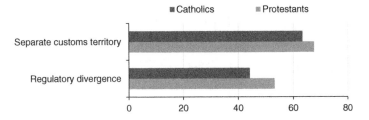

Figure 14.5 Percentage of Catholic and Protestant respondents who would find each scenario "almost impossible to accept"
Source: Garry et al. (2018).

relatively unobtrusive and could make use of existing infrastructure at ports, they caused alarm among unionist politicians over the possible long-term consequences of Northern Ireland being treated differently from the rest of the UK.

If the "backstop" were to come into effect, it would not change Northern Ireland's constitutional position in the UK. Upholding its commitments in the 1998 Agreement, the UK government insists that Northern Ireland's constitutional status continues to rest on the principle of consent; in other words, it can only change if a majority of voters in a future referendum choose to unify with the Republic of Ireland. However, for many in the Protestant community, typically aligned with support for the Union with Great Britain, the prospect of economic divergence from the rest of the UK is unsettling. A majority say they would find it "impossible to accept" different standards for goods in Northern Ireland compared to Great Britain (see Figure 14.5). There is significantly higher opposition to the prospect of Northern Ireland being in a separate customs territory to the rest of the UK, and some 68% of Protestants are against this idea. Interestingly, just as Figure 14.3 showed that a sizeable number of Protestants were opposed to new border checks on the island of Ireland, Figure 14.5 shows that a sizeable number of Catholics are opposed to a regulatory or customs border down the Irish Sea – particularly the latter prospect. Taken together with Figure 14.3, the widespread opposition to a new border regime either on the island of Ireland *or* down the Irish Sea likely explains the high level of cross-community support for the UK as a whole remaining in the single market and customs union.

Among those who would find customs or regulatory divergence between Northern Ireland and Great Britain "impossible to accept", most would support peaceful forms of protest. Echoing Figure 14.4, the clear message from Figure 14.6 is that there are only negligible levels of support for illegal forms of direct action, including violence against persons. These findings

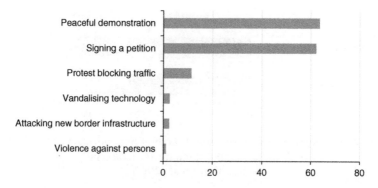

Figure 14.6 Support for various forms of protest against new East–West border checks among those who would find at least one form of check "almost impossible to accept"
Source: Garry et al. (2018).

come with the same caveats as Figure 14.4. While they demonstrate a significant degree of peaceful intent, as expressed by those who would not accept a particular Brexit outcome, the findings cannot meaningfully predict the full spectrum of future behaviour. If we can reasonably infer that over 60% of the population would find it "almost impossible to accept" Northern Ireland being in a separate economic regime to the rest of the UK, and that, of these, nearly two-thirds would support some form of peaceful protest against this outcome, it is likely that such a scenario would exist against a backdrop of deep political instability.

Conclusion

As the UK withdraws from the EU, its citizens and government have been reminded that a delicate peace process exists on its own soil – in the very part of the UK that shares a land border with another EU member state. The EU did not play a particularly active role in prelude to the 1998 Agreement, but the joint membership of the UK and Ireland helped provide a framework for constructive bilateral relations between the two states. More tangible was the EU's financial support for the peace process. Perhaps the main contribution of the EU was much less tangible all along.

If we understand Northern Ireland's peace process as the delicate cultivation of three relationships, we can see how the UK's withdrawal poses significant challenges. Within Northern Ireland, the issue of Brexit has increased the salience of the constitutional question and reinforced divisions along communal lines. In the UK's withdrawal equation, it clearly presents a dilemma: if a hard border is to be avoided on the island of Ireland, Northern Ireland will almost certainly have to exit the EU on a different basis from the rest of the UK; if Northern Ireland is to exit the EU on the same terms as the rest of the UK, a hard border would seem inevitable. Either outcome would undermine Northern Ireland's relationship with the Republic of Ireland or Great Britain; both would meet strong opposition. A return to violence is far from inevitable, and so the consequences of Brexit on the peace process should not be overstated. Similarly, however, the preservation of peace is not inevitable in a region with a recent history of conflict. The protection of the peace process in Northern Ireland rests on the continued cultivation of relationships, internal and external. Beyond Brexit, it is the responsibility of all parties to the 1998 Agreement to see that its principles and aspirations remain intact.

Notes

1 The EU was not directly involved in the negotiations culminating in the 1998 Agreement. The United States played a more influential, although not decisive, role as an external mediator (Guelke 2012).

2 After any referendum in Northern Ireland, the endorsement of a majority of voters in the Republic of Ireland would be required in a subsequent referendum for Irish reunification to proceed. The Irish Constitution no longer makes a territorial claim on Northern Ireland.

3 National identity, community background and ethno-national ideology are mutually reinforcing aspects of group identity in Northern Ireland. Those who identify as British are largely Protestant and tend to hold a unionist ideology, preferring to see Northern Ireland remain in the UK. Those who identify as Irish are mainly Catholic with a nationalist ideology, aspiring to the reunification of Ireland.

4 The 2002 edition of the NILT survey included a module of questions on people's attitudes to the EU. These questions were not repeated in subsequent iterations of the study.

5 See Phinnemore & Whitten, Chapter 12, this volume.

6 Less than a third of people in Northern Ireland say they are 'very' or 'fairly confident' that they understand what the North–South Ministerial Council does (Garry et al. 2018).

7 This is in no way to suggest that civil rights demonstrations *caused* violent conflict in Northern Ireland. However, they were symptomatic of a widespread sense of injustice by the Catholic community, providing a context for peaceful protests to be exploited by violent actors.

References

ARK (1998) *Northern Ireland Life and Times Survey*. Available at: www.ark.ac.uk/nilt/1998 [accessed 21 February 2019].

ARK (2002) *Northern Ireland Life and Times Survey*. Available at: www.ark.ac.uk/nilt/2002 [accessed 21 February 2019].

ARK (2018) *Northern Ireland Life and Times Survey* [dataset]. Available at: www.ark.ac.uk/nilt/2018/ [accessed 20 June 2021].

Arthur, P. (1999) '"Quiet diplomacy and personal conversation": Track Two diplomacy and the search for a settlement in Northern Ireland', in J. Ruane & J. Todd (eds) *After the Good Friday Agreement: analysing political change in Northern Ireland*, pp. 71–95. Dublin: University College Dublin Press.

Bell, C. (2006) 'Peace agreements: their nature and legal status'. *American Journal of International Law* 100(2): 373–412.

Bew, P., H. Patterson & P. Teague (1997) *Between war and peace: the political future of Northern Ireland*. London: Lawrence & Wishart.

Birchfield, V.L., J. Krige & A.R. Young (2017) 'European integration as a peace project'. *British Journal of Politics and International Relations* 19(1): 3–12.

Coakley, J. (2002) 'The North–South institutions: from blueprint to reality'. Institute for British–Irish Studies (IBIS) Working Paper, No. 22. Dublin: IBIS.

Coakley, J. (2014) 'British Irish institutional structures: towards a new relationship'. *Irish Political Studies* 29(1); 76–97.

Denton, G. & T. Fahy (1993) *The Northern Ireland Land Boundary, 1923–1992*. London: HM Customs and Excise.

European Commission (2017) 'Joint report from the negotiators of the European Union and the United Kingdom government'. Available at: https://ec.europa.eu/commission/sites/beta-political/files/joint_report.pdf [accessed 28 March 2019].

FCO (Foreign and Commonwealth Office) (2012) 'Award of the Nobel Peace Prize to the European Union'. Available at: www.gov.uk/government/news/award-of-the-nobel-peace-prize-to-the-european-union [accessed 28 March 2019].

Garry, J., K. McNicholl, B. O'Leary & J. Pow (2018) 'Northern Ireland and the UK's exit from the EU: what do people think?' Available at: www.qub.ac.uk/sites/brexitni/BrexitandtheBorder/Report/Filetoupload,820734,en.pdf [accessed 20 January 2019].

George, S. (1998) *An awkward partner: Britain in the European Community*. Oxford: Oxford University Press.

Goodwin, M. & C. Milazzo (2017) 'Taking back control? Investigating the role of immigration in the 2016 vote for Brexit'. *British Journal of Politics and International Relations* 19(3): 450–464.

Guelke, A. (2012) 'The USA and the Northern Ireland peace process'. *Ethnopolitics* 11(4): 424–438.

Haagerup, N.J. (1984) 'Report drawn up on behalf of the Political Affairs Committee on the situation in Northern Ireland', European Parliament Working Document 1-1526/83, 9 March. Available at: http://aei.pitt.edu/89466/1/1983%2D84.84.1526.pdf [accessed 20 June 2021].

Hayward, K. (2006) 'Reiterating national identities: the European Union conception of conflict resolution in Northern Ireland'. *Cooperation and Conflict* 41(3): 261–284.

Knox, C. (2016) 'Northern Ireland: where is the peace dividend?' *Party and Politics* 44(3): 485–503.

McCrudden, C. & D. Halberstam (2017) '*Miller* and Northern Ireland: a critical constitutional response'. University of Michigan Public Law Research Paper No. 575; Queen's University Belfast Law Research Paper No. 2018-3. Available at: https://papers.ssrn.com/sol3/papers.cfm?abstract_id=3062964 [accessed on 1 April 2019].

McCrudden, C., J. McGarry, B. O'Leary & A. Schwartz (2016) 'Why Northern Ireland's institutions need stability'. *Government and Opposition* 51(1): 30–58.

McGarry, J. & B. O'Leary (1997) *The politics of antagonism: understanding Northern Ireland*. London: Athlone Press.

McGarry, J. & B. O'Leary (2006) 'Consociational theory, Northern Ireland's conflict, and its Agreement. Part 1: what consociationalists can learn from Northern Ireland'. *Government and Opposition* 41(1): 43–63.

Meehan, E. (2000) '"Britain's Irish question: Britain's European question?" British–Irish relations in the context of European Union and the Belfast Agreement'. *Review of International Studies* 26(1): 83–97.

NIO (1998) *The Agreement: agreement reached in the multi-party negotiations*. Belfast: Northern Ireland Office.

Nobel Committee (2012) 'The Nobel Peace Prize for 2012'. Available at: www.nobelprize.org/prizes/peace/2012/press-release/ [accessed on 28 March 2019].

Police Service of Northern Ireland (PSNI) (2018) 'Police-recorded security situation statistics'. Available at: www.psni.police.uk/globalassets/inside-the-psni/our-statistics/security-situation-statistics/2018/august/security-situation-statistics-to-august_2018.pdf [accessed on 29 March 2019].

SEUPB (Special European Union Programmes Body) (2019) 'PEACE IV Programme overview'. Available at: www.seupb.eu/piv-overview [accessed on 29 March 2019].

Smyth, M. (2004) 'The process of demilitarization and the reversibility of the peace process in Northern Ireland'. *Terrorism and Political Violence* 16(3): 544–566.

Stevenson, J. (2017) 'Does Brexit threaten peace in Northern Ireland?' *Survival* 59(3): 111–128.

Treaty of Paris (Treaty Establishing the European Coal and Steel Community) (1951), in Simmonds, K. (ed.) (1980) *Sweet & Maxwell's European Community Treaties: including the European Communities Act 1972*, pp. 3–46. London: Sweet & Maxwell.

UK Government (2017) 'The Government's negotiating objectives for exiting the EU: PM speech'. Available at: www.gov.uk/government/speeches/the-governments-negotiating-objectives-for-exiting-the-eu-pm-speech [accessed on 29 March 2019].

Unwin, D. W. (2014) *The community of Europe: a history of European integration since 1945*. Abingdon: Routledge.

Wall, S. (2008) *A stranger in Europe: Britain and the EU from Thatcher to Blair*. Oxford: Oxford University Press.

Wilson, R. (2016) *Northern Ireland peace monitoring report: number four*. Belfast: Community Relations Council.

15

EU Structural Fund programmes on the island of Ireland: Interreg and the cross-border dimension

Giada Lagana

Introduction

The European narrative of peace and reconciliation has been an inspiring one for the amelioration of the conflict in Northern Ireland. Of course, the success of the peace process is to be credited primarily to the will of the actors in the conflict themselves, and to the action of the Dublin and London governments, with the assistance of the US administration. However, the EU also played an important role in facilitating negotiations, in rendering the border between the North and the South more permeable, and in making available structural and cohesion funds that helped to develop the border region's depressed economy (Lagana 2017). As a result, cross-border cooperation has increased substantially in the past several years.

This chapter will focus on the EU's Interreg programme, the initiative aimed specifically at border regions in Europe. The chapter is divided into four parts. This opening section examines the historical development of cross-border cooperation on the island. Next we look at the Interreg programme and its related economic issues and challenges. Then we examine the changes introduced during the period after the 1998 Agreement before exploring the possible consequences of policy choices that are currently being made and their likely implications for the future of cross-border cooperation on the island of Ireland.

The 1985 Anglo-Irish Agreement created the context for the development of cross-border cooperation (McCall 2014: 43). From 1985, local government reforms in Northern Ireland increased nationalist political influence in border areas which strengthened demand for cross-border links (Tannam 1999: 118). In addition, the rather different national projects of the British and Irish governments vis-à-vis European integration began to converge in support of cross-border cooperation. Initiatives for the border regions were supported by increased EU funding. Significant EU funding became available in the 1990s with the Interreg programme to assist the economies of border areas and encourage cross-border cooperation. This programme was complemented by other funding from the IFI and Co-operation Ireland (Coakley 2017).

The political talks process initiated in the 1990s further strengthened cross-border cooperative arrangements (O'Dowd et al. 1995: 276). The cessation of paramilitary violence in Northern Ireland from October 1994 removed a major constraint on the normal conduct of life, and in 1995 the EU initiated a programme unique to Ireland to promote social inclusion and reconciliation, the Special Support Programme for Peace and Reconciliation.[1] The programme covered Northern Ireland and the six border counties in the Republic of Ireland.

When the talks process culminated in the 1998 Agreement, this had a further impact on EU support for cross-border cooperation. First, the EU was anticipated to be an important factor in preserving and consolidating the initially uneasy peace on the island (Laffan & Payne 2001; McCall 2007; Tannam 1999). In addition, the Agreement's model of institutional cooperation is purposefully complex, elaborate and ambiguous, consciously fragmenting political and institutional power by creating independent institutional layers. This created space for local authorities in the border regions to become more influential, and the local allocation and management of EU funds further empowered them.

The Interreg I & II programmes

During the negotiations of the Single European Act in 1985–1986, it was argued that peripheral countries and regions with weaker economic development would find it hard to compete with other member states in a single market environment. The focus of this argument was on Greece, Ireland, Portugal and Spain (the so-called four cohesion countries) and on poorer regions in other member states. There was also a debate around the specific requirements of the European border regions. Typically, these areas were suffering from their peripheral location and had more problems of unemployment, underinvestment and underdevelopment than the less remote regions of the member states. The poorer regions would require substantial financial assistance to enable them to compete on a level playing field with the core economies. It was in this context that the Delors I package of Structural Funding from 1988 to 1992 allocated special cohesion money to Ireland. In addition, plans were drawn up for a new initiative aimed at the border regions: Interreg. The programme was perceived as assisting the competitiveness of border regions in the context of the internal market programme.

The first Ireland/Northern Ireland Interreg programme ran from 1991 to 1993. The development objectives of the programme stressed the need to tackle specific problems of peripherality and to address 'the interests of the local population' (European Commission 1991). From this point of view, Interreg constitutes the first expression and the first EU initiative specifically focused on the local. This objective is also echoed in the second of the project's aims, dealing with creating and developing linkages and networks across borders and between communities (Laffan & Payne 2001: 47). These are the beginnings of what would later become a specific EU emphasis on a "bottom-up" approach. The guidelines also stressed the importance of genuine cross-border cooperation:

> The Commission will accord priority to proposals which are made in co-operation with regional and local authorities in border areas and which include the establishment or development of shared institutional or administrative structures intended to widen and deepen cross-border co-operation between public agencies, private organizations and voluntary bodies. Where possible, these shared institutional and administrative structures should have the competence to implement jointly determined projects. (Laffan & Payne 2001: 47)

Over the course of Interreg, the two tenets of "bottom-up" mobilisation and "genuine cross-border" cooperation evolved. Interreg started to be perceived by the Commission as the Union's policy instrument to create capacity within border regions for "bottom-up" development (interview 7). The key features of its model of capacity building encompassed the identification of obstacles and limits, multi-annual programming, local mobilisation and institutionalisation. Schemas for classifying types of cross-border projects and for joint planning of programmes were developed. Each sector of cooperation was developed as a sub-programme and a monitoring committee and a related civil service network in both the Dublin and Belfast administrations were responsible for the delivery and management of the programme (Laffan & Payne 2001: 53). At the other end was the creation of lasting institutions shared between the border areas concerned. The purpose of those was to sustain coherence in the approach to development in the European borderlands. Notwithstanding clear difficulties – which will be explored in the next section – the initiative continued during the next round of funding.

Interreg II ran from 1994 to 1999 and its guidelines were almost a carbon copy of those from 1990. The thematic areas eligible for funding were development planning, aid to investment, small and medium-sized enterprises, tourism, infrastructure, environmental protection, rural development, plant and animal health, linking associations of all kinds on a cross-border basis, education, and training and unemployment. One substantial difference was found in the implementation process of the programme. While the Department of Finance in Dublin (DoF) and the DFP in Belfast held overall responsibility for the implementation of the programme in their respective jurisdictions, the Commission looked for a more decentralised management structure with development officers whose role was to enhance the capacity of potential beneficiaries on the ground to participate in activities. As a core part of the management structure, joint working groups were established (interview 6). They comprised the relevant sectoral government department officials from the Belfast and Dublin administrations. Such a complex and fragmented organisation required a policy response on several fronts, which ultimately was not adequately provided.

Four main obstacles emerged. Firstly, efforts to design and manage cross-border projects in a decentralised manner had to contend with the highly centralised nature of the Irish and UK states. Policy-making power tends to be concentrated at the centres with only a limited role for the peripheral areas (Hogwood et al. 2000: 84–85). The separate regions of the UK have some discretionary power, particularly after the creation of devolved administrations in Northern Ireland, Scotland and Wales. None-theless, such local power tends to be modest. Therefore, the Structural Funds, with their emphasis on partnership and "bottom-up" development, did not fit easily into the dominant style of public policy making on either side of the border. The authorities in Dublin and Belfast were quick to assert their role as gatekeepers in relation to Brussels (interview 7). For example, in the Republic, the Department of Finance dominated the design and imple-mentation of the National Development Plan. It only engaged in limited and largely cosmetic consultation with sub-national actors, with the result that the plan reflected national sectoral imperatives rather than regional and local ones (interview 6). In Northern Ireland, the DFP was the key actor in the elaboration of the North's Community Support Framework. There was limited consultation with local interest groups and the cross-border dimen-sion was apparently minor in the plans submitted for funding under Interreg.

The second issue was the high degree of rivalry between agencies across the border, which complicated the effort of the joint working groups. Lack of joint management at the working group level was evident and projects tended to be appraised and agreed within the department network and according to the policy priorities for that administration. The involvement with another jurisdiction was at the very least non-standard and was often seen as upsetting long-established procedures and power relationships (Coakley et al. 2005: 120–124). Only occasionally did locally designated representatives from the two administrations exchange information regard-ing sub-projects, involving very little overall joint planning and manage-ment (interview 1). With such a system, even the most determined cross-border project was always going to be threatened by the administrative difficulties this lack of cooperation posed.

Third, the difference of attitudes towards the EU and its policy regimes on both sides of the border further complicated the context of managing and implementing Interreg. From accession in 1973, the attitudes and policies of successive UK and Irish governments diverged. The Irish political elite was more comfortable than its neighbour with the pooling of sovereignty and the fragmentation of political power associated with EU membership. The EU was not a contentious issue in party politics in Ireland, whereas it caused major splits in both the Labour and Conservative parties at different times (Meehan 2014: 60–61). Moreover, divergent attitudes towards European integration were accompanied by different attitudes towards some of the EU's policy regimes. Successive Irish governments played a key part in the design and ongoing improvements to the CAP, prioritising the interests not just of farmers in the Republic but also in Northern Ireland. Successive UK governments, on the other hand, were determined to bring agricultural expenditure under control (Murphy 2014: 78–79). Different fiscal policies also had a major impact upon the economy of cross-border activity (Tannam 1999: 45). In addition, from 2002, citizens of the Republic shared a common currency with other member states, but not Northern Ireland (as part of the UK).

Finally, the potential to deliver genuine cross-border projects was highly dependent upon the relevant organisations' capacity to deliver (interview 2). At the local level, business interests needed greater access to information about potential opportunities and access to a facilitator who could help them with the administrative challenges in trying to do business in two different jurisdictions (interview 2). Likewise, the local community level was in a similar position, aggravated by a lack of common understanding of the administrative structures on the other side of the border. This situation further complicated real joint management and joint planning of the Interreg local initiatives (interview 6).

Interreg III and the 1998 Agreement

Interreg III was developed and implemented in a changing institutional environment. Three different processes need to be accounted for in this context. Firstly, in 1995, the EU Commission launched the Peace Programme, which was perceived as having strong potential for facilitating a wider partnership, particularly at the local community level (interview 7). The Commission was anxious to see a comparable widening of the policy processes for Interreg. It called for a greater role for local actors by encouraging them to form cross-border networks and to develop strategic plans for cross-border policy. Local authority networks received additional funding from the Peace Programme to establish a full-time secretariat which would facilitate the development of local partnerships and integrated area plans. This clearly also benefited their Interreg management (interview 7). Following the example of the structure of the Peace Programme, the cross-border networks attempted to reposition themselves in the policy process to gain a more central role in Interreg III.

Secondly, the signature of the 1998 Agreement made provision for an Executive within Northern Ireland and a cross-border implementation body, the North–South Ministerial Council (NSMC). The work of the NSMC was to provide a formal institutional channel, supported by a secretariat in Armagh, for the office-holders in both jurisdictions to develop consultations, cooperation and action on an all-island and cross-border basis. The provisions of the Agreement clearly identified the NSMC as a decision-making body, rather than a consultative one (Laffan & Payne 2001: 89). However, in practice, these provisions were never fully implemented, as the NSMC did not meet for three years following the collapse of the Northern Ireland Executive in 2017.

Thirdly, the new institutional environment established by the Agreement encouraged the creation of an additional implementation administration, the Special EU Programmes Body (SEUPB). SEUPB has responsibility for the management of cross-border EU Structural Funds programmes in Northern Ireland, the border region of Ireland and part of western Scotland. Given the history of EU programmes in the border region, the establishment of the SEUPB was not unexpected but neither was it universally welcomed. SEUPB is beyond the direct control of either the Irish or the Northern Ireland jurisdictions and with direct dealings with the EU Commission (interview 4). In addition, the introduction of a new body disturbed the policy cycle in the established bureaucratic apparatus in the two finance departments. The DoF in Dublin and the DFP in Belfast adopted different approaches to the body from its outset. On the Irish side, the DoF seconded its key Interreg personnel to SEUPB. Their Northern Ireland counterparts wished to keep a close eye on the development of the body and issued it with several guidance notes, reflecting the will to have a more centralised relationship with it. These differing approaches led to considerable unease among Interreg beneficiaries (interview 4). When civil servants from different administrative cultures were working together in cooperative processes on cross-border projects (interview 4), this did not always work smoothly. Conflicting interests and different views about processes of policy making were still present.

All these dynamics and their interactions altered the environment within which Interreg III developed. Networks were considerably empowered to take a more active role in Interreg III by the new institutions. Although they had slightly different structures, they operated on the basis of a calendar of meetings. Their day-to-day work included project management, financial management, servicing committees and task forces, preparation of papers and reports, networking within other organisations in the region, developing strategies for the region, and liaising with government departments, the European Commission and the media (interview 5). The effectiveness of the system relied on the capacity to leverage the political and administrative resources of the participating councils. The councils worked on the basis of encouraging partnership between the bodies responsible for different functions within the participating networks and coordinating statutory agencies within their geographical areas.

The networks wanted to create a wider regional identity and regional sensitivity among the participating councils. The aim was to get the politicians to see the advantages of a larger regional framework. The motivation was both political and economic. Politically, the lack of influence over public policies in local areas was a major grievance (interview 4). Economically, for those councils on the northern side of the border with nationalist majorities, cross-border cooperation was always regarded as a positive (interview 2). Unionist councillors, on the other hand, were willing to embrace functional cooperation that did not have political overtones, but that could bring additional funds to their areas. Inevitably, this was an unpredictable process because not all politicians in the border region were committed to this model. Moreover, not all senior officials in local governments gave priority to it or to cross-border cooperation. However, a critical mass of support for the networks developed under the aegis of Interreg III (interview 2), fuelled by the changing opportunities in the political environment and following the bottom-up approach introduced by the Peace Programme.

The success of the networks in carving out a role for themselves in the implementation of Interreg III reflects their own growing capacity to negotiate and to use their limited resources to best effect. The role of the SEUPB in this context was also one of mediating between the local and the European level. The networks' eventual success was highly dependent upon the outcome of factors such as the need for the networks to reorganise so as to involve a wider societal interest; the capacity of the SEUPB to establish and organise itself quickly enough to be an effective actor for both the management and the development of Interreg and other EU programmes; and, finally, the priority accorded to the matter at the Council level. Criticisms are often made about the SEUPB concerning its capacity to represent civil society, or to mediate between the sponsoring departments.

In the evolution of its role, the dynamic initiated by the creation of an executive in Northern Ireland and the NSMC was crucial. The addition of a political dynamic to what was traditionally an administrative framework had a profound influence on the evolution of the body and, consequently, on the impact of the programme in the border region. One UUP MEP described the programme in the following words:

> Interreg is still one of the most popular programmes of Europe and it lasts the challenge of time. We – the Unionists – were suspicious of its aim of changing the meaning of 'border'. We tried to resist while the programme persisted through the years, and I now consider it as one of the best programmes ever delivered in the border regions of the island by the EU. (interview 3)

Cross-border cooperation on the island after Brexit

Article 50 was triggered on 29 March 2017 and the "divorce negotiations" between the UK government and the European Commission opened on 19 June 2017. The narrowness of the UK vote to Leave, and the fact that a majority (56%) in Northern Ireland voted to Remain, ensured that the politics of Brexit were more problematic for negotiators than once predicted. The Remain vote had a majority in eleven of the eighteen Northern Ireland parliamentary constituencies. Of the eight Northern Irish constituencies along the border, only one (Upper Bann) voted to Leave with many of the others returning large Remain votes, including a ratio of more than 2:1 in South Down (BBC n.d.).

The shock of Brexit impacted negatively on all civil service and local council departments across the Irish border, North and South. The sources of potential friction were multi-layered. Since a majority of voters in Northern Ireland – and particularly nationalist ones – voted Remain, the Irish government felt obliged to protect the interests of these citizens. On the other hand, the UK government was obliged not to take sides in undermining nationalist interests. And once Article 50 was triggered, Ireland and the UK were not on the same side for the first time in decades. The Irish government was part of the EU27 negotiating team while the UK government was "the other side", so the Irish government was not free to bargain unilaterally with the UK even if the UK requested it. Thus, both governments could not share information in the way they once did, neither could they liaise in the neutral framework of the EU.

The European Council (2018) insisted that the negotiations would occur in three stages and that substantial progress must be made in stage one, which dealt with the Irish border, the CTA and citizens' rights. This reflected intensive lobbying by Irish officials, the objective of which was to ensure that the UK government would not link the border issue to gaining concessions in a trade deal (Tannam 2018). The UK and Irish governments' interests and preferences were consequently diverging from the very beginning. Similarly, the EU argued that it was the UK's responsibility, not the EU's, to solve the Irish border issue. Again, this reflected the Irish government's position and was at odds with UK preferences (McCall 2018: 294). More generally, Brexit means that the Irish government has lost a powerful ally with whom it shared many common interests in the EU. Instead, it is now faced with conflicts of interest emerging from economic issues (Gillespie 2017).

Economically, Brexit turned a spotlight on several regional weaknesses and vulnerabilities. It raised the possibility of border checkpoints on main arterial routes, the closure of hundreds of secondary cross-border roads, and mobile border security patrols to control the movement of people and goods. The management of the Irish border had never entirely reduced it to merely a line on the map, but the disappearance of customs posts and the removal of security checkpoints had taken much of the friction out of it (McCall 2018: 300). This freedom of movement, together with successful cross-border interactions, had helped to erode the 'border in the mind' (Gormley-Heenan & Aughey 2018: 497). The importance of cross-border trade to small firms, the integration of the agri-food industry and other sectors[2] have all been partly assisted by the form of border management in recent years (Magennis et al. 2017: 38).

One contribution of Interreg to good border management has been the creation of cross-border cooperation across the region between business bodies, higher education institutions, health services and efforts by policy networks and interest groups to facilitate cross-border reconciliation. In this sense, the new partnership arrangements in the Derry-Donegal North West City Region have been highlighted as a step in the right direction (Magennis et al. 2017: 44). Similar results have been represented by the Memorandum of Understanding between Newry, Mourne and Down District Councils and Louth County Council which was signed in 2011 (White 2011). The joint approach taken by networks and local authorities, from Interreg III onwards, was a concrete step towards the economic integration of the island of Ireland. It also shows how the EU tried to support the local level through engaging with local citizens and bringing their views to the functioning of Strand Two of the 1998 Agreement and, more broadly, to the peace process in Northern Ireland.

Solving many of the issues raised above will depend upon how the impact of Brexit on the Irish border – whatever form that takes – can be managed. The success of any future regime for the management of the Irish border needs to be judged, not only on how well it answers the political and economic dilemmas caused to the border region by Brexit but also how far it allows the current level of co-dependencies, which exist across Council areas and between policy networks, to continue unhindered.

The Interreg VA programme for 2014–2021 aims to help to create a more prosperous and sustainable cross-border region. The programme reflects priority areas for territorial cooperation in Europe. In line with the Europe 2020 strategy, the Commission requires that all of the new 2014–2020 programmes focus on a narrow range of activities to ensure that there is sufficient available funding to bring about significant change. The original guidelines stated that 'projects have to be cross-border in nature and must, therefore, involve partners from at least two member states' (SEUPB n.d.: 1). Clearly, Brexit poses problems for maintaining support from this point of view. While the UK left open the door to continued participation in some EU funding programmes, it is currently unclear what these might be. In particular, it is not clear if this will include some or all of Interreg programmes, thus potentially disrupting many of the achievements realised to date on the island of Ireland.

Conclusion

This chapter focused on the Interreg programme and the economic issues and challenges of cross-border cooperation which confronted policy makers on the island of Ireland. It situated Interreg in the context of the Irish border and it clarified why the administrative models adopted for the first two programmes, Interreg I and II, did not achieve satisfactory results and particularly lacked focus on "genuine cross-border" sub-projects. The analysis argued that the centralised nature of the Irish and British administrations, the high degree of rivalry between agencies across the border and the different attitudes towards the EU on both sides of the border, hindered the authentic involvement of networks and interest groups in the initiatives. Subsequently, the signing of the 1998 Agreement, the creation of SEUPB with its exclusive European remit and the networks' capacity to use their limited resources to create a wider regional identity and regional sensitivity among the participating councils, all impacted positively on the Interreg III programme. Finally, this chapter provided a preliminary analysis of the possible consequences of Brexit and its likely implications for the future of cross-border cooperation on the island of Ireland.

Even though the Irish border region has received significant amounts of EU funding since the 1990s, it continues to lag behind national averages. Contrary to popular opinion, the evidence presented shows a real need for the management of cross-border cooperation and cross-border initiatives to remain as close as possible to its current position, given the practical issues and political sensitivities around it. In addition, continuity in the current management of cross-border cooperation would allow networks and interest groups to keep growing and learning from their past experience. Cross-border cooperation has been integral to the European integration project because it presents a bottom-up projection for integration that offers some counter-balance to charges of undemocratic top-down Brussels polity-building. It can also advance conflict resolution because it can provide a means to open the territorial cage of Northern Ireland and promote cross-border inter-cultural dialogue for communities amenable to such dialogue.

In other words, peace, services, people and investment, and the free movement of goods, should be the goal. The EU has certainly been flexible and imaginative when it has established arrangements for the management of other borders. For instance, it has engaged in Germany and Cyprus and also between Croatia and Bosnia and Herzegovina. Recognition of the unique circumstances of Ireland, with its distinctive cross-border flows, contained within the new Irish government National Planning Framework, could also potentially provide a restart for regional policy. In this context, the continuation of EU funding to ensure not only that cross-border cooperation through Interreg continues, but so too peace and reconciliation projects funded by the Peace Programme, research collaboration in Horizon 2020 and successor programmes, and student mobility activities through Erasmus, is certainly an essential element for the future.

Notes

1 Commonly known as the Peace Programme.
2 For example, accountancy firms in the border region estimate that 30% of their staff and 50% of their clients straddle the border.

References

BBC (n.d.) 'EU referendum results'. Available at: www.bbc.com/news/politics/eu_referendum/results [accessed 12 September 2020].
Coakley, J. (2017) 'Resolving international border disputes: the Irish experience'. *Cooperation and Conflict* 52(3): 377–398.
Coakley, J., B. Laffan & J. Todd (2005) *Renovation or revolution? New territorial politics in Ireland and the United Kingdom*. Dublin: University College Dublin Press.

European Commission (1991) *Joint Interreg programme for Northern Ireland and Ireland, 1991–1993*. Luxembourg: Office for Official Publications of the European Communities.

European Council (2018) *Guidelines, 23 March 2018*. Available at: www.consilium. europa.eu/media/33458/23-euco-art50-guidelines.pdf [accessed 12 September 2020].

Gillespie, P. (2017) 'A British departure from the EU would have major consequences for Ireland'. *LSE Blog*. Available at: https://blogs.lse.ac.uk/europpblog/2016/03/15/a-british-departure-from-the-eu-would-have-major-consequences-for-ireland/ [accessed 12 September 2020].

Gormley-Heenan, C. & A. Aughey (2018) 'Northern Ireland and Brexit: three effects on "the border in the mind"'. *British Journal of Politics and International Relations* 19(3): 497–511.

Hogwood, P., C. Carter, S. Bulmer, M. Burch & A. Scott (2000) 'Devolution and EU policymaking: the territorial challenge'. *Public Policy and Administration* 15(2): 81–95.

Laffan, B. & D. Payne (2001) *Creating living institutions: EU cross-border cooperation after the Good Friday Agreement*. Centre for Cross Border Studies report, Institute for British–Irish Studies, UCD. Available at: www.crossborder.ie/pubs/creatingliving.pdf [accessed 28 October 2019].

Lagana, G. (2017) 'A preliminary investigation on the genesis of EU cross-border cooperation on the island of Ireland'. *Space and Polity* 21(3): 289–302.

Magennis, E., A. Park & L. Heery (2017) *Brexit and the border corridor*. Border Corridor Local Authorities. Available at: www.eastborderregion.com/media/uploads/Brexit%20and%20the%20Border%20Corridor%20Report.pdf [accessed 2 November 2019].

McCall, C. (2007) 'Creating border space in Ireland: an EU approach to ethno-national threat and insecurity', in A. Warwick & J. Anderson (eds) *Geopolitics of European Union enlargement: the fortress empire*, pp. 61–77. Abingdon: Routledge.

McCall, C. (2014) *The European Union and peacebuilding: the cross-border dimension*. Basingstoke: Palgrave Macmillan.

McCall C. (2018) 'Brexit, bordering and bodies on the island of Ireland'. *Ethnopolitics* 17(3): 292–305.

Meehan, E. (2014) 'The changing British–Irish relationship: the sovereignty dimension'. *Irish Political Studies* 29(1): 58–75.

Murphy, M.C. (2014) *Northern Ireland and the European Union: the dynamics of a changing relationship*. Manchester: Manchester University Press.

O'Dowd, L., J. Corrigan & T. Moore (1995) 'Borders, national sovereignty and European integration: the British–Irish case'. *International Journal of Urban and Regional Research* 19(3): 219–285.

SEUPB (n.d.) *Citizen's summary: Interreg VA programme (2014–2020)*. Special EU Programmes Body. Available at: www.seupb.eu/sites/default/files/styles/file_entity_browser_thumbnail/public/INTERREG%20Content%20Type/IVA_CitizensSummary_English_Amended_Version2.pdf [accessed 12 September 2020].

Tannam, E. (1999) *Cross-border cooperation in the Republic of Ireland and Northern Ireland*. Basingstoke: Macmillan.

Tannam, E. (2018) 'Intergovernmental and cross-border civil service cooperation: the Good Friday Agreement and Brexit'. *Ethnopolitics* 17(3): 243–262.

White, P. (2011) 'Re-thinking the border region economy: the way forward'. Presentation at the conference on *Reviving the Border Region Economy*, Cavan, 18 November. Available at: www.crossborder.ie/pubs/bre_White.pdf [accessed 12 September 2020].

Interviews

1   Andy Pollak, former director of the Armagh Centre for Cross-Border Studies, 28 November 2015.
2   Ruth Taillon, former director of the Armagh Centre for Cross-Border Studies, 10 November 2015.
3   Jim Nicholson, former UUP MEP for Northern Ireland, 27 November 2015.
4   Patrick Colgan, former chief executive of the Special EU Programmes Body and Senior Adviser Government of Ireland, 16 May 2016.
5   Roberto Speciale, former head of the EU Committee on Regional Policy, 17 March 2017.
6   Andy Pollak, former director of the Armagh Centre for Cross-Border Studies, 27 April 2018.
7   Carlo Trojan, former EU Commission secretary-general, 27 February 2019.

16

Ireland and the EU: nationalism in internationalism

Michael Holmes and Kathryn Simpson

The future relationship of Ireland and the EU

The aim of this book has been to evaluate how the Irish–EU relationship has been impacted by the "long decade" of crises that have befallen Ireland, the EU and, indeed, the globe. Our focus has included both the Republic of Ireland and Northern Ireland. So with two polities to consider and contributions covering social, political and economic perspectives, we do not intend to impose a single overarching interpretation on the analysis. Our aim in this final chapter is to identify areas of broad agreement and disagreement and to suggest what these might mean for the Irish–EU relationship.

We start by summarising the main pre-crisis interpretations of that relationship. In the second part of the chapter, we summarise some of the main findings from the various chapters and interpret how these might feed into a broader approach to Ireland's relationship with the EU. We argue that this relationship is characterised by a slightly paradoxical "nationalism within internationalism" attitude and that this has been strengthened by the various crises. In the final part of this chapter, we explore how this relationship might evolve in the future, identifying potential fault-lines that might further disrupt it. However, our general conclusion is that Ireland has become an even more committed partner of the EU over the years of crisis since 2008, even if that commitment remains firmly embedded in a self-interested approach.

Irish–EU relations pre-crisis

At the start of 2008, thirty-five years had passed since the Republic of Ireland and Northern Ireland joined what was originally the European Community. By that point, a consistent analysis of Ireland and European integration was well established. European membership was almost universally seen as a very positive thing for Ireland, North and South, though the rationale for this interpretation was different in each polity.

In the Republic, membership was regarded as an essential part of a significant and successful redirection of the Irish economy, away from a protectionist, autarchic model to an open, export-orientated one. Membership contributed to 'the economic modernisation of Ireland' (Laffan & O'Mahony 2008: 1), with O'Brien declaring it to be 'the European rescue of the Irish state' (2009: 106). O'Donnell argues that 'European integration and governance have been centrally important in the economic transformation that Ireland has experienced in the past decade' (2000: 209). Membership might not have caused all of this, but it provided the context (O'Donnell 2000: 212), and 'becoming a member state in 1973 was the culmination of a decisive shift in Ireland's domestic and foreign economic policy, a shift that embraced internationalization and economic development' (Laffan & O'Mahony 2008: 8). Europe is also associated with positive social transformations. O'Connor argues 'it is widely accepted that, legally and politically, membership of the EU has impacted positively on the position of women in Irish society' (1998: 3). Begg agrees that 'European Union social policy has been hugely influential in the progressive development of Irish social policy, particularly in the field of equality' and also notes the role of the EU in trade union rights (2004: 46).

The positive perception of membership did not occur immediately. Drudy and McAleese were slightly cautious in their evaluation of the first ten years of Irish membership, noting 'it would appear that the benefits and costs of membership have been rather more finely balanced than originally envisaged' (1984: 12). It also seemed that the Republic had joined not out of any great Europeanist conviction, but for highly practical reasons. There has been something of 'a "begging bowl" mentality in the way both the state and Irish society have looked upon the EU' (Kirby & Murphy 2011: 141). Laffan refers to a pervasive mentality about Brussels being where someone could 'get us a grant' (1989: 43). Another early analysis noted how 'our membership has been of a peculiarly passive nature' and commented that 'Brussels is best known as a source of arbitrary largesse or hardship' (Hederman 1983: 143).

However, there were losers as well as winners from membership, and this was particularly evident in the No votes recorded in a series of European referendums in Ireland. While Keogh argued that the Yes outcome in the Single European Act (SEA) referendum in 1987 was 'the "last hurrah" for those who continued to believe that there was a hope of Ireland leaving the European Community' (1990: 281), a level of significant criticism persisted, challenging various aspects of the Irish–EU relationship. This was shown in the rejection of the Nice and Lisbon treaties in Ireland. Because of the perception of Ireland as a good European, 'when Ireland voted No to the Treaty of Nice in June 2001, the reaction in many quarters was as if a good pupil had suddenly misbehaved' (Holmes 2005a: 1). The further No vote on the Treaty of Lisbon in 2008 suggested that 'Ireland's long-standing consensus on the EU is over' (Laffan & O'Mahony 2008: xiii).

The opposition came from divergent sources and raised different issues. Broadly, we can identify radical left opposition, focusing on the perceived neoliberal aspects of the EU; a more nationalist opposition, focusing on loss of sovereignty; and various forms of right-wing opposition, ranging from neoliberal concerns that the EU was over-regulated and offered too many social protections to conservative fears that the EU would undermine Ireland's Catholic social ethos (Holmes 2005b: 82–84). This means that opposition to the EU is always something of a temporary phenomenon that coalesces around the time of referendums and is not a coherent and consistent force. Nonetheless, the same could be said of pro-EU groups. Most political parties, most of the media and many interest groups (farmers, business groups, trade unions, civil society groups) are strongly pro-European. However, the "pro-Europeanness" of business groups is by no means the same as that of trade unions; that of farmers' organisations can clash with that of environmental groups.

What emerges is quite a mercenary outlook on EU integration. While there are some idealists, Ireland's enthusiasm for participation in the EU is built around specific policy benefits and advantages – market access, agricultural benefits, social benefits or whatever. In similar vein, however, the continuing criticism of the EU in some quarters also reflects a fragmented, policy-by-policy approach. What acts as a binding agent on both sides is an appeal to a presumed national interest.

If we turn to consider Northern Ireland, there is a perception that the region is "less European" than the Republic, with Kennedy noting that 'enthusiasm for European integration and for the European Union in Northern Ireland has never reached the intensity it has in the Republic' (2000: 4). The long conflict also made it difficult to foster a broad consensus in Northern Ireland. There has always been a tendency for politicians from one camp to argue that "if the other lot are for something, then I must be against it", whatever the "it" might be. In general, 'the limited salience of EU issues for the region's political parties' (Murphy & Phinnemore 2005: 151) must be noted.

However, Northern Ireland has also benefited from EU membership and 'enjoys a privileged position within the EU' (Murphy & Phinnemore 2005: 152). It has received extensive funding through the CAP, the ERDF and from various cross-border funding programmes. In general, there has been a growing appreciation of the potential benefits of the EU for Northern

Ireland and a deepening level of engagement with EU institutions and activities (Murphy & Phinnemore 2005: 165), with the region developing a distinctly 'European flavour' (Murphy 2014: 5).

The EU has also been a support for peace in Northern Ireland. As several of the contributors to this volume have noted, the EU itself exemplifies a successful model of conflict resolution, one which allows different national identities to coexist in a peaceful fashion. It also provided a setting in which the British and Irish governments and politicians from both communities in Northern Ireland could experience processes of negotiation, compromise and consensus-building. As Laffan argues, 'without the embedding of both states in the wider system of European integration and without the model of politics offered by the EU, it is unlikely that both states and other political actors could have found the political capacity and the institutional models to craft the Good Friday Agreement' (2002: 63).

However, Brexit had a significant impact on awareness of the role played by the EU in Northern Ireland. As in the Republic, much of the debate revolves around the practical, sectoral benefits of the EU. And there is a notable impact related to perceptions of "national" interest. Of course, perceptions of nationalism in Northern Ireland are quite different from the Republic. But we can see both a strong influence from Irish nationalism, and perhaps also one that comes from English nationalism, with some actors in Northern Ireland being more open to Eurosceptic influences emanating from England.

The impact of the crises

The 2008 financial crisis was a shock to the Republic's pro-EU stance. This was highlighted in Chapter 7 by Moore and Trommer on protest movements and is also evident in Chapter 6 by Holmes on political parties. The EU was seen as imposing an economic prescription on the country without any democratic accountability, and this led to 'an unparalleled growth in support for the left in Ireland' (Holmes 2019: 79). However, criticism of the EU was tempered by two things. Firstly, the Irish financial crisis was interpreted on all sides as being due to errors by the Irish government of the time, not as a result of EU policies. Secondly, while there was strong dislike of the austerity medicine, there was also an acceptance that the EU was a necessary bulwark to protect Ireland from the potentially even less tender mercies of the global financial markets (Simpson & Loveless 2017).

These themes of austerity and economic hardship are also frequently found in the narratives on the causes of populism. Ireland may therefore be regarded as potentially fertile ground for a rise in populism. Moore and Trommer (Chapter 7) and Elliott (Chapter 5) suggest that populism in Ireland was manifested in the form of a social movement consisting of interrelated waves of public protect. From household-centred contestations of housing taxes and water charges, to demonstrations and marches on issues such as austerity, asylum policy, homelessness, marriage equality and women's bodily autonomy, Irish citizens have aired their grievances through public protest and have, often successfully, demanded change in Irish politics.

This is a rather unusual story of populism. On the one hand, many of the risks associated with populism (government submission to populist demands, the lending of political parties to populist causes and a fragmentation of parliament) were experienced in Ireland. However, they were realised in a way that left the political establishment *largely* intact. Political and structural reforms were minor, concessions to populism were quite issue-specific and the political parties that guided the imposition of austerity in 2010 are back in power (see Holmes, Chapter 6). At least some of this is due to the apparently quite limited appeal of Euroscepticism in Ireland. Despite the potentially favourable conditions for criticism of the EU following the financial crisis, if anything support for the EU was strengthened.

Elliot (Chapter 5) examines how Ireland's migration policy evolved from a series of opt-outs to comprehensive solidarity with EU member states on this policy issue. While Ireland's migration policies have moved closer to EU norms, the motivation for policy change came from domestic rather than EU level politics. Social movements and the judiciary played decisive roles in some of the major changes, particularly on the right to work for asylum seekers and reforms to the direct provision system and the IPA. While Ireland remained largely unaffected by the migration crisis, it placed itself in the group of open-minded EU member states reiterating the values and norms of the EU project. And the protection, promotion and emphasis on the importance of the values and norms of the EU project (and not regarding it as solely as an economic project) is further demonstrated by the lack of debate around Irexit, as is shown by Holmes (Chapter 6), Simpson (Chapter 8) and Cawley (Chapter 9).

Populism, in the context of Ireland, is contingent and local, reacting to the peculiarities of political culture and circumstance. While populism may be sweeping liberal democracies across the globe, it is fundamentally a local phenomenon. And although there has been a growth in more EU-critical opinion in Ireland, arguably the 2008 financial crisis had less of an effect on Irish attitudes on European integration than might at first have been supposed. Simpson (Chapter 8) shows that despite some growth in critical attitudes, Irish public opinion remains strongly supportive of membership, particularly when compared with other EU member states. Gallagher et al.

(Chapter 3) also underline how the EU prescriptions were perceived as leading to an economic recovery, and they conclude that 'Ireland is choosing Europe'.

This idea that Ireland is choosing the EU also appears in several chapters that consider the impact of Brexit. Tonra (Chapter 2), Holmes (Chapter 6) and Laffan and O'Mahony (Chapter 10) note how Brexit served to "re-bind" the Irish–EU relationship, noting the development of a strong anti-Brexit, pro-EU consensus in Ireland. Laffan and O'Mahony focus in particular on Ireland's formulation of a Brexit strategy with two strong approaches. One was to build and maintain a broad domestic consensus that membership of the EU is a good thing for Ireland, and the second was to ensure that Ireland's core interests were understood both in Brussels and in the capitals of the member states. Kinsella (Chapter 11) also notes that Brexit deprived Ireland of its natural ally in the EU, but that this served to push Ireland more strongly *towards* the EU. In light of the Brexit crisis, Ireland reformed its diplomatic infrastructure and reinforced key bilateral relationships with the EU with the EU26 member states offering unparalleled support for Irish interests throughout Brexit negotiations.

While there was no quid pro quo on the part of the EU for this support for Ireland during these negotiations, Tonra (Chapter 2) argues there may have been an implied expectation that Ireland would show greater solidarity on issues such as taxation, defence, regulation of the digital economy or budgetary transfers – key issues where Ireland has remained somewhat of an outlier in the past. Killian (Chapter 4) examines one of these key issues in depth – taxation – and argues that Ireland's combative stance on maintaining a low tax rate while remaining in good standing with the EU is a delicate balance. The way in which tax policy has developed in Ireland illustrates the complexity of the Ireland–EU relationship and neither the 2008 financial crisis nor the Brexit crisis has changed that.

In light of Brexit, Ireland will have to adapt to losing the UK as an important partner and ally on many issues in the EU. One example of this adjustment is Ireland joining the New Hanseatic League – an unofficial title given to a group of fiscally conservative EU member states coordinating policies and positions on a new European architecture on economic governance and the future of the single currency on an informal basis.[1] This potential new relationship is discussed by Tonra (Chapter 2), Gallagher et al. (Chapter 3) and Killian (Chapter 4).

The Brexit crisis is also examined specifically in the context of Northern Ireland in the latter chapters of the book. Kinsella (Chapter 11) argues that it is appropriate to consider the island of Ireland as an economy in three parts with different productivity levels, income levels and sectoral strengths. Northern Ireland is its own distinct economy and one which has lagged behind the Republic of Ireland in terms of productivity, growth and living standards for the past thirty years. And as Kinsella argues, Brexit will only widen this divide. Economic disruption is certain with inevitable increased friction on east–west trade and this will subsequently have implications for politics *in* and the politics *of* Northern Ireland. Phinnemore and Whitten (Chapter 12) assess how the Brexit crisis has unsettled Northern Ireland; tensions have been revived and the constitutional question is once again to the fore. Brexit has undoubtedly highlighted Britain's constitutional arrangements and the inconsistency of political claims about them.

This in turn has created profound uncertainties about the UK's commitments vis-à-vis the island of Ireland and has undermined its reliability as a co-guarantor of the 1998 Agreement. Evershed (Chapter 13) considers these constitutional implications for Ireland, in particular the potential break-up of the UK and the renewed prospect of Irish unity. Both the economics and politics of Brexit have reminded both individuals and governments of the delicate peace process that exists in Northern Ireland and reiterated that part of the UK shares a land border with another EU member state. Pow (Chapter 14) affirms that while the EU did not play an active role in the run-up to the 1998 Agreement, joint membership of the UK and Ireland provided a framework for constructive bilateral relations between the two states, while EU Structural Funds, specifically the EU's Interreg programme and the Peace Programme, have provided tangible financial support for the peace process in Northern Ireland, as discussed in detail by Lagana (Chapter 15).

Nationalism in internationalism

The Republic of Ireland's relationship with the EU demonstrates a kind of "nationalism in internationalism". The country is strongly committed to working with the international cooperative framework. However, it does so on the basis of advancing its national interests. The same could be said of most EU member states, but there is something additional to the Irish case. There are hardly any competing visions of what the national interest should be: the pro-EU consensus also constitutes a consensus about Ireland's interests in the EU. The financial crisis and Brexit were both instances where the perceived Irish national interest was broadly similar to the main approach of the EU. Thus, there was no great tension between Irish and European interests. However, that is by no means guaranteed to be the case, as we will see in the last section of this chapter.

Of course, this "nationalism in internationalism" only applies to the Republic of Ireland. Northern Ireland has a different relationship with the

EU. However, it is not immune to the effect, since some parties and civil society groups are organised on an all-island basis. In general, Northern Ireland was not affected by the financial crash in the same way as the Republic, but Brexit had a huge impact there. At one level, it challenged the existing constitutional compromise, threatening the stability of the peace agreement and its multi-layered structures. At another, it perhaps served to underline the importance of the EU in supporting the peace process.

However, while the EU was in the past content to play a very low-key role, avoiding the kind of high-profile engagement of successive US governments, it was pushed much more to the fore by Brexit. When both Ireland and the UK were member states, the EU could function as a neutral actor in Northern Ireland. Following Brexit, the EU is obliged to defend the interests of its member states, and this could lead to problems. While the EU is normally reluctant to intervene on sensitive national political issues, rather surprisingly it did so on Northern Ireland. Following Brexit, the European Council issued a statement acknowledging that in the event of Irish unification, Northern Ireland would be automatically readmitted to the EU (Rankin 2017). While this could be seen as no more than a statement of fact, it could also be interpreted as interfering in the internal affairs of the region.

Change and continuity in Ireland's relationship with the EU

It is perhaps too soon to draw conclusions about the impact of the extended series of crises on the Irish–EU relationship. The full consequences – of the financial crisis, of Brexit, of the rise of populism, of the other challenges – are still working their way through the system. But some of the broad parameters are becoming evident.

Ireland remains a pro-European country, and indeed the net effect of the crises may even have been to strengthen this. There is a growing pro-EU consensus among Irish parties. Fianna Fáil and Fine Gael were there from the start, Labour joined by the time of the Maastricht Treaty campaign, the Greens did so with Lisbon, and Brexit marked the moment Sinn Féin also crossed the Rubicon. This leaves only a small radical left advocating any kind of Euroscepticism in parliament in Ireland. Despite the financial crisis, despite the growing growth of inward migration to Ireland, despite the possible temptation of following our large neighbour (and its important market), the far right is minuscule and largely irrelevant.

Why does this pro-EU stance happen? While undoubtedly there are economic and social benefits from membership, it is too simplistic to say, "the EU is good for Ireland", since membership also involves economic and social costs. But there is recognition that Ireland is a small state which cannot expect to set its own agenda. Therefore, it benefits from international rules and norms. But in terms of mainstream political, social and economic actors there is little evidence of a deep conviction in European integration. The pro-EU consensus in Ireland is very much an Irish nationalist one. The EU is viewed with approval because it provides benefits and helps Ireland advance its interests. Overall, there is an emphasis on support for the EU, but couched in terms of Irish interests. The debate about European integration is about who can best secure benefits and protect the country from perceived undesirable policy developments.

The situation is similar in Northern Ireland. Again, few demonstrate any deep pro-integration conviction, and while the relationship is generally positive, it is couched in terms of how the region benefits from the relationship. While there is an acceptance that it will not benefit from every single decision emanating from "over there in Brussels", in general it is in the North's interests. Of course, for both Northern Ireland and the Republic, this may not always be the case. Three broad areas of future challenges can be identified.

Firstly, whatever form it might take, the relationship with the UK will remain a central influence for Ireland. Brexit does not mean that Britain has floated off into the Atlantic like some stone raft. It is still Ireland's neighbour, there is still a huge economic relationship between the two, and of course it is still part of a sovereign state which includes some of the island of Ireland. It is particularly important for Northern Ireland, where the relationship is open to dispute and is as much about cultural identity as about economics and politics. As we have already argued, the EU might find it trickier to be seen as a neutral player in Northern Ireland after Brexit. The UK is also still very important for the Republic, which will have to adjust to a different form of association with its neighbour.

Secondly, the way that the EU and its precursors tended to respond to previous setbacks was to try to seize the moment for a leap forward in integration. If this occurs after Brexit, some of the ideas would prove challenging for Ireland. In particular, French President Emmanuel Macron (2017) has already floated the idea of deeper defence cooperation and of a more coordinated corporation tax system for the EU. Both of these ideas would threaten Irish red lines, and just as there is a pro-EU consensus, there is consensus in support of the Irish approach on these policies. Ireland's low corporation tax rate is backed by virtually all parties and business groups, while there is widespread support for neutrality. If a push for deeper integration in these areas does emerge in the EU, it will certainly create problems for Ireland's "national internationalism".

Thirdly, the sequence of crises that afflicted Ireland and Europe from 2008 has by no means ceased. Throughout this period, there has been growing concern about the challenge of climate change. Speaking about EU targets for reduced emissions, the former Taoiseach Leo Varadkar admitted that the country was 'nowhere near close to reaching our target of a 20% reduction by 2020' (McEnroe 2018). Then in 2020 the Covid-19 pandemic created even greater turmoil. It produced a far greater economic shock than the financial crisis did, and also highlighted challenges in terms of how political actors – states, international organisations and others – find an appropriate balance of resource allocation.

Ireland's relationship with the EU is unique and distinctive. The Republic of Ireland has generally shown strong enthusiasm for participation in the EU, as evidenced by public opinion, support of pressure groups and support of political parties. But at the same time, the Republic of Ireland has twice voted against EU treaties, and public opinion is marked by low levels of knowledge about the EU. And of course, the Republic of Ireland is not all of Ireland: Northern Ireland has its own distinctive relationship with the EU, one which is caught up in the ever present community rivalries there.

Note

1   The group consists of finance ministers from Denmark, Estonia, Finland, Ireland, Latvia, Lithuania, the Netherlands and Sweden, and was established in February 2018 (*Economist* 2018).

References

Begg, D. (2004) 'People, work and social change', in J. Hourihane (ed.) *Ireland and the European Union: the first thirty years, 1973–2002*, pp. 40–53. Dublin: Lilliput.

Drudy, P.J. & D. McAleese (eds) (1984) *Ireland and the European Community*. Cambridge: Cambridge University Press.

Economist (2018) 'Northern member states unite on Eurozone reform'. *Economist*, 8 December. Available at: www.economist.com/europe/2018/12/08/northern-member-states-unite-on-euro-zone-reform [accessed 1 August 2020].

Hederman, M. (1983) *The road to Europe: Irish attitudes 1948–61*. Dublin: Institute of Public Administration.

Holmes, M. (ed.) (2005a) *Ireland and the European Union: Nice, enlargement and the future of Europe*. Manchester: Manchester University Press.

Holmes, M. (2005b) 'The development of opposition to European integration in Ireland', in M. Holmes (ed.) *Ireland and the European Union: Nice, enlargement and the future of Europe*, pp. 75–93. Manchester: Manchester University Press.

Holmes, M. (2019) '"Frankfurt's way or Labour's way": the Irish left and the crisis', in M. Holmes & K. Roder (eds) *The European left and the financial crisis*, pp. 68–85. Manchester: Manchester University Press.

Kennedy, D. (2000) *Living with the European Union: the Northern Ireland experience*. London: Palgrave Macmillan.

Keogh, D. (1990) *Ireland and Europe, 1919–1989: a diplomatic and political history*. Cork and Dublin: Hibernian University Press.

Kirby, P. & M.C. Murphy (2011) *Towards a second republic: Irish politics after the Celtic Tiger*. London: Pluto Press.

Laffan, B. (1989) '"While you're over there in Brussels, get us a grant": the management of the Structural Funds in Ireland'. *Irish Political Studies* 4(1): 43–57.

Laffan, B. (2002) 'These islands and the European dimension', in B. Tonra & E. Ward (eds) *Ireland in international affairs: interests, institutions and identities*, pp. 46–65. Dublin: Institute of Public Administration.

Laffan, B. & J. O'Mahony (2008) *Ireland and the European Union*. Basingstoke: Palgrave Macmillan.

Macron, E. (2017) *Initiative for Europe*. Speech delivered at the University of Paris-Sorbonne, 26 September. Available at: http://international.blogs.ouest-france.fr/archive/2017/09/29/macron-sorbonne-verbatim-europe-18583.html [accessed 1 August 2020].

McEnroe, J. (2018) 'Ireland will miss EU admission targets for 2020, admits Taoiseach'. *The Irish Examiner*, 21 November. Available at: www.irishexaminer.com/news/arid-30886731.html [accessed 1 August 2020].

Murphy, M.C. (2014) *Northern Ireland and the European Union: the dynamics of a changing relationship*. Manchester: Manchester University Press.

Murphy, M.C. & D. Phinnemore (2005) 'Northern Ireland and the future of Europe debate', in M. Holmes (ed.) *Ireland and the European Union: Nice, enlargement and the future of Europe*, pp. 151–170. Manchester: Manchester University Press.

O'Brien, D. (2009) *Ireland, Europe and the world: writings on a new century*. Dublin: Gill & Macmillan.

O'Connor, P. (1998) *Emerging voices: women in contemporary Irish society*. Dublin: Institute of Public Administration.

O'Donnell, R. (ed.) (2000) *Europe: the Irish experience*. Dublin: Institute of European Affairs.

Rankin, J. (2017) 'Europe could allow a united Ireland to join EU after Brexit'. *Guardian*, 28 April. Available at: www.theguardian.com/uk-news/2017/apr/27/eu-to-debate-recog+nising-united-ireland-to-allow-swift-return-for-north [accessed 1 August 2020].

Simpson, K. & M. Loveless (2017) 'Another chance? Concerns about inequality, support for the European Union and further European integration'. *Journal of European Public Policy* 24(7): 1069–1089.

Index